LEADERS *and* LEADERSHIP

Geoffrey Stern

To Guy
Pina
With good wishes
from

Geoff

March 1997

i

First published in Great Britain in 1993.

The London School of Economics and Political Science,
Houghton Street,
London WC2A 2AE.

Telephone 071-405 7686

This Book is based on the BBC World Service series
Leaders and Leadership.

ISBN 0 85328 156 4

Design and production; Mike Scorer, LSE, Drawing Office.

Printed in Great Britain by Parchment Ltd., Oxford.

To John Tusa,

For his much valued friendship and encouragement during my 30 years of broadcasting.

CONTENTS

INTRODUCTION

Five years ago a chance remark at an LSE reception set in motion a train of thought that was to lead to two successful radio series and a number of apparently well received articles. The source of the remark was the late West German Chancellor, Willy Brandt, in London to promote a book on foreign aid, and in the course of a brief conversation with me he described himself as a political 'has-been', suggesting thereby regret at no longer being in power or in the limelight. It then occurred to me that the world was littered with such 'has-beens' and that here, indeed, was a potentially fruitful source of information about history, politics and international politics, should anyone care to tap it.

And so it was that I conceived and then – courtesy of the BBC World Service – embarked upon my interviews with Presidents and Prime Ministers, past and present, under the title 'Leaders and Leadership'. My main object was to better acquaint myself and my listeners/readers with the nature and role of the political leader by asking the practitioners: what precisely they thought they had been doing, why and how they came to be doing it, under what constraints and to what effect? Above all, did they consider they had moulded or were at the mercy of events? Behind my line of questioning was an attempt to produce the kind of first hand empirical evidence often lacking in decision-making studies, and to be able to make a more informed judgment about the motive force of history – is it men (and women) or movements; personalities or processes?

Though the answers to my questions were as diverse as my interviewees, I was able to amass from 13 lengthy face-to-face discussions a great deal of interesting material about political consciousness, leadership skills, decision-making processes, constraints and, perhaps most importantly, how and why particular critical decisions came to be made. From King Hussein, for example, I learned why Jordan had to commit itself to a war in 1967 it was bound to lose. From Kenneth Kaunda I discovered the thinking behind the establishment of one Party rule in 1972 and its abandonment in 1991. From Helmut Schmidt I learned why he was so keen for an American commitment to supply Cruise and Pershings, and how he came to take the decision. From Mieczyslaw Rakowski I was able to discover who took the decision to impose martial law in Poland in 1981 and why.

Anyone canvassing the views of any participant in any social process, especially those of a partisan politician, needs to be imbued with more than a modicum of scepticism. After all, complete intellectual detachment may elude interviewer and interviewee alike, while, of course, the politician tends to be more skilled than most at rationalisation, special pleading and other forms of semantic subterfuge. On the other hand, I had the distinct impression that since most of my interviewees were either in retirement or near the end of their political careers, they were treating our sessions as confessionals, getting things off their chest before the historians got to work on them.

As to the interviewees, they were a diverse array of notables, including leaders hereditary, authoritarian and democratic, appointed and elected, from political left, right and centre and from the five continents. So far as I was concerned they had to be people of a reflective disposition, not given to lighweight and inconsequential Reaganesque reminiscences, and for the most part I got what I wanted. None had any idea of what I was going to ask, though I indicated to Kenneth Kaunda's Press Secretary the general areas of discussion, explaining that each interview was meant to cover several distinct lines of enquiry.

1. A personality profile – childhood, family relationships, political awareness and the first steps on the political ladder.

2. Leadership – qualities requisite and how acquired, principles versus pragmatism, special requirements for particular countries.

3. Decision making – role models, choosing a Cabinet, drawing up priorities, how decisions are made, the degree of effective power given geopolitical and economic situation, etc.

4. Particular controversial decisions.

5. The use and abuse of power – the joys and tribulations of office, the temptation to corruption, feelings the day after removal from office, letting go, place in history.

The interviews were recorded at various times between March 1989 and June 1991 and originally broadcast in two series, one in Spring 1989 and another in Autumn 1991. In the text below all 13 interviews appear in order of transmission, but at greater length than the broadcasts which were edited versions of the originals. Though the printed texts make minor omissions and alterations by way of clarification, I have tried to make them as close to the original as possible.

In conclusion I should like to express my gratitude to all those leaders and former leaders who gave at least an hour and a quarter of their valuable time to this enterprise, to John Tusa, the recently retired Managing Director of the BBC World Service who made it possible, to Trish Williams, Kari Blackburn, Alastair Lack and Ferri Jahed who produced the programmes, to Ourania Anagnostou who helped compile the profiles and the bibliography, to Sonia Livingstone for her invaluable suggestions, to Toni Huberman, Amanda Melton and Elaine Childs of LSE who laboured on the typescripts and to Iain Crawford, Fiona Whiteman and Alex Vincenti who secured publication of this joint LSE/BBC endeavour.

An Anatomy of Leadership

There is a common thread linking the cub-mistress, the head teacher, the managing director, the orchestral conductor, the sea captain and the statesman. All hold positions of power, are entitled to deference and supposedly exercise authority. As such they are expected to possess that elusive quality we call 'leadership' – not easily defined since what is deemed to make for 'good' leadership in one context may be entirely out of place in another. Clearly, what it takes to lead a successful dance troupe will be different from what it needs to head a team of research scientists. By the same token the skills required to be mayor of a small rural community may well be different from those demanded of a head of state, even though both roles are in a broad sense political. In this study the emphasis is on those who bear ultimate political responsibility as head of state or government.

Malvolio in Shakespeare's Twelfth Night points to the variegated ways in which people acquire high office. 'Some men are born great, some achieve greatness and some have greatness thrust upon them'. To put it another way: some attain power as a result of some hereditary principle of rule; others by election or appointment, others, yet again, through some irregular, unconstitutional proceeding – a coup, for example, or a revolution. However, one can also give to Malvolio's observation a further, perhaps more interesting interpretation – that there is no single or simple answer to the question as to how the more distinguished leaders acquire the qualities differentiating them from the merely mediocre or the downright bad. The source of 'greatness', it seems, might lie in nature, nurture or in effort, adaptability and flair. But what is it about a politician that merits the ascription of 'greatness'?

Though there may be disagreement as to whether or not particular personalities deserve to be considered 'great', there would seem to be general accord amongst both scholars and lay observers that the mark of 'greatness' lies in part in the ability to impose, as it were, an individual stamp on history – changing, speeding or stemming in dramatic fashion the flow of events. In this sense the ascription rests on some conception of the situation prior to the advent of power of the leader in question and implies the existence of some antecedent need, want, spiritual or material void subsequently to be filled. Perhaps the leader's 'greatness' lies in moulding and unifying a nation out of diverse groups, or, alternatively in liberating one people from the oppressive rule of another. Perhaps it lies in giving a sense of direction and purpose to a people who have lost their way, or, alternatively, in helping to preserve a sense of direction and purpose despite all the odds. Perhaps it lies in bringing peace and prosperity to a troubled and impoverished country or, alternatively, in bringing hopes of peace and prosperity to a turbulent world. In short, the leader may need to be a successful warrior or an accomplished conciliator, an innovator or a preserver of tradition, an orator or an organiser, a visionary or a pragmatic operator depending on the circumstances. Though assessments may change over time, ultimately the 'great' leader is one perceived as having displayed unusual skills in meeting the needs and fulfilling the expectations of his or her followers.

But beyond giving satisfaction to followers, does a leader have to be a benefactor in a more general sense to be considered 'great'? Since the list of 'great' leaders would probably have to include people like Xerxes, Attila the Hun, Genghis Khan, Napoleon, Stalin, Mussolini, Hitler and so forth, the answer would appear to be 'no'. On the other hand, in drawing a distinction between politicians and statesmen, the latter comprising people who have made a mark in international as distinct from domestic affairs, we have an opportunity of identifying the 'great' with the 'good'. For we can ascribe 'statesmanship' to those leaders whom we feel may have contributed to the sum of human happiness and consign to the lesser role of 'world politician' those we believe to have had a significant but generally malign influence internationally.

Not that it should be assumed that the President or the Prime Minister is always as important as the office would suggest. For while some leaders acquire the status almost of demi-god, others are content to play a merely ceremonial role, leaving the real work of government to people working behind the scenes. It would be rash, for example, to infer from an inventory of formal positions and qualifications the degree of effective power held by those in high office. On paper, for example, Hua Kuo Feng, the successor to China's Mao Tse Tung, held an array of political and military posts making him even more powerful than his predecessor. That he lost office after little over two years indicates just how precarious in fact was his hold on power. Meanwhile Hua's rival in the Soviet Union, Leonid Brezhnev, was acquiring an ever expanding number of titles, awards and accolades at a time when his physical capacity to hold effective power was fast diminishing. And we learn from both China's Teng Hsiao Ping and Burma's General Ne Win in the early '90s that a country's effective ruler can shed one official position after another and yet maintain control long after he has disappeared from public view.

The extent to which political leaders can exercise effective power depends on a number of separate but related factors. Their inherent skills must, of course, come high on the list, as must their own conception of what the role of leader requires. This in turn will depend on the nature of their respective country's political system together with its policy-making process, and on the perceptions and expectations of its citizens. But there are also all manner of political, social and economic constraints – both domestic and foreign – affecting the ability of a leader to wield the power that is supposed to go with the office.

In a book, *The Anatomy of Power*, written in 1979,[1] the late James Margach pointed to the importance of personality in the political process and singled out a number of characteristics he regarded as indispensable to aspiring politicians. These included 'ambition, courage, ruthlessness, the pursuit of fame, character, vision, judgment, patience, stamina'. But he also pointed to an additional asset which he saw as in some sense prior to all the others – 'luck', defined as being 'blessed with incredibly good fortune... coinciding with the misfortunes of their rivals and sometimes of the country as well' (p.2). In his view it was luck together with good timing – the ability to exploit successfully sudden good fortune – that helped propel a leader of the Opposition, such as Harold Wilson, or a member of the Cabinet, such as James Callaghan, into 10 Downing Street. By implication it was bad luck as well as bad timing that deprived a man like Neil Kinnock, who once appeared to have Number 10 within his grasp, of the premiership. By extension, any leader unfortunate enough to hold power during a recession or slump – as, for example, Messrs Major, Bush, Mitterand, Kohl and Yeltsin – is likely to stand accused of 'a lack of leadership', and, of course, President Bush has already had to pay the political price for failing to give the kind of 'lead' the Americans were looking for at the end of 1992.

Though the Margach checklist referred specifically to the British political scene and made no distinction between the characteristics needed to get to the top and those

7

required to stay there, some of the qualities it highlighted must surely form part of the armoury of any upwardly mobile politician under virtually any system. Certainly in none of those leaders interviewed below were the bulk of the qualities listed by the veteran columnist absent, and in many, most of the 'political virtues' he identified were combined in considerable measure. Almost all were also in possession of two further qualities not listed by Margach, but I should have thought of particular importance to a politician in the television age – plausibility and charm. After all, even the most dictatorial and disreputable leader must expect nowadays to have to face the press or the cameras from time to time.

On the other hand, in a world so politically and culturally diverse, what is sought and expected of a political leader must differ from one country to another and from one time period to another. It is one thing to preside over the fortunes of a democracy, another to be in charge of an autocracy, oligarchy or one Party state. And, of course, there may be significant differences regarding leadership roles as between one democracy and another. In countries such as Britain and Germany, the constitutional position of head of state is largely ceremonial, whereas in France the head of state, who serves a fixed term, normally exercises far more effective power than the prime ministers, who tend to change with monotonous regularity; while in the US the very extensive presidential role is nonetheless to a degree limited by the separation of the powers. Further, in many democracies, especially those with proportional representation, the Prime Minister has to be adept at forming coalitions, a quality not normally required of a leader of a country such as Britain with a first-past-the-post electoral system. And, of course, there are federal states which limit the power of central government, and unitary states with prickly minorities whose interests the power-holders disregard at their peril (as Britain tended to do in Ireland for centuries).

But the respective roles of head of state and head of government are determined not merely by constitutional structures but also by the tension between traditional practice and changing fashion. The shadow of the past, in other words, will often serve to limit the extent to which significant shifts in the exercise of political authority occur. One has only to consider, for example, the aftermath of the many revolutions in the name of Marx, which far from ushering in the 'withering away of the state' tended merely to reinforce state power. Admittedly Lenin could at first justify the increasing concentration of power in Soviet Russia on the grounds that the revolution was endangered by civil war, war, intervention and blockade, but in tightening political controls still further after his country was no longer at risk and establishing a pervasive network of bureaucrats, censors, secret policemen and spies he was drawing on earlier patterns of rule and laying down structures of authority that other so-called Marxist revolutionaries would emulate. In a parliamentary democracy, on the other hand, it clearly matters whether the prevalent economic ideology is liberal and non-interventionist or social democratic and interventionist and whether politically power is supposed to be centralised or devolved. For any leader wielding more power or less than is acceptable to either the ruling team or the electorate puts his or her position at risk. Yet what is acceptable is often grounded in traditional notions of responsible leadership. If Lord Home's colleagues thought him too weak to continue as Premier, Margaret Thatcher's colleagues came to think of her as too strong and rejected her, just as the electorate had rejected Winston Churchill immediately after the Second World War.

What, then, is the relationship between the individual and the political role he or she feels called upon to play? In a perceptive paragraph in one of his books, the American scholar Kenneth Boulding suggests the existence of a dynamic interchange: 'The individual... never merely passively fits a role. He reorganises the role through the operation of his own peculiar image. When a square peg is fitted into a round role...the peg becomes rounder, but it is also true that the role becomes squarer'.[2] In other words, no matter how compelling the constraints of political office they are rarely, if ever, so constricting as to stifle initiative altogether. Politicians are thus free within certain prescribed limits to explore to the full the range of possible options and behaviour patterns, though, clearly, the more colourful, imaginative and dynamic are likely to be more adventurous than their more conservative colleagues in identifying and pursuing the opportunities for choice. As against this, certain kinds of situations, for example, a domestic political or economic crisis, revolutionary developments in a neighbouring state or a threatened invasion, may severely narrow the framework of perceived options. But what determines the limits of political behaviour? How, in other words, do political roles originate and acquire definition?

Unlike most actors in the conventional theatre, the 'actor' in the 'theatre' of politics does not generally work to a given text. However, like the actor in an improvised drama, the political 'actor' usually works to a sub-text or scenario derived from history and tradition. What establishes the parameters of the political role – whether that of local mayor, revolutionary agitator, opposition leader or, indeed, of president or prime minister – are the widely shared perceptions and expectations in the political community, based on either explicit rules or understandings emanating from custom. In its approach to government, each political community, that is, inherits a framework of conventions, precepts and notions that defines the characteristics of legitimate authority, identifies the boundaries of acceptable behaviour and prescribes standards of competence and conduct. On the other hand, what is deemed to constitute 'legitimate' authority varies from one society to another, so that what is considered tolerable political conduct in one society may be dismissed as unacceptable in another. For example, the abuses

9

known as Watergate, which drove Richard Nixon from the American presidency, might well have been regarded as standard practice elsewhere and thus well within the bounds of acceptable political behaviour. Sadly, by the same token, the political experience of, say, Haiti, gives its people few grounds for the belief that political leadership can be other than oppressive. What manifests itself as 'normal' political behaviour in that poor unfortunate country would be considered well beyond the pale in most others.

As in improvised drama, the way the political *dramatis personae* play their allotted roles will be a matter for critical judgement, and the 'actors' designated 'great', 'mediocre' or 'bad' according to whether or not their 'performance' carries conviction. As for the criteria by which the citizen 'audience' judges that 'performance', they will be shaped to considerable extent by the nature and modalities of the political system itself. Though political 'actors' may be evaluated ultimately in terms of their contribution towards the security, welfare and prestige of their respective societies, how that contribution is understood will depend to a degree on whether the leader 'plays' or is supposed to 'play' the ceremonial head, the chairperson, chief, demagogue or demi-god. This, in turn, will depend on whether the country in question is a parliamentary or presidential democracy, under an ideologically grounded Party dictatorship or ruled by monarch, sheik, military officer or civilian despot.

On the other hand, conditions change and with them political expectations. In an age of what the German sociologist, Max Weber, calls 'traditional' authority, such as absolute monarchy, the best that the concerned citizen could hope for was wise and considerate leadership that would provide a framework of order and justice within which the people could conduct their lives and livelihoods. In an age of what Weber calls 'legal' or 'rational' authority, as exemplified by representative government, the leaders are expected to respect and reflect community interests and values and, where possible, further them. Where the leader exercises what Weber calls 'charismatic' authority[3] – a reference to figures such as Hitler, Mussolini, Gandhi, Roosevelt, Mao, Soekarno, Nkrumah, Nasser and Castro – the followers in effect abdicate their own individual powers of choice and respond to whatever the leader does with 'devotion, awe, reverence and blind faith'.[4] To those whose feelings of awe and reverence are manifested through thick and thin (feelings which, incidentally, may be promoted and enhanced by modern media technology) the 'performance' of the leader invariably measures up to or even exceeds expectations.

However, what people expect of their leaders is one thing: what they get may be something else, and in practice the crucial decisions affecting people's lives may be determined in a variety of different ways. In a classic study of 1939, social psychologist, Kurt Lewin, distinguished between three different types of decision-making – 'autocratic', 'democratic' and 'laissez-faire'.[5] The 'autocratic' leader gave orders, discouraged criticism and lacked objectivity in his judgement of others. The 'democratic' leader made suggestions, listened to the suggestions of others and worked for consensus. The 'laissez-faire' leader gave no orders and made no suggestions unless specifically asked – in effect, opting out of the decision-making process. More recently, the Harvard economist, Graham Allison, in *Essence of Decision* produced a decision-making typology of particular, but not of exclusive relevance to foreign policy making.[6]

Allison dubs his first and more conventional decision-making framework the 'rational actor' model. Here policy is the outcome of a calculated, purposeful and, above all, rational process in which all options are considered by a unitary policy-maker in pursuit of stated goals and objectives. His second framework, the 'organisational process' model shifts the emphasis from the individual decision-maker to the complex procedures by which policy may be arrived at. Here, decisions are the product not of deliberate choice but of 'pulling and hauling' between the representatives of different government departments, each functioning according to 'standard operating procedures'. It is a process which produces a policy which no-one strongly objects to even if no-one is particularly happy with. In Allison's third framework, the 'bureaucratic politics' model, policy is, again, the product not so much of deliberate choice but in this case of a power struggle between key individuals in the bureaucratic élite whose several objectives, personal as well as professional, may be incompatible with one another. Here, again, policy, therefore, has to be the product of various complex bargaining strategies, in the process of which the leader's individual preferences and prejudices may be submerged.

That presidential or prime ministerial designs may be buried in collective decision-making raises the key question as to the relationship between the leader and the broader political, social and economic environment within which he or she has to operate. While in some countries constitutional or decision-making procedures may enlarge and enhance the effective power of certain leaders, in others they may reduce it, while unfavourable domestic and international circumstances may further circumscribe their freedom of action. Clearly, in societies where there is serious civil disorder, heavy indebtedness and a threat of mass starvation as in Ethiopia and Somalia in the early '90s, even the most dominant and authoritarian political personality can be politically diminished. By the same token a country's unenviable geographical circumstances can often seriously erode the power of its leader to determine effective policy, so that, as is evident from the texts which follow, the leaders of countries such as Poland or Jordan are often at the mercy of international events over which they have little control. At the same time, of course, external commitments such as alliances, treaties, investments and trading arrangements, together with a nation's solicitude for its nationals in hostile foreign terrain may tie the hands of even leaders of countries generally more favourably placed than either Poland or Jordan. And, of course, legal and diplomatic considerations as well as calculations of relative abilities can further constrain effective action.

So what are we to conclude? Was the nineteenth century literary historian Thomas Carlyle right to see 'great men' as the motive force behind history or was the late British prime minister, Harold Macmillan, nearer the mark when he claimed that the most difficult things an administration has to face are 'events'. Did Neville Chamberlain reflect or mould Britain's appeasement of Hitler? Was Churchill's role in Britain's war effort critical or did he merely, as he claimed, give the 'roar' to the 'British lion'? Did Gorbachev kill European Communism and with it the Cold War or was he the instrument of an historical process already under way? Such thorny issues will doubtless long continue to be the subject of debate, even if Professor John Garnett in *Common Sense and the Theory of International Relations* has taken some of the heat out of the discussion with his claim that 'policy makers are never as free as their critics think they are'.[7] So how free are they? Are political affairs determined by will or by fate? Do particular men and women gain significance only when they understand, respond to, reflect and evoke the temper and spirit of the times? It is to be hoped that the interviews which follow will at least help readers to clarify their minds.

NOTES

1. James Margach, *The Anatomy of Power*, London: 1979.

2. Kenneth Boulding, *The Image*, Ann Arbor: 1959, p.60.

3. See for example Reinhard Bendix, *Max Weber: An Intellectual Portrait*, New York: 1960.

4. A R Willner, *The Spellbinders: Charismatic Political Leadership*, New Haven: 1984, p.7.

5. K Lewin, R Lippitt & R K White, 'Patterns of Aggressive Behaviour in Experimentally Created 'Social Climates', *The Journal of Social Psychology*, No.10, 1939, pp.271-99.

6. Graham Allison, *Essence of Decision*, Boston: 1971. See introduction.

7. John Garnett, *Common Sense and the Theory of International Relations*, London: 1984.

Helmut SCHMIDT

CHAPTER 2

Stern: Herr Schmidt, you were a teenager when the Weimar Republic collapsed and the Nazis came to power. Could you or anyone else have predicted then that one day you'd be Chancellor of a Social Democratic Germany?

SCH: No of course not, I was fourteen when the Nazis came to office.

Stern: So what were you like in those days; were you just one of a crowd, or someone that stood out ?

SCH: No, some little boy in the crowd.

Stern: Would you say that you were a happy child?

SCH: Neither happy nor unhappy. I was a very normal boy except for one thing. My father was, in the terminology of the Nazis, a half-Jew and under the Nuremburg laws I was a quarter Jew, and this of course led my father and my mother, and to some little degree also my brother and myself, to be afraid of what might happen to us.

Stern: But if you are a quarter Jewish, how did you manage to conceal that from the authorities?

SCH: Well, my father had been an illegitimate child. He was born out of wedlock, and he pretended that his father was unknown, and we even got somebody who was willing to give us a paper on which it was stated that the archives of Hamburg did not show his father's name. Of course he knew his father, but, with that little paper, we got away with it.

CHAPTER 2

Stern: What was your attitude to the regime which you served with distinction? You were in the forces for eight years, got an iron cross, and ended up as an Oberleutenant.

SCH: Well I would reject the word 'distinction'. It was a rather normal career for somebody who had finished senior high school to become a reserve Officer in the course of a year. After all, many of the people of my age had become Captains and Majors. What was my attitude? Well, of course naturally I was not a friend of the Nazi regime. On the other hand I believed that one had to serve one's country and that, like millions of young people in those years in Germany, one had to find one's own way.

Stern: During the war you must have had precious little opportunity to read about Social Democracy.

SCH: No, *no* opportunity. You didn't have access to any political books other than Nazi books and they didn't interest me.

Stern: So how did you become a Social Democrat?

SCH: I became a Social Democrat tentatively in the beginning, in a British POW camp on Belgian soil, in the last weeks of the war, not under the influence of English non-commissioned officers, who were the ones who dealt with us, but of a German university Professor who like myself had been captured. He was, I think, a religious socialist, a very well educated man about 20 years older than me.

Stern: And he converted you, did he, to Social Democracy?

SCH: The word 'convert' is wrong. I didn't hold any particular political convictions thus far, except that I was against the Nazis. I didn't know what to be in favour of, I only knew what I was against. So 'converting' me is the wrong word.

Stern: But when did you decide that you were going to go into Social Democratic politics?

SCH: Immediately after my release from the camp, in Autumn '45.

Stern: And what were you going into politics for? Did you want to change society?

SCH: I didn't go into politics. I became a member of the party and attended meetings in the place where we then were living in the vicinity of the city of Hamburg and when they soon found out that I was quick in perception, quick in argument, in some particular fields they used me as an instructor.

Stern: But you were willing to be used.

SCH: Yes of course, but this doesn't mean I went into politics. I was earning my living otherwise, and was also attending university.

14

Stern: But when did you decide you were going to have a political career as such?

SCH: I never decided that.

Stern: You mean other people decided it for you? I don't think you're like that are you?

SCH: No no. I ended my studies in '48 or '49, I don't recall exactly now, and then started working as an employee of the City of Hamburg in the economic administration. And I had just started to make a little career in that authority when after four years, at one and the same time, three different constituency parties asked me 'wouldn't you like to stand as a candidate in our constituency'. I did choose one because I thought it might be a very interesting experience for a couple of years to see how democracy works from the inside. I never took the decision to become a politician – I just went there because I was invited, and thought it might be interesting.

Stern: So it was a kind of scientific experiment was it ?

SCH: Not scientific – practical.

Stern: A practical experiment, but you went into politics without any idea of saving Europe or the world?

SCH: I had many ideas of what was to be done in my own country, but these were not the reasons for joining parliament. I had had these ideas before that and I had never thought of having a parliamentary career. But it was offered to me and I thought I would take it just for a couple of years – maybe for one period of legislation, maybe for two. Certainly not for a lifetime.

Stern: I must say I find it a bit difficult to believe that, in the end, you were a reluctant Defence Minister, a reluctant Finance Minister, and a reluctant Chancellor – is that what you're telling me?

SCH: This I didn't tell you as yet but you seem to have read it elsewhere, and it's true. I was not very eager to become a Minister. For example when the Social Democrats for the first time since 1930 provided the nation with a Chancellor, which was Willy Brandt at the time, it was clear that the Defence Ministry had to be occupied by a Social Democrat again. But the Social Democrats didn't really have somebody who was fit, by his former studies, speeches and experiences, other than me. So they thought I would be the ideal man for that office, but I didn't want to become Minister of Defence. For two reasons: number one, I was Floor Leader for the Social Democratic Party and would have liked to have stayed on; secondly, I knew the ideological history of my own party. It was none too friendly to the idea of defence or with the armed forces. So I thought it was a rather hot stool on which I was going to sit. They needed about a fortnight to persuade me to overcome my reluctance.

Stern: But didn't you have political ambition at all?

SCH: Well I don't know. Everybody has some ambitions and vanities – politicians, artists, painters, actors – and certainly I was equipped with a normal amount of that, but I was most happy when I was the Floor Leader of the Social Democrats in Bonn, which was in the period between '66 and '69, and would very much have liked to have stayed on in that capacity. The most gratifying thing about it was the fact that you had the confidence of your own colleagues. You were the one to make the front bench speeches. But if I had said something which my people wouldn't have liked, they would have scolded me immediately thereafter. The most rewarding thing at the time was to have the feeling of being borne by a great majority of one's own political friends, and my ambition was to maintain that status.

Stern: When you finally became Chancellor, what qualities do you think you brought to that office?

SCH: I think what matters more than my own opinion was the opinion of the people who made me Chancellor, and it seems that they felt that what was needed at the time was a down-to-earth man, a pragmatic man, a man who could define the problems and solve them as far as they were solvable at all.

Stern: Does that mean a man without principle?

SCH: A few of them in the beginning seem to have thought so, but of course I never was a man without principles, but I didn't like the idea of carrying around my moral principles like a preacher every Sunday. I followed my principles without placating them.

Stern: What are your principles?

SCH: Looking at it with hindsight there were different sets of principles in my thinking then. On the one hand the principles that were laid down in the German Constitution which we inherited in the course of the 19th century from Philadelphia and from the American Constitution in the main and before that from natural law as had been developed in England and in France.

Stern: Freedom of speech, freedom of worship and all the civil liberties and so on...

SCH: Yes, civil liberties, the liberty of the individual. And secondly there was the principle stipulated at the end of the last century by a German social scientist and philosopher, Max Weber, who taught that a political leader, or indeed a politician or anybody in public life, has to be responsible not only for his good intentions, but also for the factual outcome. Because of that principle, I never indulged in fantasies or in utopias or in ideological dreams. I always felt the responsibility for what was going to be the consequence of what I was doing today.

Stern: Does that mean that sometimes you had to either abandon principle or trim your principles in order to suit the circumstances.

SCH: I did not have to abandon my principles, but sometimes I had to abandon the ideologies of my party.

Stern: Which didn't make you very popular with the Party sometimes.

SCH: Later on. At the time when I became Chancellor I was rather popular, because they had just had undergone a period of four and a half years of indulging in great ideas and in which, for instance, the financial management was not very down to earth.

Stern: Now you've said that pragmatism is the quality which you were able to bring to the Chancellory. Is this a quality that all leaders should have ?

SCH: Well if you are talking of leaders in general the answer would be no, not necessarily. If you are talking of statesmen governing a country and being responsible for what happens within that country or between that country and its neighbours, the answer is yes.

Stern: What other qualities do you think are necessary for leadership?

SCH: It depends on the specific situation in which a leader is born, is raised, in which he lives. It depends on the environment of his society, nation, country, international environment, which may change from time to time. It depends for instance on the constitution. If you have a democratic constitution you have already narrowed in a way the necessary qualifications of that leader, before you start to define them in particular. Then you have different types of democracy. For instance, the American democracy needs a different type of leadership as compared with, let us say, French or Italian democracy. In America you have a two-party system, practically speaking. In France, in Italy you have some six, seven, eight parties. So a French or an Italian leader needs to be able to form a coalition and hold it together. An American President never has to think about it. I use this as an example in order to make clear what I say when I said it depends on the constitutional circumstances and environment. It also depends on the time. Before you had television and broadcasting, the qualifications that were needed were quite different from the qualifications which somebody needs in the television age. Reagan obviously had enormous talent for using television and reaching the nation. This wasn't necessary in the times of Lord Palmerston or Disraeli.

Stern: So in the television age does a leader have to be popular, does he have to be likable, does he have to be televisual?

SCH: He does not necessarily need to be likable, but he needs to be understandable and to be able convince his audiences – at least the majority – and hopefully not alienate the minority.

Stern: So what is leadership? Is it a skill, is it a craft, is it an art?

SCH: It's not just one art or one craft, it's a set of things and I think one facet of it that has more or less not changed from the 19th century to the 20th century when we went from a newspaper democracy to a television democracy, is the credibility of the person. People must be convinced to a fine degree. They must be convinced that he really thinks what he says or that he really will do what he says today, tomorrow or the day after tomorrow. That he is a dependable man; that she is a dependable woman.

17

Stern: Do you need to have a degree of human magnetism for that, to be able to attract people?

SCH: I don't know what the overtones of the word magnetism in English would be. The Americans normally use the word 'charisma'. It's difficult to define what it really means, but perhaps a certain irradiation is necessary, especially in the television age. If a leader doesn't bring this charisma he may not really meet the expectations of his nation.

Stern: When you wrote about Ronald Reagan, whom you didn't think much of, you said he had charisma. Yet here was this man with charisma pursuing policies which, in your view, were not very appropriate.

SCH: I think his charisma was much greater than his judgment.

Stern: When you find yourself Chancellor, leader, it's pretty lonely isn't it?

SCH: That is true. And I was afraid of it, before I started out.

Stern: Is that one of the reasons that you say you were reluctant to take the job?

SCH: Yes, quite so.

Stern: What did being lonely at the top mean? Did it mean that you could have few friends?

SCH: The German Federal Chancellor, in a way, has to bear the final responsibility, like the British Prime Minister or the American President; unlike the French Prime Minister, unlike the Italian Prime Minister, unlike the Dutch Prime Minister. So I think that if compared with the Prime Ministers in Paris and in The Hague or in Rome a German Federal Chancellor, like an American President, like Margaret Thatcher today in England as Prime Minister, is more lonely than other Prime Ministers in other democracies. As regards France, I have to add a footnote because since De Gaulle's re-writing of the French Constitution, the French President, if he so chooses, may matter more than the Prime Minister. And the French President if he really wants to lead the country, like De Gaulle, like Giscard, is a very lonely man again. In West Germany the Federal Chancellor is the man who matters. The Federal President has no decision-making in the political field.

Stern: Now you've written about 'Men and Power.' But surely the qualities that you've itemised: pragmatism, dependability and so on, are qualities that are possessed by women as well as men.

SCH: Well, let me first correct the false image which has been created by the English translation of the German word 'Menschen'. Menschen in the German language means male and female alike. So, a correct translation would have been "Human Beings and Power" but this would have been too long a title and not very eye-catching for prospective readers.

Stern: But why do so few women make it to the top?

SCH: Because women, over the ages, have been at a great disadvantage in public life and the prejudices of the public still are not really overcome against women in public office. We are in the process of overcoming these prejudices, but they haven't really been overcome as yet.

Stern: When they do make it to the top, is their behaviour noticeably different from that of men?

SCH: I don't know. I have seen Indira Gandhi from afar only. Also Mrs Bandaranaike and Mrs Aquino. I have seen only one lady from close by which is Margaret Thatcher, and I think her behaviour is a little different compared with her predecessors like James Callaghan, Harold Wilson, Ted Heath or Harold Macmillan. More than her predecessors she seems to feel it necessary to again and again and again establish her position of power.

Stern: So what does that tell you?

SCH: It may be that it is sort of compensation for the aforementioned deep-seated old prejudices. It may be from time to time that a female leader may bring some typically motherly attitudes. It has not happened as yet, but as regards Margaret Thatcher again, I remember that her son once was lost in an automobile rally in the African desert, and I called her by telephone to express my sympathies and this was the only time when I understood that she, as a mother, was deeply troubled. She even wept on the telephone, but obviously was eager to conceal this from the British public.

Stern: We've had a look at what leadership is, but what's it for? The cynics say that it has to do with ego trips and personal ambition, the Marxists that it's about serving the interests of the ruling class, and the idealists that it's about serving a higher purpose – that the leader is a kind of mystical embodiment of the state. What do you think?

SCH: I would not subscribe to any of these alternatives. To me the sense which always has played a great role in Germany since Immanuel Kant is duty, to do one's duty.

Stern: But where does this 'duty' come from? Is it God given? Is it man given? Is it tradition given? Is it foisted on you by pressure groups?

SCH: No, not by pressure groups. No, it must come from your own moral convictions on the one hand and from the analysis of the situation on the other.

Stern: In your time you've been bitterly critical of certain leaders, for their lack of judgment or for their reluctance to take bold or unpopular measures or whatever. But didn't you find as Chancellor that the leader, at least in a democracy, often has less room to manoeuvre, less freedom of action, than his critics suggest?

SCH: I would reject the introduction of your question. When I was in office I didn't harshly criticise other leaders publicly...

Stern: No, but you have done since haven't you?

SCH: Afterwards. After I left public life I have made some criticisms, yes. Now as regards the core of the question. The freedom to operate is sometimes greater than the public understands. In most instances it is much narrower than the public seems to understand. This is true in all the democratic countries. It's even true in Communist dictatorships. Within the group of democratic countries it again depends on your constitution and the political habits of your country. For instance, in the main, the American President, by the Constitution, has enormous freedom to operate. He is the executive. On the other hand he can not appoint a Foreign Secretary or a Secretary of Defence, as we have just seen in the instance of former Senator Tower, without the consent of the Senate. Whereas in Britain or in Germany the Prime Minister or the Federal Chancellor of course is the only one who decides who becomes Foreign Secretary, Lord Chancellor, Finance Minister or whatever.

Stern: He can choose his own Cabinet, that's right, but what about the policies? You were in office when the oil price rise occurred, which fuelled inflation throughout the west. Did you not find that that was a major constraint on what you could do at home?

SCH: Price 'rise' is a very kind word. What you really are talking about is an explosion. We had two oil price explosions and if you compare the oil prices of 1981 with the oil prices of 1972 you will find that they were twenty-five fold, which meant the beginning of the so-called debt crisis of the developing countries on the one hand and the mass unemployment in the industrialised countries on the other hand. This was of course an enormous problem, and quite a few leaders at the time, let us say in '73,'74, did not understand what was building up. They didn't have enough economic insight to enable them to perceive what the consequences were going to be, and what had to be done as early as possible to make these consequences smaller, easier to bear. Of course the two oil crisis explosions hampered the budgetary policies, the tax policies, the monetary policies of almost every government in the world, though for some they seemed to broaden the scope for operation. For instance, the scope for operation for the Prime Minister of Saudi Arabia was broadened enormously. And also for Brezhnev, because the Soviet Union was a net exporter of petrol and of natural gas, whose prices went up with the oil prices. The oil price explosion was not of Soviet making but they were great beneficiaries of the whole thing and therefore could all of a sudden earn much more hard currency than hitherto and import much more from the world markets.

Stern: But you in Germany of course had to import a lot of oil.

SCH: Oh yes, we had to import all of our oil. We didn't have one drop of oil in our own soil, nor a litre of gas. It hampered us very much and it took quite a bit of time to make the public understand that the times of beautiful economic weather were gone and that we were living in a different period now. It takes some time to make your public understand that the situation has changed and that you have to take measures quite different from those they had been expecting only a quarter of a year earlier.

Stern: And yet you were pretty successful in keeping inflation reasonably low. You were more successful than most of the other western countries. How did you manage to do that? Were you pretty ruthless?

SCH: Well we were ruthless in a way, but we explained to the people that the time of enormous annual increases in real wages had gone, that the time of enormous increases of real profits from corporations had gone, that there was no use in printing the money in order to pay the higher price for oil because this would have led to inflation, as it has done in other countries. In order to make the people, the entrepreneurs, the trade unions understand the different setting in which we were operating, it was necessary to call them to your table. I had an enormous number of meetings in my place, at night, first dinner and then discussion, where the trade union leaders and the entrepreneurs and the bankers and the politicians were sitting around one and the same table. Something which never happens in Britain, France or in America, or Italy. But this was the main instrument to convince the lobby groups, the pressure groups, the great organisations of the necessities of the period and to make them aware of the far narrower corridor within which decisions could be taken or not taken.

Stern: So this was the hallmark of your leadership. You let people understand what were the constraints of your own position and the difficulties you were facing.

SCH: I tried to make people understand, yes, and to some degree it was a success. But after a couple of years they became wary; they didn't like it any longer. They did not understand that the second oil price explosion of 1980-1 did even greater harm to our economies than the first one. We had just overcome the deficits on our balance of payments from the first oil price explosion, now the second one had fallen upon us...

Stern: But why couldn't the Schmidt magic work the second time as it had worked the first time?

SCH: Well as I said people became fed up with that. Within my own party some people were fed up with my pragmatic handling of economic problems. They would have liked to have got back to what I call Utopias, ideas for improving the world, you know.

Stern: So you saw your role in a sense as an educator to explain to people.

SCH: Partially, yes, and it is the task of any leader of a state, to educate his public to understand what he is doing and why.

Stern: Your political career spanned the oil crisis, the creation of the European Monetary System, the transition from East/West detente to what's sometimes called the 'second cold war'. How do you calculate that elusive concept that we call the national interest?

SCH: To take into account what is in the interest of your neighbours is very important for a country like Germany that has more neighbours than almost any other nation in the world, maybe except the Chinese and the Russians. That's one of the reasons there have been so many wars in which Germany was either entangled or in which Germany was overrun like under Napoleon at the beginning of the 19th century, or in which Germany has lashed out onto the soil and territory of her neighbours. So it is also in the interest of one's own nation to take into account the interests of the neighbouring nations.

Stern: But is it you, as Chancellor, who evaluates these things and in Cabinet?

SCH: No, not necessarily in Cabinet, but not in the solitude of your own drawing room either. I have always depended heavily on discussion with knowledgeable people, many of them from the ranks of politics, the entrepreneurs, the trade unions, the sciences and from the churches – Catholic as well as Protestant.

Stern: But did your Cabinet object to the fact that you were bringing in all these outsiders?

SCH: No. I didn't bring them in. I had private discussions with them in small groups. And some cabinet members would also participate.

Stern: That raises an interesting question. You were in coalition with the Free Democrats, who didn't always agree with you on policy. How did you choose your Cabinet?

SCH: Well, if you have to form a coalition – something rather alien to British democrats – you have to engage in compromises before you start out.

Stern: You do deals, do you?

SCH: I wouldn't call them deals. 'Compromises' I would rather say, and you have to engage in compromises every day thereafter. For instance, you may be strong enough to reject some candidate of your coalition partner for a certain ministry, but in the main, you will have to accept those persons whom your coalition partner presents as ministerable.

Stern: Did you always consult your cabinet colleagues prior to a decision and consider yourself bound by what they said to you?

SCH: Only two decisions of the German government during the eight and a half years of my Chancellorship were ever taken outside the Cabinet. Inside Cabinet, some people come to the Cabinet table much better prepared than others, and in most cases I was the best prepared. On top of that, I had a certain ability to argue, which leads to a situation where the Federal Chancellor, in the end, can be seen as having been the one who made the decision. By the German Constitution it's not necessary to have a Cabinet decision. The Constitution says that the Chancellor gave the directives of policy. I never in a formal way given a directive as I could have done. With two exceptions I always convinced the Cabinet.

Stern: What were the two exceptions?

SCH: One was the double-track decision, which I entered into together with the Foreign Secretary, but not with the Cabinet. They had to accept what we had decided, in conference with the British, the French and the American leaders. The other one was after Hans Martin, Schleier the Chairman of the Employers' Federation, had been murdered together with his policeman and his driver. I made the decision not to give in to the demands of the terrorists.

Stern: I want to look at this so-called double-track decision, where you called for the deployment in Europe of nuclear weapons of intermediate range, the so-called INFs, in response to Moscow's deployment of the SS20s. Now was it basically your idea that the Americans should supply Cruise and Pershing missiles to their European allies?

SCH: This is putting it a little bit too simply. In the first place it was not I who detected that the Russians were building the SS20 missile fleet, which I understood to be in the main politically directed against West Germany. It was detected by American satellites, but they of course shared their knowledge with their allies. I immediately understood this as a possible instrument to blackmail my country and to single out Germany from the rest of the alliance. And therefore, I asked my American allies to be included in their ongoing Salt 2 talks. Gerry Ford was willing to do so, Jimmy Carter was not willing to do so, which was the beginning of the differences of opinion which occurred later on to a greater degree between the Carter administration and myself.

Stern: But what was the point? Did you think that the Soviets would dismantle their SS20s, or was this a way of strengthening the European wing of NATO?

SCH: The main point was to enforce upon the Soviets the necessity to engage in negotiations for limiting this kind of missilery on either side by treaty and I said publicly already in '77 or '78 that the best outcome of these negotiations would be a zero solution on either side. I called it a double-zero option. It had nothing to do with strengthening the alliance. I didn't think that the Pershings and the Cruises were strengthening the alliance. I thought that they were a necessary counter force against the SS20s.

Stern: But you knew Brezhnev very well, you'd met him several times. Did you think that he would yield in response to this kind of pressure?

SCH: Yes I did.

Stern: But this decision of yours evoked a great deal of opposition on the Left of the Party, and I think in the Cabinet too.

SCH: Not in the Cabinet, no.

Stern: How did you deal with the opposition?

SCH: Well, by talking to them, by answering their questions, going to an endless number of Party conferences and making my point understood. It wasn't liked, but it was accepted. It was repudiated only after my Party and I myself had left office.

Stern: Looking back on the decision, do you think it was the right one?

SCH: Oh yes of course, and as you have seen the outcome was, in the end, exactly as I had thought the best possible outcome would be. We got to a double-zero solution in the end.

Stern: Of all the decisions you had to take as Chancellor, what was the most difficult?

SCH: The decision which cost me the greatest amount of moral persistence – taking great risks and not really knowing what the outcome was going to be – was to send an aeroplane full of armed specialists from Cologne first to Cyprus, then to Djibouti at the border between Africa and Arabia, and then to Somalia to regain another German plane that had been abducted by some terrorists – German terrorists in the main – full of totally harmless civilian passengers.

Stern: This was the hijacking at Mogadishu.

SCH: Yes, if it had gone wrong, which could have happened, we could have ended up with a hundred dead people. I was prepared to resign next morning, and this was the period during my time in office which cost me the greatest amount of energy.

Stern: Did you agonise about that? Did you have any sleepless nights?

SCH: Sleepless nights I never had, but it was an agonising experience, yes.

Stern: Did you ever entertain doubts about any of your policies?

SCH: Oh yes, oh yes.

Stern: ...or indeed your fitness for office?

SCH: Oh yes, oh yes, a thousand doubts, but I overcame these doubts a thousand times.

Stern: When people called you names, like 'Schmidt the lip'...

SCH: This is much earlier...

Stern: Yes, but did you just shrug it off, or...

SCH: Yes I did, yes, yes.

Stern: Was your view 'they can call me what they like, I don't care'?

SCH: Yes.

Stern: Over your career, you've held immense power, in the Defence Ministry, the Finance Ministry and finally as Chancellor. Now there's that famous phrase by Lord Acton: 'Power tends to corrupt'. Were you ever corrupted by power?

SCH: I don't know what Lord Acton, whom I do not know, meant by that phrase.

Stern: Can't power go to one's head?

SCH: Oh certainly it can.

Stern: Did it go to yours?

SCH: I don't think so. I was happy at being relieved from office.

Stern: Did you never get withdrawal symptoms, did you never feel very irritable at being no longer at the top?

SCH: No.

Stern: Wouldn't you like to be back at the top again?

SCH: No, not at all.

Stern: So what are the drawbacks of office?

SCH: The only regret I have about my period in office was that I didn't resign a year earlier.

Stern: Why do you say that?

SCH: Because then it would have been totally my own decision and not the decision of my coalition partner. I don't like situations in which my fate is being decided by others.

Stern: But if you don't want to go back into politics, would you still like to give advice ?

SCH: Lots of people come privately to seek advice. On the other hand I quit parliamentary life years ago and am quite happy to be out of the daily routine.

Stern: But did you quit it because you had to, or because you wanted to?

SCH: No, I didn't have to, I wanted to.

Stern: Have you achieved all the things you set out to achieve?

SCH: When I became Chancellor I did not set out to achieve a lot of great things. What I understood to be my duty then, having become Chancellor all of a sudden – not having planned for it at all – was to keep the ship on an even keel, and this is what I did.

Stern: Of all the leaders that you've met over the years, and you've met so many of them, whom do you most admire?

SCH: The man whom I admired most was Anwar Sadat, the Egyptian leader, a military man by profession, but also a peacemaker. If he had had somebody in Jerusalem or Tel Aviv like Moshe Dayan or like Golda Meir I think they might have been able to bring peace to a great deal of that region. He was a very religious man, deeply convinced that Judaism, Christendom and Islam did stem from the same roots; that all of us were sons and daughters of Abraham. All of us had been given the laws of God through the hands of Moses at Mount Sinai. From this belief he derived the insight that it must be possible to bring peace about between the three great monotheistic religions in the world and he believed this and lived up to this belief knowing very well that he was risking his life, which he lost in the end, due to his policies of peace-making.

Bulent ECEVIT

CHAPTER 3

Stern: Bulent Ecevit, you have been a poet and a journalist as well as a politician. And it is sometimes said that unhappiness is a spur to creativity. Is that true?

ECE: Well of course, if you are working in politics or fighting in politics for a cause you must be dissatisfied with the way things are going or with the system in your country. And if one may describe this as a sort of unhappiness your observation is certainly true. I also wrote most of the poems that I like personally during periods of extreme trouble and tension in politics. Otherwise I felt I would be lost in politics and alienated from myself. It was a sort of constructive escapism for me.

Stern: Were you unhappy as a child?

ECE: No, we had a very simple and happy family life. My father, who was a professor, was interested both in politics and writing and my mother was a professional painter, so the conversations at my home centred around politics, arts and literature and that was really educative for me. And, though I was the only child of my parents, I was not a child with problems.

Stern: What about as an adult? Can I ask Bulent Ecevit the journalist to profile Bulent Ecevit the man?

ECE: It's very difficult for a politician, or indeed anyone, to analyse oneself, but I'll try to. My characteristic as a politician I think is this: I am not interested in personal political power. I don't enjoy power. I even consider it as a sort of affliction that may distort one's mind and vision. But at the same time one has to hold on to power in order to achieve things. Yet I often give up my political positions. In fact, I have never been ousted from elected office. I always chose to resign when I thought I should, but I never gave up fighting. As a journalist, I suppose I would not consider this as normal, because usually the motive psychological force of a politician is attachment to power or positions of power, particularly in the east. I think it's seldom in the east that politicians leave their posts of their own will, although that's quite common in established democracies in the west.

Stern: So what do you want power for? Is it for Turkey? Is it for the world? Is it for yourself?

ECE: No, definitely not for myself. I said I do not enjoy power. I consider it even irksome or bothersome, leaving very little room for private life etc. And I have no personal ambitions. But there are certain causes for which I have the urge to fight and one has to have power to achieve things, but I rather like sharing power with the people and try to see to it that the power thus shared should not be used as a factor of coercion.

Stern: Someone once said that you were rather too nice to be a politician. What do you think they meant by that and was that a compliment or an insult?

ECE: Well, both I think. Usually, the kind of remark made politely by politicians to indicate my deficiencies as a politician. But I think I surprised politicians who thought like that when I took very challenging positions when I thought there was a need to do so.

Stern: But it's an awesome job you let yourself in for. Don't you have to be either very arrogant or a little crazy to want a job like that?

ECE: Well, I don't know. I don't think I have ever been arrogant, and it depends on the definition of craziness, but either one must have a very great passion for personal power or a great passion for a cause and I think I have the passion for a cause as a Social Democrat and democrat.

Stern: So what qualities did you think you could bring to the premiership?

ECE: I try to be a conciliatory person. I think that reconciliation and compromise are essential to make democracy work. Building up a consensus provides reliable grounds to tread on and one of the things I admire most in the Scandinavian social democrats is their ability to compromise with others when necessary.

Stern: Do you have to be intelligent to be a leader?

ECE: Well, I suppose so, although it doesn't seem very modest to say so. I think to be good in any job requires a kind of intelligence.

Stern: But intelligence in what sense?

ECE: Having judgment and the courage to take risky decisions.

Stern: But a risky decision may involve lives.

ECE: Yes, but you must weigh the possibilities. If the cost would be more lives unless you took the risk, then you have to take the risk.

Stern: What is leadership in your view?

ECE: I suppose an art. An art that one possibly has to be born with to some degree, although you acquire some of the qualities of leadership through practice.

Stern: Can I just ask you whether these are qualities which women can have as well as men?

ECE: Certainly. Why not? Women sometimes have a stronger will than men. And they can be more uncompromising and sometimes even ruthless, and what is interesting is that some of the strongest women leaders have emerged in societies where women socially and culturally have an inferior position, as in the east.

Stern: So why are there so few women leaders?

ECE: The life of a politician is very taxing; a politician does not have much time for his home. Yet if a woman is a housewife she has to look after the husband, the house, the children etc. So relatively few women have the possibility of participating in politics. But the fact that very strong and able female politicians have emerged in India for instance, or more recently in Pakistan, and previously in Sri Lanka, indicates that even in societies where women have a relatively lower position socially they can prove themselves.

Stern: People who criticise their leaders assume that leaders have great scope for independent action and that they could do otherwise. Now did you find that you were as much a free agent as your critics suggested, or were you constrained to a considerable extent by circumstances?

ECE: Of course every politician is constrained to some extent, and there are limits to the degree to which you can break through the constraints. But sometimes a leader, particularly if he has no personal ambitions, has to take the risk of challenging the constraints, particularly if he wants to introduce and promote a new movement, as I did when I was one of the persons who initiated the social democratic movement in Turkey.

Stern: How would you describe your style of leadership? When you took decisions was it with or without consultation?

ECE: I always consulted, but I didn't consider myself bound by the results of the consultation.

Stern: Well, if you didn't always listen to what people were saying to you, what about your democratic principles?

ECE: I have always kept in mind the problems and aspirations of the people at large, but I

29

don't think it is necessarily democratic to feel too much bound by the decisions and inclinations of the few politicians around you. What is important is that a political leader should not lose intellectual and psychological communion with the people.

Stern: When you had a coalition government you had to take some of your opponents into your cabinet, people that didn't always see eye-to-eye with you. Do you think that differences of view in cabinet are a help to good policy-making, or should you have people in cabinet that think as you do?

ECE: Well, it varies from situation to situation. If you are heading a single party government of your own, then of course you expect cohesion and harmony. But, if you are heading a coalition, compromise is essential.

Stern: Were you good at delegating responsibility?

ECE: Some of my former political friends wouldn't say so, but I think I always tried to delegate, yes.

Stern: So you didn't take all the decisions yourself.

ECE: No, but when it came to a hard decision that involved risks that I believed had to be taken, I didn't hesitate taking those decisions.

Stern: Did you ever turn to literature, poetry or philosophy when you were making a decision?

ECE: Yes, I always either wrote or translated, read poetry or philosophy at the most difficult periods of decision. During the second military intervention in 1971...

Stern: You're talking about the intervention within Turkish politics?

ECE: That's right, yes. My leader Ismet Inönü, whom I revered very much and to whom I had been very close, decided to compromise with the military to some extent and I refused to co-operate. I objected. So I resigned from my post as Secretary General and took a sharply critical line against the military intervention and against my leader's decision. I thought my political career had ended because I had alienated all the main forces in the country having left my post as Secretary General. But after a short while I realised that as a result the democratic left movement, which I had helped to start in Turkey, would be endangered. So I decided to continue fighting for the movement, but tried to refrain from challenging Inönü himself until one day at a public meeting, when I was trying to explain my complicated attitude, a worker took the microphone from me and he said "Ecevit, we are willing to take all the risks following you in your struggle, provided you promise that if need be you will challenge Inönü himself. If you are not willing to do that, please leave us alone". I thought for a minute and I said "Yes, I'll do it". But again, it was very difficult for me. Then I remembered *Bhagavad-gita*, which I had read many years ago, and I thought I could find a solution there.

So I re-read the conversation between Arjuna and Krishna. Arjuna had at one point led an army against his adversaries but on the battleground he realised that many in the opposing columns were his highly esteemed elders and friends, and he didn't have the heart to fight them. He said "I have no ambitions personally. I have no interest in victory. I would rather they should defeat me than that I should try to defeat them". At that point Krishna intervened – obviously Krishna represented one aspect of his conscience – and said "There are certain things that one must do. You can't get away from your responsibilities by refraining from action. What matters is that you fight in a selfless way, that you are not interested in the fruits of your victory if you gain victory, that you do it out of a sense of duty". As a result of that very interesting conversation Arjuna takes up his arrows and bows and fights. And that solved my psychological problem, and I fought and I'm afraid I won.

Stern: Given the numbers of military interventions, and the fact that you yourself were imprisoned by the military in the latest intervention, does that suggest perhaps a degree of political immaturity - that Turkey isn't ready for democracy?

ECE: Of course it's very difficult to make democratic roots in any developing or underdeveloped society and Turkey is a developing society. And it's not the immaturity of the people that causes the military intervention in Turkey, it is rather I would say the immaturity of the self-styled intellectuals in the elite classes. During the Ottoman history the Turkish people were to a large extent excluded from political participation. For instance, for over two centuries after the conquest of Istanbul there was not a single Turkish-born prime minister or Vizier. They were all appointed from among Christian renegades. The Turks, the founding nation, were legally free and could share the Sultan's power and limit it, but the Sultans wanted unlimited power so they found all sorts of means to exclude the Turks almost completely from administration and politics until the disintegration of the Empire. So, the people remained de-politicized. But there is definitely much greater attachment to democratic ways and attitudes among the masses in Turkey than among the majority of the intellectuals either on the right or the left.

Stern: What are the special problems in governing a country like Turkey?

ECE: Turkey is a rather complicated society. It is ethnically very mixed for historic reasons, and although nominally heading an empire for six centuries, the Turks were among the most neglected parts of the subjects of the empire. And because of the high rate of population growth, economic development must be rapid, yet this creates certain problems also.

Stern: I wonder if we can look now at perhaps your most controversial decision - sending the troops into Cyprus. How did you come to that decision. Were you responding to pressure, and if so from whom?

ECE: No, not to pressure, but to events. You see, the Turks in Cyprus had been very badly treated by the Greek majority for nearly two decades. From the end of '63 onwards they were subjected to periodic massacres, many of them had to leave their lands although they were farmers and remain in ghetto-like places for many years. They were deprived of possibilities of participation in the administration, in spite of the constitution, which was shelved by the Greek administration, and finally on 15 July 1974 the military junta in power in Greece at the time manufactured a coup in Cyprus which would certainly have resulted in the extermination or extradition of the whole Turkish population. Cyprus would certainly have been annexed to Greece, which would have caused irreparable damage to Turkish-Greek relations, and dictatorship would have been extended to Cyprus and would have been further entrenched in Athens (in the event of annexation). So, if we had not intervened, there would have been two great tragedies and the risk, the cost of the intervention, was minimal in comparison to what would have happened if we had not intervened as a guarantor power. It was certainly one of the most difficult decisions of my life because I hate wars and I love the Greeks. But I felt I had to take the decision.

Stern: Would the Greeks feel that you loved them?

ECE: I know that some know I love them. Others might not believe it, but I even wrote in my younger years a love poem to the Greeks, and by a strange coincidence, a few weeks before the action we had to undertake in Cyprus, a member of parliament in another party came to the rostrum and said, "Here is this man Ecevit, who had written a love poem about the Greeks, and is the Prime Minister now. How can we expect him to defend our rights?"

Stern: Can you remember how the poem goes?

ECE: *We become aware when we are homesick*
That we are brothers with the Greek.
One should see a native of Istanbul
Hearing a Greek song when abroad.

We swore at each other in the free manner of Turkish,
We drew daggers like enemies,
Yet love lies hidden in us
For the days of peace.

What if in our veins
It is not the same blood that flows?
From the same air, in our hearts
A crazy wind blows.

With the warmth of the same sun,
With the grace that the same rains bring,
Goodness surges in us,
In armfuls of spring.

From the same water and flavour
Our sins take their root.
Harmful and tasty as any drink, our vices
Are distilled from the same climate's fruit.

A blue magic between us,
A warm sea,
Two peoples on its shores
Equals in beauty.

The golden age of the Aegean
Through us will revive,
As with the future's fire
The heart of the past comes alive.

First their laughter
Touches your ear,
Then Turkish words
In Greek accent you hear.

Hear reminiscences
Of the Bosphorus;
You recall the raki
With cheer

And you feel homesick,
And you become aware
That you are brothers,
The Turk and the Greek.

Stern: And yet as a result of your decision of 1974 you were called a "second Ataturk" and "conqueror of Cyprus" and so on. Are you proud of titles like that?

ECE: No, no. In fact when, after our military action, my pictures wearing a military helmet appeared in Turkey on the buses and the coffee houses, I sent messages to all the governors that they should be taken out of sight. I didn't like those sorts of titles. I didn't do it for heroic purposes, you know. It was to save the lives of the Turks there and to ensure the existence of a separate state on the island.

Stern: Yet some people would say that as a result of this decision you have blood on your hands. How do you live with that kind of accusation?

ECE: No, I don't think so, because before the Turkish action in '74 there was continuous strife and conflict on the island. Not only the massacring of the Turks, but continuous conflict between Greek guerilla groups and the Greek people. Yet since mid-1974 there has been uninterrupted peace on the island, both between the two communities and

33

within the Greek community. If we had not intervened, bloodshed would have continued on immense scales. I felt desperate of course. I didn't like it at all. That's why when the United Nations pressed for a ceasefire I immediately accepted, although our coalition partners of the time strongly objected.

Stern: But you were in a position of power, which is presumably why you accepted the United Nations recommendation. You'd got what you wanted.

ECE: Yes, but I didn't want the conflict to continue. In fact, I gave one single military order to the army before the operations started: You mustn't open fire unless you are fired at. And they obeyed, although it was very risky for any army to do so. So I took every precaution that there would be as little bloodshed as possible. In fact, although the Turkish military action took place in mid-summer when Cyprus was full of tourists from all around the world, not a single tourist as far as I know was hurt as a result of the Turkish action.

Stern: Can you remember your mood at the time? Did you have sleepless nights?

ECE: Certainly, particularly the first two nights after the operation when I feared that some of those colonels in Athens might do crazy things.

Stern: Do you ever have any regrets about what was done?

ECE: No, as I said, I weigh it always in my conscience but I reach the conclusion that but for that action much greater tragedies would have occurred. You see, I did my best to prevent the second phase of the military intervention. We just needed security for the Turks on the island, so I suggested at the second Geneva conference, early August 1974, that a small part of the island, only 17%, should be demilitarized and turned over to Turkish transitory rule, under United Nations auspices, where Turks could live in security. Only when that was rejected did we have to continue with the military operation. But we checked ourselves. Two more days and Turkish troops could have conquered the whole island, but we just didn't want to do it.

Stern: But the island is still divided, and do you ever stop and say to yourself "I did that"?

ECE: Well before it got divided I made another proposal to the Greeks that there should be a confederation, that there should not be mass removals of population, but that was also rejected.

Stern: Can we turn to another aspect of Turkish politics, this time a domestic aspect, its human rights record. Now Turkey is often under attack from not only its foes but also some of its friends as well. Do you think Turkey's critics have a point here?

ECE: Yes, I think so, I am afraid. There may be occasional exaggerations certainly, but there has been torture and too many limitations on the possibilities of mass participation. But what makes me optimistic is that there has emerged in recent years a consensus in Turkey to get rid of the tradition of violation of human rights. Turkish society is becoming increasingly more open. It is the result of the need felt for introspection among the people. What's wrong with us? Why do we have so many military interventions? Why do we have so many violations of human rights? Before 1980, when constitutionally there was much greater freedom of expression in Turkey, there were certain social and cultural taboos, certain subjects which could not be debated for social reasons. All those taboos have been demolished in recent years. Everything, including the reasons behind the military interventions or religious fundamentalism or atavism, is now being freely aired and debated, and this makes me believe that thereby we can cure many of our problems in the field of human rights and democracy.

Stern: What should Turkey's friends do in this respect - exert open pressure on Turkey or pressurise behind the scenes?

ECE: During the military intervention, in spite of the fact that I knew I would be put in prison if I was outspoken, I was very outspoken to my European Social Democrat friends about the situation in Turkey. I never mince words, but when they asked me what line, what attitude, they should adopt I said "that's your problem. My duty is to tell those who are interested what the situation is in Turkey, but what policy you should follow, that's up to you". So, if you don't mind, I won't answer your question for that reason.

Stern: If there are countries - the Soviet Union, Turkey, South Africa, Israel, or whatever - whose human rights record a government disapproves of, should it go public and exert public pressure which could be counterproductive, or should it work behind the scenes?

ECE: No, no. As a democrat I believe in openness. The more public it is, the more effective it can be. In Turkey there was never a popular reaction against criticism from our friends in the West. But people do expect greater fair play. They expect the same countries to show as much concern about the extreme violations of human rights in Bulgaria for instance, against the large Turkish minority there.

Stern: You've had the power of life and death over people. Now you know Lord Acton's phrase "power tends to corrupt". Have you ever been corrupted by power?

ECE: I don't think I gave myself time enough to be corrupted, because whenever I felt it best to resign from positions of power I did so, as Chairman, as Secretary General, as Prime Minister.

Stern: Henry Kissinger once confessed that "power is the ultimate aphrodisiac". Does it have an almost sexual quality about it?

ECE: Well, as I said, I personally disliked personal power. I don't enjoy it. I regard it as a kind of bondage and as a freedom fighter I don't like bondages.

Stern: But you like an audience, don't you?

ECE: Sharing with the people, I would say.

Stern: All right, but didn't you enjoy the attention and the accolades?

ECE: No, not that.

Stern: The motorcades?

ECE: Definitely not. I don't even like being photographed, you know.

Stern: What about the frustrations then, the sacrifices. What's the worst of it?

ECE: Well, the routine of a political leader leaves one very little time for private life and for private interests and I have a lot of private interests. So, I had the longing sometimes to be in a place where I would not be watched, but I would be the watcher of other people.

Stern: I imagine that one of the frustrations of office is that you can be so easily removed from it, or in your case resign from it. What does it feel like the day after?

ECE: The feeling of freedom. Relatively speaking at least.

Stern: No withdrawal symptoms?

ECE: No. And good conscience that you haven't stuck to the position of power at all costs.

Stern: And yet you still want to be in politics?

ECE: I have always continued fighting.

Stern: Would you like to be back on top?

ECE: Well, that has never been my objective. What I want to do is continue fulfilling my contribution to the political movement to which I am attached, and what matters is that I should hold the position which is most suitable for my continued co-operation under changing conditions.

Stern: Who were the people who influenced you most in your political career?

ECE: Ataturk certainly was a great source of inspiration for me. Then I worked for many years very close to Ataturk's friend, close associate and successor Ismet Inönü. He was an influence on me. And also some thinkers who were not politicians. For instance philosopher Karl Popper, in his refutation of historicism and in his insistence that people should always question what is supposed to be the truth or reality.

Stern: Did you do that as a politician, did you question yourself? Did you question your own motives?

ECE: Well, whenever I had to take a decision I always thought in terms of what might happen if I did not take certain decisions or risks.

Stern: Were you ever uncertain, were you ever unsure of yourself in taking decisions?

ECE: There has to be an element of scepticism. If you are over confident then you can make mistakes easily.

Stern: Tell me why you admire Ataturk and Inönü so much.

ECE: Well, they did miraculous things. Not only during the war of liberation but changing to a modernistic society in a very brief time, and by initiating those reforms which would pave the way for democracy. In fact Ataturk during his lifetime tried to introduce a multi-party democratic regime twice but then thought, rightly or wrongly, that his reforms would be endangered with an early transition to democracy. But remember that Ataturk chose to work with a parliament - and a very critical parliament - throughout the war of liberation because he wanted to prove that the war of liberation was not being fought by the military in essence, but by the people and for the people. Then, at a period in world history when many leaders with no military background donned marshal's uniform, Ataturk took away his well-earned marshal's uniform when he became the President.

Stern: And who are the politicians you admire today?

ECE: Well, I admire the determined way, for instance, Benazir Bhutto has been able to come to office. I admire that not only for the possible personal or family reasons for which she gave the fight, but that she fought at the same time with the objective of democratizing her country. Also, I must express my admiration for Yasser Arafat. You know, a few years ago when the PLO was expelled cruelly from Lebanon everybody thought that the political career of Yasser Arafat had ended. But a stronger Yasser Arafat emerged.

Stern: Looking back on your career do you think it's been a success or not?

ECE: Well, you see, I have been trying to promote democracy and social democracy in Turkey. And they are both processes to which there is no end. So you keep working. If a person felt he or she had reached finally the objective of his or her efforts then the world would stop.

Stern: What's your proudest achievement?

ECE: I wouldn't talk about a single achievement, but the fact that even under the greatest obstacles I have continued to work and fight for what I believe to be good for the people.

Stern: And the most embarrassing thing that you've done? Something that you look back on and say "I wish I hadn't done that"?

ECE: It's difficult to say retrospectively, but I formed in the beginning of '78 a very shaky government with the inclusion of some independent members of parliament who had come from other parties. It was obvious from the beginning that with such a shaky and incoherent government I couldn't take steps in the way of implementing our social democratic programme, but I formed it because I believed that if we hadn't formed a government at that time Turkey might end up with a kind of fascist rule. There was at that time in office a so-called nationalistic front (and you can guess what that implies), and in order to put checks to the process I thought I had to form a government. But I paid dearly on account of it, personally and in the party, so sometimes I wonder whether I should have formed it. But I cannot decide whether I did the right thing or the wrong thing. Another thing about which I debate in my mind is this: during that shaky government in '78/'79, which I headed, the whole world was passing through an economic crisis and Turkey was particularly adversely affected by that crisis. There was terrorism, conflict and polarization, and government work and responsibilities were very heavy. During that period I chose to neglect my functions and tasks as a politician and concentrated, possibly too much, on state affairs. And I later reached the conclusion that a politician cannot afford to do that. It looks like the proper moral choice, but you have to remember that you are a politician before being a statesman.

Stern: When the history books come to be written, what would you like to be remembered for?

ECE: For what I did during the military intervention period in Turkey, because I took the risks of challenging the military rules, and criticizing the military interventions, and of course my contribution to initiating the social democratic movement when as Minister of Labour in the '60s I helped introduce very liberal and democratic labour rights and legislation - freedom to strike, collective bargaining and free labour unions.

Malcolm **FRASER**

CHAPTER 4

Stern: Malcolm Fraser, you've frequently been described as being rather aloof and disdainful. Is this how you see yourself?

MF: I can't comment on how I appear to other people because whatever I say is not going to alter the judgment that they have already made.

Stern: You are, of course, immensely tall. What are you, about 6ft 4, 6ft 5?

MF: Yes.

Stern: Some of the world's most authoritarian leaders – people like Julius Caesar, Napoleon, Hitler and Stalin – were of small stature. Do you think that their size affected their personality?

MF: Certainly. They would have wanted to be impressive, and if they were not tall they would have consciously thought, "what do I do so that I impress?".

Stern: I wonder if your height has affected your political personality? Do you for example see any parallels between yourself and General de Gaulle who was also blessed or cursed with being taller than most people around him?

MF: That's an interesting parallel which I hadn't thought of, but I doubt if the General ever had to think about how he was going to impress this audience or that.

Stern: But he too was regarded as aloof and disdainful, and I wonder if that goes with being tall?

MF: I think that it does in part, but it also can go with shyness and with preoccupation. If you are thinking about a certain thing and devote your full attention to it, it is very easy to miss other things that just fly by your shoulder.

Stern: Whether or not physique does affect personality, there is not much doubt that upbringing and childhood experiences do. Your childhood seems to have been pretty unusual. You lived on a remote estate, seem to have had almost no contact with other children of your own age and you didn't go to school until you were nine. Why was that, and what effects did this rather isolated, sheltered background have on you socially and intellectually?

MF: That wasn't entirely true. I went to a boarding school when I was nine at the beginning of the war. I had been to other schools, but I had pneumonia rather badly when I was five or six and my parents were obsessed with trying to have me, not unnaturally, in a healthy environment and out of a major city on a remote farm. I think that it contributed to shyness, to not easily being able to talk with other people, not easily being able to fit into a social arrangement with your peers.

Stern: When you started going regularly to school, were you able to make friends and keep up with the work?

MF: I worked hard, generally did pretty well in ordinary classroom activities, and could play tennis, cricket and rugby as well as other people around me. I don't think I made many close friends, but I still meet a lot of people from those days and count them among the people I like to see.

Stern: Yours was a wealthy and in some ways privileged background. Was it also political? Did your parents talk much about politics? Did they have political friends?

MF: They had political friends, and, remember, my grandfather had been a founding father of the Australian constitution. He had been in the Victoria upper house and then in the Australian Senate for nineteen years until he died. But ours wasn't a political household, though it would have been conservative in outlook.

Stern: So when did your interest in politics start?

MF: Probably in late school life, when I found that I could get in to Oxford. The question was what to study, and the choice was law or modern Greats – philosophy, politics and economics. I deliberately chose philosophy, politics and economics because I thought it was broader and had a wider compass than a legal education and so I suspect that there was a latent political interest at that time.

Stern: Had your parents and teachers said that you were born, as it were, to rule?

MF: Heavens no. People don't say that. Most teachers in my country would think that if somebody had been to Melbourne Grammar and to Oxford and came from a large grazing property, they would be totally unfit to rule.

Stern: But why did you want to go into politics? What were your ambitions at that time?

MF: I came back to Australia having seen what was happening to Britain in the early post war years which I thought quite disastrous in terms of British power, influence and position in the world. I could understand the social requirements for establishing a fairer society, but at the same time strongly opposed nationalisation, ever increasing government expenditure. In Australia we had a Labour government until 1949, which had tried to socialise, to nationalise the banks, which terrified a great part of the population. It was doing many quite extreme things. The philosophical and ideological differences between Left and Right in Australia were as great as in Britain at that time, and I felt strongly about the kind of Australia that I'd like to see and help build.

Stern: And the key to it was power, influence and prestige, was it?

MF: I think it would be a very barren exercise pursuing political power just for the sake of it, and while I can see that would attract some people it had absolutely no attraction for me. It was what you could do with that power, the values you could advance with that power, and if you couldn't advance some values that were worthwhile well then as far as I'm concerned, let somebody else do the job.

Stern: Well let us return to the period when you leave Oxford, with not a very good degree. A third class, yes?

MF: I didn't work hard enough in my last year.

Stern: You leave Oxford, you return to Australia and you plunge into politics and at the age of 25 you are elected as a Liberal MP for a seat in Western Victoria. Now you had had very little experience, and I wonder whether the fact that you were a wealthy son of a prominent family with political connections helped in your political advancement?

MF: No. It would have been a positive hindrance because in the customs and psychology of Australia, the person who was going to succeed in public life was a self made man born of totally impoverished parents, won all his education through scholarships (which were very hard to get in those days), and came to the top through sheer hard work, being of far above average intelligence and imbued with a desire to want to achieve. If somebody is born allegedly with some advantages, in political terms that is a hindrance – something that one had to overcome.

Stern: So you got into politics on your own effort, but when did you first begin to think that you might have leadership potential, that you might actually make a good Prime Minister?

MF: That would have been very much later. My general approach to any job in politics was, " do it as well as you can". The first job that I had was to turn what had for more than half its life been a Labour seat into a seat which at least was going to be secure for Fraser. Shortly after going into politics I got married and decided that travelling about a thousand miles each week between sittings of the parliament was rather silly, and so I moved to Canberra for the parliamentary sitting. All my colleagues said

41

"Bye bye Fraser, that is the end of you. You won't hold your seat". Well I increased my majority more than anyone else. That rather mystified them. Ten years after I'd been in the parliament as a backbencher doing a number of things on government committees, I went to Harold Holt, who was shortly to be forming a government, and said, "I've had a reasonable grounding, starting to have some parliamentary experience, and I want to know whether you think I've got the capacity to be a Minister in your government or not? If the answer is no then I will retire from the parliament and make way for somebody who I hope will have ministerial capacities. It is up to you." A couple of weeks later he asked me if I'd join his government in the one portfolio that probably terrified me more than any other, as Minister for the Army.

Stern: Why was that terrifying?

MF: Well I hadn't been in the services. I'd been the wrong age and I didn't really understand the mores and customs of the services and there would be a great deal I had to learn. I just sat down in the army headquarters for six weeks and didn't undertake any public engagements or make any speeches or whatever, trying to get to grips with things such as what the various badges of rank meant. (Rather important for a young Minister of the Army!). That led to other appointments. I don't think through any of this I ever consciously thought that I should try and become Prime Minister, though some people started to write about it, I suppose, in the late 1960s, early 1970s, especially as the party's fortunes started to wane.

Stern: What did you say to that?

MF: That I'll do whatever job I have at the moment as well as I can. At the end of the day, when Sir William (Billy) Snedden was leader of the party, people came to me and said, "it doesn't matter what you want, what you say, you can't stop us from making you leader of the party," and so things went on from there.

Stern: You didn't object to that?

MF: I didn't object to it, but I didn't initiate it.

Stern: But you'd had rows with two of your own leaders. One was John Gorton who I think you accused of "stubbornness" and insisting on "getting his own way".

MF: You have to relate that actually to the issues. One involved the call out of troops in Papua New Guinea, which was a reasonably serious act; and the other involved a series of personal relationships and what the office of Prime Minister was trying to do to one of the senior ministers.

Stern: You also quarrelled with Billy Snedden, and having said that you weren't going to stand against him, you did stand against him.

MF: No I never said that I wouldn't stand at any time. I had said I would support the leader, but the words that I used did leave the options open.

Stern: These rows then, were not part of a Fraser game plan for power?

MF: Not part of a Fraser game plan for a minute. The Gorton arguments were more about values and about the way in which the government should conduct itself than about actual policy issues.

Stern: What about the even more spectacular rows over your party's refusal to appropriate the funds to enable the Labour government under Gough Whitlam to run the country. Were you intending to bring his government down in 1975?

MF: When I came into office as leader of the Opposition in May of that year I would probably have preferred the easier choice of letting the government run on to the election, because it was a doomed government and had been scandal ridden. It had deceived the Governor General, the Queen's representative over executive council meetings, it had taken acts which would have been justiciable if they had ever been followed through and which would have been struck down in a high court. There were a number of personal ministerial scandals which involved ministers lying to the Prime Minister, and the Prime Minister as a consequence misleading the Parliament because he had been misled by his own ministers.

Stern: But the Government had a mandate to govern didn't it?

MF: Oh, what is a mandate? You see, this is where we come apart from the Westminster system. We happen to have a democratic Senate and our Senate is built on the lines of the United States' Senate, and quite deliberately so because the United States constitution was very closely studied by the founding fathers before Australians decided what should be in the Australian constitution. So you can't draw an analogy between our Senate and the current powers of the House of Lords. I'd be totally opposed to a hereditary or a Canadian style appointed Upper House having any significant power. But if it's a people's house as is the House of Representatives, and if power is shared between both democratic houses, then you have to get your budget through both houses, and if the Senate says, "no" and the House of Representatives says, "yes", the logical way to resolve that difference is to put the country into an election.

Stern: So you don't think that Gough Whitlam was right to feel aggrieved or cheated when the Governor General handed over premiership to you after you had made it virtually impossible for the Labour party to govern. Was that fair play?

MF: It would be fair play for a democratic majority in the House of Commons, or for people who changed allegiance because a government had done some terrible things in Britain, for example, to reject the budget of an English government would it not? What is the difference? I mean, the government has got to keep its majority to be able to get its budget through above all. If it can't get its budget through it can't, as the Australian government did, produce some phoney documents and say, "the banks must pay our bills". Quite unconstitutional! Lord Hailsham wrote an interesting little paragraph in the foreword to Sir John Kerr's book, saying that Mr Whitlam was really rather a lucky ex Prime Minister; all he did was to lose office and then the subsequent election, when the person who'd acted in the same way previously – was it Charles I or II? – lost his head.

Stern: At the end of 1975 therefore, you are handed the premiership and you are able to keep it for nearly eight years. What qualities do you think that you brought to that office?

MF: We brought an entirely different set of policies. Before President Reagan and Prime Minister Thatcher, we said what governments can do is limited; we have to cut government expenditure hard.

Stern: So monetarism was a key issue.

MF: I don't like that word because "monetarism" is taken to mean just one set of policies or one approach to government, and you can't govern sensibly if you have just a one-eyed view of the sort of policies you ought to pursue. We would have believed that the environment, women's issues, equal opportunities and education were important, so whilst we cut expenditure in many things there were some areas where quite deliberately we would have spent more.

Stern: You brought a philosophy to government; but what about your own personal qualities? What were they?

MF: I suppose whatever qualities were needed to persuade first, my own party to elect me leader after they have suffered defeat and humiliation and secondly, whatever qualities were needed to achieve by far and away the two largest popular votes in the history of Australia. You have to know where you are going, to be able to express your views clearly in ways that can be understood, you have to have a media that will at least give you a reasonably fair go and is owned by a great many people and not one who can determine this or that. You need a commitment, a capacity to stick with a particular course, you need to be able to persuade your own colleagues that what you are doing is right and at least to carry a majority of them, and that involves listening to them. You don't just come from on high and say, "this is the policy". You have to consult with your own cabinet, your own party, listen to other people in the community. Out of all this, build a policy which at least has the support of the majority of the nation.

Stern: Are you a good listener?

MF: I think so when I need to be. There are some people who think that I can't listen, but they just don't know the extent of the hours spent in listening in cabinet to one's colleagues or in listening to the Australian Council of Trade Unions when they are putting views.

Stern: Does leadership not also involve an element of ruthlessness as well?

MF: Oh yes. The sort of decision which was always uncomfortable was where you have to make a choice between a political colleague and friend and values which you think are important. One thing you have to understand above all of a leader is that if you don't uphold values which are important to the government, the country, to the community as a whole, nobody else will and values can fall very sharply.

Stern: So what is leadership, would you define it as an art or a skill?

MF: In the end I suppose it's something in that comes from within a person. Obviously leadership qualities can be developed, and people do need experience. You can't just take someone from an alien environment and say, " run a major corporation", "run the government","run the country". Experience and background in terms of the things that you have done are obviously important, but none of that is going to be enough unless someone has a lot of the qualities which are difficult to define except in terms of the capacity to make up your own mind, the capacity to listen, to persuade, to keep a team together in spite of whatever difficulties you might have along the way.

Stern: So the potential is there right from the beginning, and then you acquire certain skills on the job.

MF: Well most of them you have probably acquired before you become leader – as a minister or whatever. But no job is anything like the job of Prime Minister, where you have to be able to give full and total concentration to, say, twenty subjects a day. And with the parliament sitting you can't necessarily choose your own timetable. If a crisis comes up and you have to give a lot of time to it , you still have to do all the other things, or else work falls behind. So a capacity to work hard, but selectivity is also important. President Reagan once described Mr Carter in very apt terms. He was like a person who could describe all the pieces that went into making a car with great accuracy and detail, but he just didn't know how to drive it. Hard work alone is not enough.

Stern: Is that the difference between a politian and a statesman?

MF: At some stage people start to say so-and-so is a statesman, probably when he has stopped being a politician. Maybe it's something that comes when you have been out of office for a while. I would have thought that someone who governs their own country well, which after all is the real test, should deserve that accolade.

Stern: So a country like Australia, which some people see as being on the periphery of world politics, can produce statesmen. Would Robert Menzies be one of them?

MF: In my book certainly. He was by far the best of our Prime Ministers, and he also won Australia a reputation in the world which I think by and large was a very respected one. Because values and approaches have changed, the Menzies' years have lately come in for a bit of criticism, but you have to judge against what was relevant at the time. You can't make ex-post judgments about a government's behaviour and then say that's the judgment that should have been made in the middle 'fifties.

Stern: Are politics in Australia rather different from politics in Europe, since it is a long way from Europe?

CHAPTER 4

MF: It is a long way from Europe and the determining feature I suppose is its relatively small population in a large island continent. In some ways politics has been more personal. People expect to see the Prime Minister around, so that involves an enormous amount of travelling.

Stern: Is that another way of saying that in Australia perhaps the job of Prime Minister is not quite as lonely as it is in other countries?

MF: Well it's always been possible, generally because of the lesser need for security, to get out and to speak to the ordinary people and that is really what it is all about in Australia. But you can't prevent the head of government position being a thoroughly lonely one. From the nature of things you have to manage a team, you can't play favourites with people that you like or if you do you endanger your government, so there is a loneliness there that you just can't avoid.

Stern: You've picked out a lot of different qualities needed for leadership, the ability to listen, to persuade, to conciliate, to hold a team together and so on. These are presumably qualities women have as well as men. Why do you assume that so few women get to the top?

MF: I've often wondered in Australia why more women don't go into politics because my own political party, the Liberal party of Victoria, had a very advanced party constitution. On all the important committees of the party you had equal numbers of women and men, you had to have a country woman vice-president as well as a male one, you had to have a city woman vice-president as well as a male one, and so in terms of the organisation of the party one would have thought it was ideally placed to select women as good and able candidates. We have always had one or two notable women senators, but in the Lower House generally not. Though the idea of equal opportunity through all walks of life has pervaded society from the middle of the sixties onward, women representation is still not as good as it might be. We don't have many women standing for pre-selection in the party ballots, and when we do, I'm not at all sure that women vote for women as readily as they vote for men.

Stern: What does this tell you about the way that society is organised?

MF: I don't think that it tells you anything about the way society is organised. I think that it does say something about peoples attitude to each other.

Stern: You have talked about the importance of values. Who shaped your political principles and influenced your thinking? Or did you work them all out for yourself?

MF: Nobody works everything all out for themselves. Whatever you do is a product of not only your birth but all your own experience and there is no doubt my time in Oxford helped me to, I think, isolate the important from the unimportant – knowing that this document is not worth reading, having just looked at a bit of it, and being able to make the right judgment.

46

Stern: What is the value of a degree in Politics or, indeed, in International Politics? Should an aspiring Prime Minister take a course in one of these subjects?

MF: No, nothing is essential because all people are different. If someone hasn't got a degree maybe they can learn all they need to learn by reading and talking with people. There are no absolute rules.

Stern: As a Prime Minister you had to translate your values into policy. Now in domestic policy, you were constantly warning of the dangers of self indulgence, constantly preaching the virtues of self restraint. What was all that about?

MF: Again it needs to be put in the context of Australia in 1975/76. We had had a government which had increased government expenditure by 46% in one year and in two adjacent years by 23%. Quite plainly the economy was going mad, inflation was up to 19% at one point, wages blew through the roof. Australians had been led to believe that they could have it all and keep it all and not have to work quite so hard to keep it, and we had to do something to turn that around. So the basic requirement I suppose was to get the government's finances back into order and to have people's ambitions at least restrained.

Stern: Did you restrain your own ambitions? Were you a shining example of virtuous self-denial?

MF: I doubt if anyone fulfils ones own aspirations as well as he sometimes should. I took some decisions that were at the time described as extravagant which in context I think were necessary. There was one incident where the defense department bought two second hand 707 aircraft which had quite an extensive defense use, and defense wanted them. This was, however, an opportunity for the Labour party to say here was the Prime Minister, "just indulging himself". They did not know the full details of some of the security problems that we had flying internationally by commercial aircraft. In Singapore on one occasion everything was off-loaded from one aircraft that I and my party were supposed to be on and checked again as it was going on. A delay of many hours followed simply because a Red Guard person was seen in the vicinity of the airport. Now there is a limit to the amount of inconvenience or danger to which Prime Ministers should put other people in the international travelling community. Our decision, taken on security grounds, was seen as a good political opportunity to say that Fraser was "self indulgent". It would have been much easier to have just gone on flying commercial. But it was the right decision to have the aircraft.

Stern: Let's move to your foreign political aims. You had a reputation for not just being a cold warrior but also a merchant of doom. You were constantly making gloomy predictions about Australia being dragged into a third world war by Russia. Before that you thought it might be dragged into a war by China, and even Indonesia. Looking back over those years don't you think that you might have gone just a little over the top?

MF: I don't know what you've been reading.

Stern: Some of your critics.

MF: Some of my critics are not always particularly accurate. Again you have to put some of that criticism against the background of journalists who didn't entirely like Fraser because Fraser had destroyed their God – Gough Whitlam. I did make a speech in July/June 1976 about foreign policy, saying that if the Soviet Union wants peaceful co-existence it is time for the Soviet Union to give a sign or a signal and not just use empty and meaningless words. There was a great build-up of Soviet activity in the Indian Ocean and in the Pacific. They had continued to support Vietnamese activities – an anti-Chinese gesture as much as anything else – but it wasn't a peaceful move as far as our part of the world was concerned.

Stern: But the Soviet Union, which was expanding in this way, also had a lot of enemies didn't it? You mentioned China, there was militant Islam, there was the West and other enemies too, and at least four of them had nuclear weapons. So is it at all surprising that the Soviet Union should try to secure its interests, just as Australia, the USA, etc would want to secure theirs?

MF: The Soviet Union had nuclear weapons and there was only one country that could match it, and I don't really see the others' possession of nuclear weapons as posing a separate and independent threat to the Soviet Union. The West had not expanded its influence in the post war years, but the Soviet Union had, and under the Brezhnev Doctrine put down a hard and fast policy; once Communist always Communist, and anyone who challenged that in any part of the world really challenges the Soviet Union. I think that too many people up to the time that Thatcher and Reagan took office had been prepared to make excuses for the Soviet Union, saying that they had had a terrible history, they'd got enemies all around and therefore needed to have a very large army. But whenever the West reduced its expenditure on military armaments up to that time the Soviet Union spent more. They had done nothing up to the middle 1970s that indicated a firm determination to work for peaceful co-existence. Today's world is quite a different one, a more hopeful one.

Stern: So how did you arrive at your judgment at what Australia's national interest was? What were the criteria?

MF: Well you have certain documents you work from. There's a military document, the strategic basis of Australian defense policy, there is all the input from the departments of foreign affairs. Then you have judgments which inevitably have an element of subjectivity attached to them, and you have to be as constructive a player in our part of the world as possible. A priority was to repair the alliance with the United States because the Whitlam government had damaged this relationship in a very serious way. Another was to restore Australia as a credible financial nation, well run and respecting international financial institutions, which was something which under Mr Whitlam had not been done. Also to develop to an extent a new sense of independence or separateness from the old world. I believed that with the trade arrangements emerging in Europe and in North America, Australia's future, more than ever, was bound up with Asia. So, instead of coming

48

to Britain or Washington first I went to Japan and China, just as a symbol.

Stern: So your conception of what the national interest was was dependent to some extent on what you were advised by the foreign office, by the ministry of defense and on what former leaders of your country had done. Is that right?

MF: It depended on a whole lot of factors and your judgment of those factors at the time. For example, I established with the agreement of the Commonwealth as a whole regional meetings of the Commonwealth, in particular, what is called the South Pacific forum, which was Australia, New Zealand and a dozen or so very small, fragile Pacific island economies; but I wanted them if possible to rub shoulders with a larger group from South East Asia, India, Bangladesh, Sri Lanka. It was an odd mix, but to see how the interests of Indian villages in part coincided with the interests of small island states was quite an interesting revelation for everyone involved. It started to bring these small countries into the wider world community, and as a result of these early moves the Commonwealth has now established an office in New York which enables them to keep tabs on the law of the sea and on other things in the United Nations that affect them. Now, this was all part of Australia trying to play a more active and constructive role regionally in the area of greatest importance to us.

Stern: I'd like now to come on to your style of administration. Some of your critics have said that it was pretty authoritarian. Was it?

MF: I don't think it was authoritarian, and if the critics had listened to the long debates in the cabinet they wouldn't have believed so either. I never made statements on policy if I knew that that policy was up for grabs and going to come up for government discussion.

Stern: Did you choose a Cabinet that would let you get your own way?

MF: No I deliberately believed that one should choose a cross section of views from the party so long as the people chosen had the basic ability to contribute. Because I have a lot of views that other people don't have, I needed to hear the answers, or arguments against a particular line of action before making a decision.

Stern: You consulted, did you, before every decision?

MF: Well our Cabinet office would look at all the submissions coming in from ministers – the generators of Cabinet business – and say to me that they thought that these should go to cabinet committees because they were not of major importance, that those of greater importance should be taken by Cabinet – and for the most part I would accept that recommendation. The committees would take decisions binding on the Cabinet as a whole. I chaired the foreign affairs and the defense committee, and the major economic committee. But that against the background that Australia was in quite severe economic difficulty. But when ministers advanced their submission, whatever they wanted to argue for, it was debated in Cabinet.

Stern: Did the Cabinet or the committees ever persuade you to change your mind about anything?

MF: Oh yes they did, but I probably wouldn't have said what was in my mind until after the discussion. Often I would be changing my mind on an issue, and my cabinet colleagues wouldn't know. I tried quite deliberately on most instances to encourage other ministers to speak first on an issue before I did.

Stern: So you were like the chairman of the board?

MF: Yes, but you also need to know what is in the submission, and to have an idea of where you want to come out. I believed that you could best get the agreement of the Cabinet by allowing all to express a view and then if you see arguments being missed you put those arguments to them. I'd try and make sure that the discussion was a full one, covering the full range of matters relevant to a particular decision. However, if I thought Cabinet was likely to go strongly against what I believed essential for Australia, I'd maybe delay Cabinet discussion a little while and say "I'd like to come back to this because I've a strong view and I'll want to be convinced that I'm wrong, and I'm not at the moment". At the end of the day if I felt strongly about an issue, I was able to persuade Cabinet that I was right. It wasn't a question of ever laying down the law and saying "because I'm Prime Minister you've got to accept my view". I didn't like ministers who altered their own view because of what they perceived to be mine. I wanted people to speak their minds.

Stern: But why did your foreign minister Andrew Peacock say about you what you had said about John Gorton, namely that you insisted upon getting your own way and that you were not consulting enough?

MF: Well the short answer to that is that it wasn't correct. He was very fully consulted. It wasn't the first time he'd considered resigning. There were others which I hadn't known about and you really have to get into that in some depth, which involves his character and mine.

Stern: You've talked a lot about your political principles. Should leaders always stick to principle or modify them according to circumstance?

MF: It depends. I could conceive of a circumstance where something should be suppressed in the national interest, but such occasions should be as few and as far between as possible.

Stern: Did you sometimes suppress information?

MF: No not deliberately, but there are certain categories of information that you don't really want blurted abroad; but maybe there is a conflict of principles there. One that says that there are certain things relating to national security that should not be made public, which is in conflict with the principle that as much as possible should be public.

Stern: You talk about the dilemmas of policy . What was the most difficult decision that you had to take?

MF: Supporting the Camp David accords by sending troops to be part of the peace keeping force in Israel. Now it wasn't a United Nations operation and it was at a time when Israel had made its encroachment in the Lebanon, and politically I knew that it was going to be very difficult to take the decision. Other senior ministers were against an involvement, and after an initial discussion about it I just put it on ice for about six months. On the positive side, the Camp David accord was the best thing that had happened in the Middle East for a very long while and still is. But the trade minister was frightened of losing trade from other Middle Eastern states if we participated. But then President Sadat of Egypt was assassinated. My deputy Prime Minister, Doug Anthony, went to the funeral and I can remember ringing him when he was in Egypt saying, "look I think we ought to discuss the Camp David accords and the role we've been asked to play." He said, "Malcolm I think that we are going to have to participate". I don't think that he would have said that six months earlier. Then we had information from our soundings that if we did participate, it wasn't going to affect our trade one iota. Those concerns relieved, we were able to take the decision. It probably took six to eight months from the time we were asked to participate to the time in which we were able to participate.

Stern: You have held enormous power. You've been Army minister, Defence Minister, Minister of Education and Science and finally Prime Minister, Were you ever corrupted by all that power?

MF: I don't think so.

Stern: How did you avoid it?

MF: Well, if you see people trying to do things you think are wrong you make it plain that you are not going to have any part of it. For example, in the late '30s and early '40s people who funded the party determined far too much policy and attitude. Now Menzies broke the link in the Constitution of the party. The money wouldn't come through to him; he wouldn't contol its disbursement. I'm in favour of that approach absolutely. I didn't want to know if a company was asking for a change in policy, whether they were major donors or whatever.

Stern: Were you never corrupted in any other sense?

MF: I don't think so. I have no doubt that my political enemies would say that I abused power and pursued policies in many ways that were wrong, but there is a difference between having a legitimate debate about what is the right policy for the country and using power for corrupt purposes, to give a benefit to a company that your friend is chairman of. Nobody would have asked me for a benefit of that kind. They knew the answer they'd get.

Stern: Is there anything that you disliked about being in power?

MF: In retrospect I would say that I travelled too much around Australia, accepted too many engagements and probably allowed myself to get too tired at times, which is a mistake for any leader. Your own party is the most voracious user of a Prime Minister's time and I should have said, "no" to at least half the party functions I accepted.

Stern: After nearly eight years as Prime Minister, suddenly one day in March 1983 it was gone. How did you feel?

MF: Well I wasn't surprised, because the previous couple of years had been extraordinarily difficult.

Stern: You were close to tears, weren't you, when you appeared on television after you'd lost?

MF: Well that was at the end of an exhausting period. "Yes" the answer is. I don't make a habit of that. But even though it might have been expected, it was a reasonably traumatic experience. I really did believe that the policies under which Labour went to the election would be absolutely disastrous for Australia and my concern was for the country. But by the grace of God, Prime Minister Bob Hawke and Treasurer Paul Keating, the party has not really followed the policies in which it went to the election. Almost immediately the language and the rhetoric of economic management, for example, was the language and rhetoric that Fraser had used eight years earlier, That was miraculous.

Stern: So you don't need to go back into Australian politics, Bob Hawke is doing it for you?

MF: The Labour government is doing some things that I'd do and quite a number that I wouldn't, but that is by the way. I'm out of politics, it's not a practical option, and I don't see anyone asking Malcolm Fraser to go back. But, remember, I was actively involved in politics for 28 years, and that is a fair chunk of your life. You asked me earlier if there was any part of politics I didn't like. The main reason I wouldn't want to be part of it again is that so much of the political debate in Australia seems to be trying to demonstrate that so-and-so is not a fit and proper person to be in the parliament, to be a minister, Prime Minister or whatever, and that really is very unpleasant. There was one occasion when somebody came into the parliament and made claims about me which I thought were outrageous, and I just walked out of the parliament. Any reasonable editorial the next day would have said how outrageous for anyone to make these claims without a shred of evidence. Instead they said it was outrageous that Fraser didn't immediately prove his innocence. You can get too much of that.

Stern: You've held so many political jobs. Are there any other posts that you would like that you haven't yet had?

MF: There would have been an element of passion with my involvement in Australian politics and over a long period. But today I'd sooner live quietly on my farm with my wife Tammy, who has always been tremendous support. If there is passion involved, that is where the passion lies. Intellectually there is one position I believe I could do reasonably well. Two or three years ago I was asked, if Sonny Ramphal doesn't stand again would I make myself available for the Commonwealth? I spoke to Bob Hawke, and about a year ago he said, "if you want your hat thrown into the ring we'll do what we can to support you". So I did and he has.

Stern: Looking back on your career what is your proudest achievement?

MF: I wouldn't want to pick on a particular example. I want people to say in retrospect that Australia was well governed in his time.

Stern: And your greatest folly?

MF: There are so many I couldn't possibly name one.

Edward **HEATH**

CHAPTER 5

Stern: Edward Heath, you seem to have had two consuming passions in your life, music and politics. Do you think that there is any logical connection between the two?

EH: No I don't think there is, even though the great pianist Paderewski became Prime Minister of Poland and Helmut Schmidt, who was Chancellor of Germany, plays the piano. When I was once asked how I could combine politics and music given that politics is reality and music is fantasy, I said, "You really must get it right to begin with. It's the politics which is the fantasy and the music which is the reality".

Stern: Is it important for a leader to have an escape like music or art?

EH: I don't regard it as an escape, but I think it's very important that leaders should have a wide variety of interests. If you are just a politician and nothing but a politician, you gradually drive yourself into the ground. You become very inward looking, very narrow-minded and then you don't look after the electorate. But if you've got other interests, you come back to problems with a fresh mind and you can serve your electors much better than you could otherwise.

Stern: Where did this interest of yours come from? Was yours a musical family?

EH: It wasn't musical in the sense that Mozart's father was a professional musician and Bach had brothers and sons who were musicians. On the other hand, my mother and father both wanted to encourage me in music and my brother as well. He became a violinist whilst I was a pianist.

Stern: But your parents weren't very well off, and yet they bought this piano for you and paid for you to have piano lessons. That must have been quite a sacrifice, mustn't it?

EH: Yes it was, and I was very grateful to them for having made the sacrifice. I remember so well the day we went to buy the piano. We went over to Margate to a shop called 'Bobby's' and I think it cost £44, which we paid for in 24 monthly instalments.

Stern: Does that suggest that you were rather spoilt as a child?

EH: I don't think so, because the discipline of becoming a pianist was really quite strict and often I would have much preferred to have been out in the evenings, swimming or playing tennis when in fact I was practising scales and arpeggios.

Stern: What about politics? Was yours a political family?

EH: It wasn't at all. My father, I think, would have described himself as a Liberal. We certainly had the 'News Chronicle' as our paper, and a look of abhorrence would come over his face if anyone ever mentioned 'The Daily Mail'. I became interested in politics at school, very largely through a debating society. I've always enjoyed debating and arguing with people.

Stern: It is one thing to be interested in politics: it is another to want a political career. Were you interested in that even before you went to university?

EH: Well I became seriously interested in politics towards the end of the war, not in a party sense but in a general sense: that we couldn't allow Europe to tear itself apart again. If we were going to survive then we ought to do something about it after the war.

Stern: So you went into British politics in order to change European politics?

EH: Yes but also because of my views about domestic politics. You see at Oxford, where I was an organ scholar, I became chairman of the Conservatives, chairman of all the university Conservative associations and President of the Union, which is a political debating society. During the famous Oxford bye-election in 1938 after Munich, I joined those who wanted a common front against the (pro-appeasement) Conservative candidate, Quintin Hogg.

Stern: I am not quite sure, though, why you are Conservative, given that in the thirties you were against appeasement and also against privilege?

EH: Because I believed above all in freedom. The socialists wanted a state-orientated system, which I believed interfered with freedom, and so for me the choice was really to support a Conservative party, but to move it away from a Chamberlainite policy, and of course there were many people who wanted to do the same at that time – Churchill, Eden, Macmillan, Duff Cooper. These were the people who were giving the lead for the new Britain which was to follow after the war.

Stern: Now you became a Conservative member of parliament in 1950. How did this come about? How did you actually get into politics?

EH: After the war I took the Administrative Civil Service examination and passed out at the head of the list, which had the advantage that later on in life I could always say to the Permanent Secretary, "Now, you behave, because if I had wanted to I could have been in your post"; but I found that I couldn't get anything done in the Civil Service, so I finally decided to leave it and try to get a seat in parliament. I had to fight the 1950 bye-election against an existing Labour member, but I won by the very narrow majority of 133.

Stern: Once on the political ladder were you determined to get to the top of it?

EH: Well, I wanted to achieve a number of things and you can only do that by getting into some position of power and authority, and that means becoming a member of government. I had been in the House less than a year when I was invited to become a whip. We were in opposition, Mr Churchill was leading and a political friend advised, "Wherever you find a bottom rung put your foot on it and move up". So I said, "All right, I'll become a whip."

Stern: But when did you start thinking to yourself that you might make a good Prime Minister?

EH: I didn't really think about that very much in those days. In fact I don't think I thought about it at all. I was really far more interested in foreign affairs and becoming Foreign Secretary. I remember, in 1938 when the bye-election came about in Oxford, they sought invitations from people who wanted to become the candidate and I sent my name in. I was just over 21, and when asked why I wanted to become the candidate I said, "Well I think that Lord Halifax is a very bad Foreign Secretary and that I 'd make a very much better one". They didn't take my advice, but afterwards when I was in the House I was really far more interested in foreign affairs than I was in thinking about Number 10.

Stern: But you didn't come into Number 10 by accident. You must have had ambition?

EH: Of course I had ambition, but it was concentrated in different places in different times. While chief whip what I wanted to do was not just to hold the party together but also to influence the Prime Minister of the day on policies which I thought were the right ones for the country. Because I had a deputy whip who was very good at getting the votes I was able to spend a considerable amount of time with Anthony Eden and Harold Macmillan, influencing them on policies. Afterwards, when Macmillan asked me what I wanted to do in 1959 I said, "I'd like to become Minister of Labour, because we have very many troubles on that front; but if you do send me there I'll want to have five years – a full parliament – in which to do it", and he agreed. But, after only ten months, he took me away and put me in the Foreign Office, asking me to carry out the first negotiations for our membership of the European Community. Well that was something that I did want to do. After all, my maiden speech in the House of

Commons in 1950 June 26 was a plea to take part in negotiations to create the European Coal and Steel Community – the first of the European communities. But negotiating to enter the European Community was really a full time job and it was very difficult to concentrate on other things.

Stern: Are you saying that you became a Prime Minister with reluctance?

EH: No. What I'm saying is that this developed stage by stage. After the Foreign Office I went to Trade and Industry and I asked Lord Home to add to it Regional Development because there were parts of this country which had never really had a fair deal and I wanted them to get it. This gave me an opportunity of producing the plan for the North East which led to an era of much greater prosperity in the North East. We did the same thing in Scotland, and we'd started to do it in the North West when the 1964 election came along.

Stern: But then you became leader of the party and in 1970 your party won an election and you became Prime Minister. What qualities do you think that you brought to the Premiership?

EH: This is a very personal question isn't it? I think first of all that as a shadow cabinet we had planned what we wanted to do, and how it could be implemented. So when we came to government we were able to sit down straight away to work on the reforms which we wanted to bring about.

Stern: So foresight would be one of them, and planning and thinking ahead?

EH: Oh undoubtedly yes, and more and more as I come to consider these things I think taking the long term view. The problem with so much of the West today is that it is taking a shorter and shorter term view. The United States takes a three month view; and here we just take a three second view. Well, you can't be successful in those circumstances, and this is the contrast between the United States and ourselves with the Japanese. The Japanese always take a long term view – 12 to 15 years – and that is the basis on which one ought to plan.

Stern: What about qualities like flexibility and tact and sensitivity? Are these important for leadership?

EH: They are very important indeed if you believe in our form of Cabinet government, which is that all these things are thrashed out by the Cabinet and you reach a consensus which is then going to carry the policy through.

Stern: So what is leadership?

EH: There are some people who would say either you are a leader or you are not a leader. I think that that is an over-simplification. People develop their capacity for leadership as they go along, but there comes a limit to that capacity for development. You can see people in positions of whom you can say, "He can do this very well, but it would be a mistake for him to go any further. It would be over-promotion and end in disaster."

Stern: How did you go about selecting your Cabinet? Did you choose people that were going to agree with you?

EH: No. Not at all. If you look at the Cabinet of '70 to '74 from Quintin Hailsham, the Lord Chancellor, to Lord Home, as Foreign Secretary, (Sir Alec Douglas-Home as he was then), Keith Joseph, Reggie Maudling, Tony Barber and his attitude towards the economy, it covered a very wide range.

Stern: And of course Margaret Thatcher.

EH: Yes, Margaret Thatcher.

Stern: How did you come to choose her as Secretary for Education?

EH: Well she had been in the Shadow Cabinet in various fields and I thought that education gave her the best opportunity, and of course, she did a number of important things. She was the first Education Minister to bring the National Union of Students into consultation over everything we did in education. I agree that I suggested it to her, and it worked very satisfactorily. From the point of view of schools organisation she created more big schools than anyone else has done in the history of this country.

Stern: Withdrawing free school milk. Was that her idea or yours?

EH: That I think was part of the general policy. The other problem, of course, was charging for museums, which I've always believed is a sensible thing to do. As a musician, if I want to go to a concert, I pay. Not very much perhaps, after all a lot of my orchestral education came from going to the promenade concerts and in those days we paid two shillings a night. I've never understood why people who want to look at pictures or anything artistic or historical shouldn't also pay a small amount. But it aroused such fury that I agreed it should be dropped.

Stern: You've had many disagreements with Margaret Thatcher since she became Prime Minister. Did you always see eye to eye when she was in your Cabinet?

EH: Not always. No.

Stern: Did you see her as a future Prime Minister?

EH: I don't think so, no. I don't think that we thought in those terms as far back as 1970.

Stern: Or party leader?

EH: No. I must make the point that we didn't spend our time thinking and talking about these things. Such questions just didn't arise.

Stern: I'd like to ask you about delegating responsibility. Was that something that you were good at doing?

EH: I used to delegate a great deal of responsibility. You appoint people whom you trust to do a particular job and you let them get on with it. We had the advantage that we'd all agreed on our manifesto and on what we were going to do, and everybody understood what was happening.

Stern: Did you always consult them before you made a decision?

EH: Oh yes, of course.

Stern: Did you consider yourself bound by what they said to you?

EH: It depended what the matter was, but in general, yes.

Stern: So you were sensitive to the views of your colleagues. Were you sensitive to the views of the people who had elected you? I mean did it matter to you that the public remained indifferent or even hostile to the European idea to which you were so committed?

EH: Well they didn't remain hostile. You are quite wrong on that. Perhaps it was too long ago and you weren't born at that time.

Stern: Perhaps I was.

EH: There was very strong support for membership of the European Community. After all, when we had the final vote we had a majority of 112, whereas our own majority as a government was only just 40.

Stern: But your own party was split. The Labour party was split. Even the Liberals were divided.

EH: In our own party I think that we had 12 out of 300 odd who didn't support us. Well that is negligible. You can't say the party was split. I'm trying to think if there is any issue on which you had everybody absolutely agreed on everything. It never happens. The Labour party was split, and they showed that because they insisted on having a whip. We had had a free vote, so you can't say that our people were forced to vote for it.

Stern: Was it really a whole hearted commitment?

EH: Yes it was, absolutely.

Stern: You don't think that it was *faute de mieux*?

EH: No, no.

Stern: So what about things like interest groups? Did you take any notice of those? Were there any particular interest groups or lobbies that were important?

EH: Well I don't think that there were interest groups or lobbies in the way that they operated in the United States, and I don't think that we ever felt that because a particular member had somebody lobbying for a new road or port or something that they necessarily had to be satisfied. That's not how the system works, but if you take an interest such as agriculture, well the Conservative party until recently had always recognised that it is very important to this country and the views of people engaged in it are also important and ought to be taken notice of.

Stern: Of course, one interest group – the miners – with their prolonged strike pretty well brought down your government in 1974. So what are the special problems in governing a country like Britain?

EH: As far as the miners were concerned, we had a general election in which the electorate gave us more votes than the Labour party, but under our system we got fewer seats.

Stern: Does that mean that you believe in proportional representation?

EH: Well, on all logic, proportional representation is a better system, yes. So it wasn't actually the miners who brought us down. What happened was we didn't get the support of the electorate for carrying on a policy which was being fair to all sections of the community. But when you talk about special interest groups in general, I think that they have far less influence in this country than they do in some others.

Stern: Earlier on you were talking about consensus. What sorts of decisions are there that only a leader can make?

EH: Very very few. You see, under our system we have a Cabinet committee system and most committees are presided over by other cabinet ministers and not by the Prime Minister, though the Prime Minister will probably preside over the Defence or the Foreign Affairs committee. True, the organisation of the committees depends on the Prime Minister, and he can arrange what committees he wants, but I've always believed that the objective of a committee was to reach agreement over as broad a front as possible, and it's then reported to the Cabinet. If any Cabinet members want more information they get it in discussion and if they want to object they can object; but one shouldn't accept as normal that a committee disagrees and refers it to the Cabinet for decision.

Stern: But did you not have some hobby horses that you wanted to ride?

EH: I don't think I've ever had hobby horses. What I found was that having delegated to committees I expected them to settle most of the problems, but I could see if there was something big, like the decision to suspend Stormont in Ulster, that was bound to come to the Cabinet, and we had to discuss it several times in the Cabinet. But on those occasions it is the job of the Leader of the House of Commons, Leader of the House of Lords and the two chief Whips to keep the Prime Minister and the Cabinet informed about the feeling of the party in both houses, because there is no point in surging ahead with a proposal if you are not going to get the support of the members in one or other House.

Stern: When you became Prime Minister did you have a role model in mind?

EH: No, I tried to work out for myself what I thought was the best way of operating. I'd served several Prime Ministers – Churchill, Eden, Macmillan and Home – and I like to think that I'd learnt a great deal from them. But each was unique. Churchill could do things other people couldn't; in foreign affairs Eden could do things other people couldn't; in economic affairs Macmillan could do things other people couldn't. I had to learn the hard way as to how use my own abilities and knowledge and experience in handling the Cabinet.

Stern: Your political career spanned the fiasco of Suez, when the British and French were obliged to call off what was effectively an invasion of Egypt, to the successful negotiations to enter the European Economic Community. How do you calculate that elusive concept that we call the national interest?

EH: The national interest is always bound to be a matter of judgment. The first thing that I should say is that you mustn't believe that the national interest and the government's interest are always the same thing because they are not, and when a government gets in the position of thinking that they are, it is very dangerous. A government is bound to try to take an overall view of the interests of all the people in the country. Here I think a knowledge of history is invaluable because you can reflect on previous episodes in history. None of them are exactly the same, but you can learn from similar occasions, and a knowledge of world affairs shows you how some governments have managed to achieve their purposes and others have got into trouble. So the broader one's knowledge the better.

Stern: Yet in going into Europe, as you were keen to do, you were going against the tide of history. I remember Mr Gaitskell, who was then the leader of the Labour party, saying "Are we to throw away a thousand years of history?"

EH: Yes it was a very silly remark. He may already have been ill at the time or he wouldn't have made it, and of course he was born in India and that probably had an effect on him, and he was a Socialist. Well, you say I was going against the tide of history. But the whole tide of history since 1940 had been going my way. In 1940 Churchill offered to France a common unity. He called it "an indissoluble unity". Well, when Churchill talks about "indissoluble unity", it means that you become one nation, one parliament, one government, one Prime Minister, one financial policy, one defence policy, one unity. If the French had been in a position to accept it in 1940 then the whole course of the war might have been different.

Stern: But as against that there is the British tradition of no permanent alliances.

EH: But that wasn't our position. These are very odd things that you say. We had an alliance with Portugal since 1372 and we've always regarded the Commonwealth as an alliance, and the colonial empire as being a polite form of alliance. And at times of difficulty we always formed an alliance. In 1939 we formed an alliance and it was because we had an alliance with Poland and France that we went to war.

Stern: But Britain also had a tradition of "splendid isolation".

EH: No that is the United States. You are getting mixed up between the two sides of the Atlantic. We've never had a tradition of "splendid isolation". Our history has always been based on the fact that, as Kissinger once pointed out to me, we always joined up with the weaker power or group of powers in Europe against the stronger powers. That wasn't "splendid isolation" at all. I remember having a discussion with Henry Kissinger about the war between India and Pakistan, and he said that we were wrong to support India which was also supported by the Soviet Union because India was the stronger power. He had supported Pakistan and China because they were weaker, and that was really what Britain's policy had always been. But I had pointed out to him that we never supported the weaker power when we thought they were going to lose. Well, Pakistan and China lost, so we were right. No I think that you have got a bit mixed up there.

Stern: People say that you were keen on the integration of Europe because the other major props of British policy – the Commonwealth and the "special relationship" with the United States – were beginning to disappoint. Is there any truth in that?

EH: No, I don't think that we visualised in 1946 when Churchill made the Zurich speech and talked about a United States of Europe or in 1948 at the Hague conference that formed the Council of Europe, that we were going to lose the whole of the colonial empire. The Dutch and the Belgians and the French realised it earlier than we did, but at the end of the 50s this began to happen but by that time three communities existed. Our trouble was we hadn't got into any of them, and then of course when the colonies became independent countries they shopped around quite naturally on their own and nobody could blame them. In the meantime Australia, New Zealand and Canada still had their trade with us which had been based on the Ottawa agreements of 1931/32 and they did extremely well out of it and we didn't do so well. That is where the adjustment was necessary when we went into the European community.

Stern: I would like to turn to another of your foreign policy initiatives when you were Prime Minister. The decision to resume arms sales to South Africa after the embargo by Labour. Was it worth antagonising a good deal of the Commonwealth in order to send a few helicopters to Pretoria?

EH: Well, what we did was to say that we wouldn't sell anything to them which could be used for aggressive purposes either externally or internally as far as South Africa was concerned, and that was a perfectly reasonable decision to take. The Commonwealth countries, or a lot of them, were, of course, hostile to this, particularly southern Africa, but one couldn't possibly have a situation in which Britain was just being told where to go and what to do by the remainder of the Commonwealth countries.

Stern: Perhaps we might move on to a policy in which you seem to have made, if I have understood it rightly, something of a U-turn. When you were in opposition, you were bitterly critical of the Labour Government's decision to remove British troops from the Gulf, from Singapore and so on and yet in office you didn't reverse the Labour decision as you had pledged to do. Why did you make the initial criticism and then retreat?

EH: No, we did reverse the policy, and we carried out our defence arrangements with the members of the Gulf; and the same applied to the Far East. The first thing that Lord Carrington did when I appointed him Secretary of State for Defence was to go out to the Far East and arrange with Australia, New Zealand, Singapore and Malaysia a common defence policy that went on for as long as they wanted it. So it is wrong to say that we made a U-turn in that respect. In the case of Iran, the Shah said that he'd now based his policy in the light of the Labour Government's decision to leave the Gulf and he couldn't change it. But we said we would help those states in the Gulf which wanted our help, and we did.

Stern: Can we turn to a decision closer to home. The introduction of internment without trial for alleged terrorists in Northern Ireland. Was it on reflection a wise decision and did you have any qualms about making it?

EH: Well, it wasn't our decision. It was the decision of the government of Northern Ireland which had been running the country ever since 1921, and we felt that we shouldn't try to interfere in their affairs. At this time, if you remember, it was very soon after the outbreak of terrorism in Northern Ireland. But looking back on it, it was an unwise decision by the government of Northern Ireland. We didn't realise at the time how out of date all their records were and how incompetently it was going to be carried through, but it emerged very quickly that all sorts of people had been interned who really were no risk at all, and that was one of the factors which lead us to intervene. We were quite prepared for the government of Northern Ireland to go on running its own affairs, except for defence, security and dealing with terrorists. The Northern Ireland Prime Minister said he wasn't prepared to accept that: it was all or nothing, and that left us with no alternative but to say, we'd have to take over the whole show.

Stern: Since leaving office you seem to have devoted perhaps more time and energy to North-South issues than you did before. Did you, as one of your friends has suggested, have, as it were, a sudden conversion?

EH: Not in the least. In 1964 we had the first UNCTAD conference in Geneva – the United Nations Conference on Trade, Aid and Development. And I led the British delegation which in fact spearheaded the proposals for setting up the permanent UNCTAD and also the measures which were carried through. So I'd been doing this long before I became Prime Minister.

Stern: During your career, you've held immense power, the power in some cases of life or death. Now, remembering Acton's famous phrase, that power tends to corrupt, were you ever corrupted by power?

EH: I don't think so. I wasn't there long enough. But I think there's great force in what Acton said. What he really said, of course, was that "absolute power tends to corrupt absolutely." That tendency is undoubtedly to be observed.

Stern: Does it go to one's head?

EH: It may do.

Stern: Did it go to yours?

EH: We wouldn't know.

Stern: Did you enjoy the trappings of office, the applause, the attention, the accolades and so on?

EH: Well, it is something which you come to accept, isn't it? It is very pleasant, but it's not the real purpose of life.

Stern: Does having that kind of power involve sacrifices?

EH: Yes, in some ways it does. There are a considerable number of things which always have to be done and you can't say, "Well, I don't feel like doing this today". So to that extent, it is a burden, I suppose. And you can't expect to have any real private life. In some ways one gets less private life here than the President or the cabinet ministers of the United States do. When I'm over there I'm often invited to lunches or dinner parties where there are very distinguished members of the Press. Everybody discusses everything perfectly freely and nothing is ever mentioned outside. You can't do that in this country.

Stern: Did you realise at the time that one of the penalties you were going to pay was that you were going to be shadowed by policemen for perhaps the rest of your life?

EH: Well, one doesn't think about these things beforehand, and then again, nobody thought that we were going to have terrorism in Ireland for more than twenty years. That's the tragedy of this situation.

Stern: I imagine that one of the frustrations of office is the comparative ease with which you can be removed from it. Can you remember what your thoughts were as the removal van arrived at No. 10 Downing Street to take away your belongings after you had lost the election?

EH: Well, I wasn't there to watch it because I'd already left.

Stern: How did it feel?

EH: Well, obviously it was a tremendous shock and I had nowhere else to go: a friend very kindly lent me a flat.

Stern: Did you begin to get withdrawal symptoms?

EH: Well, I never know what withdrawal symptoms are.

Stern: Well, did you get very irritable?

EH: I don't think so, no. There was an enormous amount to do in reorganising ourselves as an opposition.

Stern: Since you've left office, you've crossed swords many times with your successor Margaret Thatcher. Why are you so angry with her: is it her politics or her manner that annoys you so much?

EH: I never discuss the Prime Minister.

Stern: Nowadays you seem to be more popular with the opposition parties than with your own. Does this worry you?

EH: Not in the least, no.

Stern: Are you amused by it?

EH: Amused? Um, yes, I think we are amused.

Stern: Since you disagree with many aspects of government policy, do you still consider yourself a Tory?

EH: Oh yes, very much so.

Stern: You're not a closet Social Democrat?

EH: No, not in the least.

Stern: Would you like to back on top? Does Britain still need you?

EH: One would always like to have the opportunity of carrying through one's policies and trying again to achieve one's objectives. But there's no point in spending all one's time bemoaning the fact. The thing is to get on with it, and that's what I've done.

Stern: What are the objectives that you've not been able to achieve?

EH: Well, I want to see us further and further in unity with our colleagues in the European Community. I want to see that prosper, I want to see us get an economy in this country which is really strong and has got advanced technology, instead of having an enormous balance of payments deficit, and over two million people unemployed: all of these things I want to change.

Stern: Looking back on your career, has it been a success or a failure?

EH: Oh, that's for historians to judge.

Stern: And what do you think they will say?

EH: Ah, this is one of the problems. I shan't be there to read it.

Stern: What do you see as your proudest achievement?

EH: Well, I suppose historians will say, the day he brought Britain into the European Community, because we're there for the rest of history and it's part of the development of the world in its new form.

Stern: And what do you see as your greatest mistake?

EH: Well, I know what it was, but I won't discuss it publicly.

Stern: Can I ask you whether there's a kind of trade union of leaders, because you got to know Mao Tse Tung very well, and every time you came back you'd say that he was fit and well, and yet we discovered afterwards that he was not fit and not very well. Now, why did you do that? Were you protecting him?

EH: Yes, I see no reason why one shouldn't.

Stern: And you weren't alone in doing that, Nixon did the same, didn't he?

EH: I never actually used the words "fit and well". I was rather more qualified in what I said. But the fact was that he was able to carry on a wide-ranging discussion for two hours and his difficulties were physical difficulties. The second time I saw him, three or four months before his death, he found it difficult to get to his feet without being helped. Well, quite a number of people in their 80's find that, but from the point of view of carrying on a political discussion, on both occasions when I saw him, he was absolutely on the ball.

Stern: Which of the leaders in the world do you most admire?

EH: There is a handful of leaders – Churchill, Adenauer, de Gaulle, Mao Tse Tung, Teng Hsiao Ping and Tito. By the time I knew them, they'd all moved far beyond all the pettiness of party politics and were thinking on a world scale. They didn't all produce the same answers. But one felt that they were looking at the world as a whole, trying to find an overall solution to the world's problems, because they recognised that today we are interdependent and nobody can look after themselves alone. They all had this characteristic and I think it's one which one should try to emulate.

Olusegun **OBASANJO**

CHAPTER 6

Stern: Olusegun Obasanjo, it's now well over a decade since you left the military. And yet you still seem to cling to the title of General. Why?

O.O: I don't cling to the title. In fact I prefer to be addressed by my first name – Olusegun – or 'Olu' for short. But people out of politeness or whatever prefer to call me General. In fact I would rather be called "a chicken farmer", as I've said many times.

Stern: I'll bear that in mind. You are clearly a dominant personality. As a child, were you as strong-willed as you are now?

O.O: Yes, I remember on a number of occasions, because of my strong-will I was often smacked by my mother, who was more of a disciplinarian than my father. And whenever I felt that I was wrongly treated, I used to retaliate by refusing to eat. And my mother would initially say, "well if you won't eat, too bad". But that very day she would get worried because she knew that if I wouldn't eat at home I wouldn't eat elsewhere either, and she would soften and, of course, I would be petted and only then would I give in. I never really got the wrath of my father, but my mother was the one who often ticked me off.

Stern: So you got your strong will from your mother?

O.O: Quite a bit of it.

Stern: Well, you've now become an intensely political being. Now, where did that interest in politics come from. Was your family interested in politics?

O.O: My father was not a political animal, in the way I have been. He was just a simple ordinary village farmer. But he acquired a reputation for kindness and generosity and was trusted in the village. If they wanted a representative he would be picked, not as a politician, not even as a village head, just as a representative. My grandfather was also a community leader, a very responsible and respected one, again not a chief as such, but a community leader of repute. Now if you regard that as something that can be inherited or derived, then I probably did.

Stern: So there was the aura of politics in your background?

O.O: Well, it was more like community service and military service, because on my mother's side they were warriors. My great maternal grandfather was a warrior of some repute.

Stern: Is that why you chose to go into the military rather than into the political arena to start with?

O.O: No, I think I went into the military for lack of something else to do. And because with my type of background, good secondary education and all that, the military just appealed to me.

Stern: Well, you trained in Britain and when you were at the Royal Military College of Science, where you graduated, I think, in Engineering, they said that you were the best Commonwealth student they'd ever had. What had you done that so impressed them?

O.O: Actually it was the Royal School of Military Engineering, where I did what they call the Young Officers' Post-graduate Course. And among about 22 or 23 other young officers, I was the most senior. I was a captain, most of them were lieutenants. But, as always when I have something to do, I really put all my effort to it and I did put all my effort to that course. And I think the Commandant and the instructors were so impressed that they wrote the type of report you have just read now.

Stern: What effect did that report have on you? Did it change the course of your life in some way?

O.O: Well, to the extent that your military reports are not totally ignored in your military career, it had some effect in the progress I had later on in the military. It did not swell my head, however. If anything it made me feel that I had a certain ability which should continue to be developed.

Stern: Let's look at those abilities, because you rose very rapidly in the military hierarchy after you got your commission. What were those qualities that led to this rapid promotion.

O.O: One of the first reports that I received as a young officer talked about my 'agility', 'ability', 'rectitude', 'being a bit impulsive', 'being a go-getter', 'respecting his senior officers', 'loyalty'. These are the sorts of words which kept cropping up in my reports.

Stern: And are these the kinds of qualities that you look for in a military officer?

O.O: Well, naturally, you want an officer to whom you can give a job and be sure he will do his damn best to get the job done. You will look for loyalty, honesty, integrity and that sort of thing. Naturally, you want a dependable officer who will stand his ground, who knows his onions, who knows what he's doing.

Stern: But are the qualities that make for good leadership in the army, the same qualities that make for good leadership in politics – because you've had top posts in both, haven't you?

O.O: I think that the qualities for leadership whether in politics, in the army, in business, in diplomacy, even on the farm, don't differ much. You need a leader whom you can rely on, who will take you from A to B, who, if things go wrong, will be there. You need a leader on whose judgment you can rely. So, though there may be a difference of emphasis here and there, the qualities are essentially the same.

Stern: One quality which I detected in reading your book, *My Command*, which is your account of your exploits during the Nigerian Civil War, is supreme self-confidence, someone with the courage of his convictions, someone with faith in his own judgment. Yet, was there never a moment of self-doubt when you wondered whether you'd taken the right decision or even questioned your fitness to command?

O.O: No, I never questioned my fitness to command, not at all. I have confidence in myself, in my ability. There are, of course, occasions when I have sought other peoples' views, and when I am dealing with issues that affect me personally I want a second opinion. When I'm dealing with issues in times of command, well, don't forget, I will have made use of my staff officers, I will have got a lot of information in, I will have considered all the factors, and so what you see at the end of the day is a processed product. If that product elicits confidence and courage and all that, it is because you are sure of your product. It's like a manufacturer. When you are sure of the quality of your product you feel confident.

Stern: But can't that assurance sometimes make you a bit complacent?

O.O: Not really, because in the army, particularly, there is no room for complacency, because the situation changes and you must be able to change with the situation. New factors come to light, new information is brought out and as these things change, so must you change with them. In fact, that's one of the qualities of leadership – flexibility, not in terms of principle, but in terms of practice. Your goal is still the same, but if you have decided to go left flank into an attack and you suddenly find the enemy you never expected to be there, you don't go on stupidly and foolhardily on the left. You might then decide to either move to the right or provide a force to deal with the unexpected enemy, before you go on with your objective.

Stern: There seems to be a paradox, though, about you and about your career. Nowadays, you advocate disarmament, and you've taken part in mediation efforts in Angola, in Sudan and in South Africa, and you sit on various committees whose object is to try and bring about a more just and peaceful world. Yet, you'd originally opted for a profession which was likely to involve you in taking lives, and in the end you did.

O.O: I don't see any contradiction. Don't forget, you don't join the army to be a killer. I joined the army because I love peace. Now, the military must be seen as an insurance. You don't insure your car because you want to wreck it, do you? No, you insure your car because if the worst comes to the worst and you have an accident, you want to be able to have another car. I believe that that is the same with the military. You have a military force not necessarily because you are bellicose. You have a military force for security, for insurance, for peace, and so what I am doing now is not necessarily different from what I have done. I have always been a man of peace, but, of course, if you have to exercise a little bit of violence to maintain peace then you do it. But it must be just the right amount of force, not too much, not too little.

Stern: But in the end you had to kill fellow Nigerians, didn't you, during the civil war? What did that do to you, what did it feel like to take other mens' lives, especially other Nigerians?

O.O: I very much believed, as a Nigerian, in the unity, the integration of Nigeria. If you could bring this about by talking, so much the better. But if it meant, as it did, that we had to bring a certain amount of violence to hold Nigeria together, so be it! You will have read about my own prosecution of the war that it was so humane that even people on the other side felt that if I had been in the war front earlier, maybe the war would not have lasted as long.

Stern: But when you say it was humane, quite a lot of people who weren't involved in the fighting, like women and children, starved to death.

O.O: No, in fact, to the contrary. I gave food from my side to women and children on the other side who were starving. And that changed the style of the war and again this is also a sign of the quality of leadership. Now, civil war is one of the most difficult wars to prosecute, because when you are fighting international war you are fighting to destroy. But in a civil war you are fighting to unite, to build, to integrate; you cannot afford to be irresponsible in the way you prosecute the war and engage the other people. The day the war ended and I saw my colleagues on the other side, we started embracing and holding each other. To those with no shoes, I gave shoes; to those with no food, I gave food. I put my troops on foot and I gave vehicles to move refugees, to move children to their respective villages and places to live. So civil war is not like any other war, and, without being immodest, I believe that the way that war was prosecuted especially towards the end by the troops under my command made the process of reconciliation much, much easier.

Stern: You took the surrender after that war. How did you feel when you approached your antagonists?

O.O: Well, of course, we were colleagues. We'd lived in the same barracks before. We knew each other by first names in fact, we were brothers, not strangers.

Stern: Was Colonel Ojukwu who led the Biafran secession, your brother?

O.O: Of course, Emeku was my friend, a good friend. We'd lived in neighbouring rooms and at that time he had a car. You know, Emeku comes from a family background that had the means; so we used to go out in his car before the war.

Stern: And after the war?

O.O: After the war he left the country so I didn't see him. But if he had stayed, what used to happen before the war would have happened after – the same kind of camaraderie.

Stern: As someone interested in the nature of leadership, who do you think was the better leader; General Gowon, who was the Nigerian Head of State, or Colonel Ojukwu who led the Biafran secession?

O.O: Well, there's no comparison between them because they were doing two different things. I respect Gowon for standing firm for the unity of Nigeria. There are other areas where I would criticise him, but for that I would doff my hat for him any day. Now Emeku Ojukwu on the other hand believed, and I think to some extent he was right to believe, that the Ibos after the first coup had been badly treated as a people. For although some of them in the army or in politics had done things they probably shouldn't have done, the acts of a handful of people in a race or nation should not be taken as a judgment on the whole race or nation. But I don't believe that secession was the only answer for the Ibos to get redress as a people.

Stern: Even though they had been persecuted?

O.O: Yes, but if you take up arms and the other side takes up arms then you get more persecution and that's what was happening. But at the end of the day, when the war was over, we resolved our differences by identifying the concerns of the Ibos and trying to meet or satisfy them.

Stern: Let's move from military to political leadership. You'd seen heads of state come and go – many of them violently. When did you begin to think that you could do a better job than many of them?

O.O: I didn't actually seek political office. It was one of those cases where as Shakespeare said, power was "thrust" upon me, and I believe that once you accept a particular position, you must do your best in it. That's what happened in my case.

Stern: But when you were Chief of Staff at Supreme Headquarters in the mid-seventies, the then Head of State, General Mohammad asked you to work with him in drafting a new constitution. Why did he ask you? You're not a constitutional lawyer.

73

O.O: No, I was particularly lucky. You see, I'd spent the whole of 1974 in Britain at the Royal College of Defence Studies and had had the opportunity to interact with fairly senior officers both military and civil from other countries and to reflect on a number of issues that affected Nigeria. When I got home, I was told at first that I should go on leave, that there was nothing for me yet. Well, I thought that I was on my way out as a military man. But by the time I came back again I had been appointed a Minister at the Federal level – Minister for Works. Then close to the middle of 1975 a coup had been carried out, and claiming that the country was adrift, the boys who masterminded the coup invited General Murtala Mohammad, Yakubu Danjuma and me to "put this country right".

Stern: Did you yourself have anything to do with that coup?

O.O: No, I didn't.

Stern: But you knew the people who did it?

O.O: Oh yes. They were all junior officers to me who knew the type of man each and every one of us was and is. The first thing we had to tackle was to retrieve the reputation of the military which was falling to zero because Gowon had reneged on his own freely given promise to hand over to civilians in 1976. He'd come back and said 1976 was "unrealistic". Now, that dented the reputation of the military very seriously.

Stern: But didn't having another coup also dent the reputation of the military?

O.O: Well, to the extent that the leaders of the coup then gave their word and carried it out; that retrieved the reputation and honour of the military. One of the things we had to do was to contrive a constitution that would bring civilian rule in a new Nigeria, avoiding so to say the aberrations or the unwholesome elements of the first republic.

Stern: So you are saying that the coup was designed really to restore civilian leadership in Nigeria?

O.O: Well, if you like to put it that way. It was designed to retrieve the reputation of the military. I don't know whether we are saying the same thing.

Stern: We may be, and yet tragically General Mohammad went the same way as many of his predecessors. He was killed in the course of an attempted coup. You were on the same death list as he was, weren't you, but you survived.

O.O: In fact, I was assumed to have been killed. The coup makers announced my death. What happened was this. The day before the coup when I was going home from the office, my ADC said that he had refused access to a particular officer that wanted to see me. But this was a senior officer. I said to my ADC, "how dare you tell another senior officer he couldn't see me. When we get back, you 'phone him and say he should come and see me". So that officer came to me the following morning – the morning of the coup – to tell me that his wife had just had a baby boy and wanted my permission to name this child after me. And I told him to go and sort out the christening of the child and then come back after that. But because I was delayed in my house, I missed the bullet that was meant for me. Another officer who was mistaken for me was in fact shot.

Stern: Did you expect to become Head of State after General Mohammad?

O.O: Not at all, and, as I'll tell you, I did not want the job. The day after the attempted coup, we met as the Supreme Military Council – the highest law-making body in the country – and I said, "the first thing we have to do is to tell the nation that the Head of State has been assassinated. Before we do that we have to inform his family and then appoint a new Head of State. Now I want you to exclude me from this because I'm not in the frame of mind for this type of job, especially having worked very closely together with the late of Head of State". But then all my colleagues said, "we have no new Head of State other than you". I resisted for almost two and a half hours, but eventually gave in and at that point made what you may call a sort of impromptu acceptance speech.

Stern: But given the life expectancy of a Nigerian Head of State, weren't you nervous?

O.O: Not really, though I never knew that I would pull through. Pulling through was a by-product, doing a good job was what I set out to do. I kept saying to my own colleagues, I would always do my best and that they would be free to make their contribution. We ran as far as possible, a representative government, a very open government, democratic in terms of those who were there. It wasn't "you take it or leave it". I didn't ram anything down their throats. My job was to convince people or to make them see my point of view, and on a number of occasions I took a memo to Council and my colleagues were not in the mood to go along with it and I'd say "withdraw my memo". So doing a job well was my main objective. Survival came as secondary.

Stern: But so many other governments in Nigeria, though not yours, had ended violently. Do you know why? Do you have a theory about that?

O.O: I don't know. Insensitivity may be one.

Stern: Whose insensitivity?

O.O: The government's. Losing touch with the grassroots, with the goings-on at the ordinary level of the nation.

Stern: I wonder if the country is too big, too diverse to be really governable.

O.O: No, I don't agree with that. I governed it. For instance I used a military division composed of Ibos even when we were fighting the Ibos.

Stern: As a military man who found himself in politics, when do you think military intervention is good and when is it bad? Is there any general rule?

75

O.O: Not really. I am one of those who believe that there's no perfect government.

Stern: Not even yours?

O.O: Oh no, there's no perfect government, just as there's no perfect human being. Until you can create a perfect human being, (maybe out of test tube), then you cannot talk of a perfect government. The best government would be one that does things in the best interests of the majority of the people, most of the time. If a government does that – which again is an outcome of leadership -and is honest with itself and with its people, I believe that by and large, even if that government has problems, people will tend to understand.

Stern: You suggested somewhere that Africa needs strong leadership. What exactly did you mean? Unyielding leadership? Unbending leadership? Inflexible leadership?

O.O: No, being strong does not mean inflexibility. Inflexibility to my mind is a sign of an inferiority complex, of inadequacy. You should be able to take account of other people's point of view and when you have new information you should be able to use it. As I illustrated earlier, you must be objective, and you shouldn't sacrifice principle. But you can sacrifice method.

Stern: You've launched an Africa Leadership Forum for, amongst other things, the training of people with leadership potential. What do you look for as constituting that potential and how do you train people for leadership?

O.O: I believe that most people have innate ability, innate leadership qualities. And what I am trying to do in the Africa Leadership Forum is to identify a successful generation of leaders in all walks of life – in business, in politics, in the military – and to give them exposure to each other first, and to other accomplished leaders, so that they can interact and learn from them, because there's nothing as good as learning from the experienced. You can ask them, "why did you do this? How did this happen? What are the factors you have to consider?" And that sort of thing remains vivid in the memory. At the Forum's first meeting, as you probably know, we had Helmut Schmidt who openly talked about some decisions he took which he felt were not quite right but which he had to take for political reasons. For instance, the Common Agricultural Policy of the EEC. He also gave some examples of other things he believed in and carried out. Now this is the sort of thing we are trying to do. We take issues that are relevant, about which people have points of view which they want to share with incumbent leaders who will be able to do something about these issues. If all goes well, we'll be able to breed a successful generation of leaders who will have learned from their exposure to others.

Stern: But yours is an Africa Leadership Forum. Does it require different qualities of leadership to be a leader in Africa as against Europe or the United States?

O.O: Well, don't let the title mislead you. We don't want inbreeding. We invite successful leaders from Europe, from Latin America, from North America, from Asia but essentially this is targeted through African leaders. We didn't call it

African but Africa Leadership Forum because is centred on Africa. I don't believe that there are differences between the leadership qualities required of African leaders and leadership qualities required of European or Latin American leaders.

Stern: So, do you have a model in mind? Do you have an idea of a really excellent leader?

O.O: Well, even though I am a Christian I don't believe that Jesus Christ, as a human being, was perfect. So I don't have a hero. There are people certain aspects of whose life are admirable, and I believe those aspects that one admires should be cultivated, should be inculcated. But why should I take the bad aspects of their life? If I can take the good part of you and the good part of another man, and of another and put them together maybe I will mitigate the bad parts in those people to whom I am trying to expose these other leaders.

Stern: Well, you may not have a hero but you have a lot of people whose leadership performance you despise. You have accused a lot of African leaders of wasting opportunities and squandering resources and so on. But realistically, aren't the activities of many African leaders really constrained? Aren't the cards, foreign and domestic, really stacked heavily against them?

O.O: Oh yes, and I have said that too. Let's be honest with ourselves. The odds are heavily against them, but if they don't understand as well as they should the world they live in, how do you expect them to perform? And that is the sort of exposure that the Africa Leadership Forum is supposed to give. And without being too repetitive about this, at the first Forum that took place in Nigeria, Helmut Schmidt came to tell us: "You are on your own. Don't expect that the world will listen to your lamentation and put everything at your feet. You have to get yourself up". That was straight forward talk and that is the way it should be. Now if anybody has any illusion that "the world owes us a living", hearing that from a leader of Chancellor Schmidt's stature will make them think again, and some who attended that Forum thought again. But there's no doubt that there have been missed opportunities. There's no doubt that African leaders have not, in totality, performed as they should have performed. The performance has been inadequate, some of it due to their own fault, a lot of it due to things beyond their control. But if they know what is within their control and what is beyond their control maybe in the totality of their performance they will do better.

Stern: I was thinking that one of the constraints, particularly in Africa, might be tribalism. I know it's something that you took no notice of because you don't think that tribalism is important. At least it's not important for you, but it has been important for a lot of other leaders. So isn't that a constraint?

O.O: Well as you rightly said, it is not important for me, so why should it be important for the other people? We cannot, of course, wish tribalism away. It is a part of existence, part of our life but if your tribe tries to put undue pressure on you and they know that you will stand firm, they will learn to either ignore you or to call you names and leave you to get on with the job. I don't believe that tribalism per se is a difficult thing because these people who resort to tribalism only do it when they are in trouble. If a politician wants to gain political power, he goes home and he says "well look, these people are against me because I am of this tribe". Otherwise he invariably forgets that he's of a particular tribe. Tribal consciousness is used by those who are looking for power to attain positions of power and is used to maintain it, especially when they are in trouble. But I think that we should see the tribe even as a source of strength because diversity is good and my own experience is that since other tribes believe that you will deal fairly with them, that you will deal honestly with them, they won't even look at you as belonging to a particular tribe.

Stern: And is that what happened during your period of office?

O.O: Yes, that's what happened.

Stern: Let's look at some of the things that you did during that period from 1976 to 1979. First of all, on what basis did you choose your Cabinet? Did you play the General and want a Cabinet that would obey orders or did you want people who'd argue their corner.

O.O: I believed in persuasion, making your case and winning the other man round with force of argument.

Stern: Could they ever win you round?

O.O: If they had strong force of argument, why not? As I told you, I've taken many memos to Council which I had to withdraw because either it didn't get the type of support that I thought it would get, or else some people came with superior argument. One thing I tried to do was to make the Cabinet representative in terms of different areas of the country, and in fact the sort of thing we practiced became enshrined in our 1979 Constitution: that the President of Nigeria should have Ministers from all the states of the country, even if the state does not vote for him, again to bring about a Federal character so that people can feel that they have a stake in the country.

Stern: But your Government was noted not only for effecting this new Constitution which returned the country to civilian rule but also for a proliferation of policies – many encapsulated under a kind of slogan, "Operation feed the Nation", "War against economic sabotage", "Indiginization" and so on. What do you think was your greatest achievement during this period?

O.O: Let me first deal with the "proliferation" that you talk about. In a country like ours, a developing country, there's virtually no aspect of national life that does not require attention and what I am not noted for is ignoring things that I believe require attention. So what you would regard as proliferation means that I saw a perceived need somewhere and tried to do something about it. I wouldn't say that in all cases what we tried do about the perceived need turned out for the best. You asked what I would regard as the most important achievement. We laid the foundation of a good sound economy on which our future could have been built. Now that to a larger extent was destroyed...

Stern: Do you feel that you have been a failure really, since a lot of things that you have tried to do have not come about?

O.O: Let me finish. Now again, we brought about, peacefully, orderly and systematically a civilian regime. I would not regard the fact that you do something which does not endure as a failure. The present administration is going about things in more or less the same way, except the blanket banning of politicians. The fact that you build a bridge over this stream or river and then somebody comes and destroys that bridge – would you regard that as a failure?

Stern: You are saying that the bridge can be built again?

O.O: It can be built again, but if an act of sabotage, an act of war, an act of hostility leads to that bridge being broken or destroyed, you wouldn't blame yourself for it.

Stern: But why did you give it all up? Why did you give up politics and become a farmer? Shouldn't you have stayed in there and made sure that your ideas were going to be carried out.

O.O: No, I told you that we came in to retrieve the reputation and the name of the military, and we would not have been able to do that if we came in to perpetuate military rule. We came in to say "well, look, if the military gives its word, no matter what, that word *will* be its bond". Now, you don't then do that and then come back and say "well, I want to stay on. I want a plebiscite". In a thousand and one ways I could have stayed on. There was enough internal and external pressure to stay on but I don't think it would have dignified the reputation of the army or my personal reputation.

Stern: Would you like to be back in politics?

O.O: Not really. You see I come from a part of the world where we have a saying – once we say 'goodbye' in one night, you don't go back in the same night and say 'good evening' again.

Stern: How do you see your career going from now on? I mean, do you have any unfulfilled ambitions?

O.O: Not really. I am quite happy! I am here with you doing the interview and over this period for instance I have meetings in London, in Stockholm, in Geneva and in Brussels. I will go home and within a week I think I am going to the US for a meeting. Now, I enjoy that and I also enjoy the work I do now. I am practising what I preached when I was in government. You referred to 'Operation Feed the Nation'. I believe the aim of that was to create awareness for agriculture, for food production, and I when left public office I thought "well, what else can I do? I have preached something, let me practice it". And I went into farming as a full-time job and it takes my attention and it exercises me. Physically and mentally it gives me enough problems to solve. I also write, and I go to these international and local meetings. I learn from all of them and I always want to learn; learn new ideas from people or even examine my own old ideas. Do they still stand the test of time? How do the new situations affect them? So there is a lot to do without being in the presidential house.

Stern: So when the history books come to be written, what would you like them to say about you?

O.O: Oh, that I am Olusegun Obasanjo who had the opportunity to hold the fate of Nigeria in my hands, did it to the best of my ability and left it and went to the farm.

Stern: And what would you like them to leave out?

O.O: Nothing really because there is always good and bad in anything I've been into. If you want to leave out the good and take the bad, as some people will want to do, then good! If you want to leave out the bad and emphasise the good, well and good!

Stern: What do you see as your good characteristics and what as your bad ones?

O.O: My good characteristic? When I believe in something I pursue it. My bad one – people say I speak my mind. I am not diplomatic. When I have things to say I say them. Maybe it's a good thing I didn't join the diplomatic corps, though I think there are occasions when you have to be tactful. I don't believe, however, that you should lie. If you don't want to say something keep quiet, but if you have to speak then you should say what you believe, and if I say what I believe in and people feel that I say it too bluntly, I really don't have to apologise for that.

Stern: You've had a lot of power – military power, political power and so on. Does it tend to corrupt? Can it go to one's head?

O.O: It may. You see what I found was two things. Number one: your greatest enemy in power are the sycophants, and there is no man or woman in power that will ever be short of sycophants. What I say to people is "look, don't tell me what is good, I want to hear what is bad because that is what will help me". The second problem stems from that. There are times when even with the best will in the world, the advice you get from bureaucrats or your colleagues in the Cabinet or technical people is tainted, tailored advice. And only God and your ability to seek advice from more than one direction will help you out. If you want to take a decision, get advice from as many directions as possible and either cross check or bounce that advice on other bodies that can react or give you other information or other pieces of advice.

Garret **FITZGERALD**

CHAPTER 7

Stern: Dr FitzGerald, your political opponents, as well as your friends, speak of you as gentle, modest, absent-minded and professorial. Aren't these rather unusual characteristics in a politician?

GF: Well, they are perhaps unusual characteristics. I don't think that's the sum total of my personality however. I hope I have some other qualities that qualify me rather more for politics than the ones you have mentioned.

Stern: You have also been dubbed Garret the Good, an honest politician, a man of integrity. But are you really suited to the rough and tumble of politics? Aren't you really a rather academic person, more interested in research?

GF: No, I am basically a very combative person, and always have been. I have always involved myself in controversy, argument and debate. I have challenged the establishment in a university, and am really much more of an activist and troublemaker than an ordinary quiet academic doing research.

Stern: You are not the first academic to have gone into political life. But do you think an academic background is a really suitable preparation? After all, as an academic you don't have to make crucial decisions affecting people's lives, do you?

GF: I think there perhaps are some problems arising from an academic background in terms of a tendency to see both sides of questions and that makes it sometimes more difficult perhaps to be decisive. On the other hand, I think that the objectivity one can

81

bring from an academic background is important in a discipline where the nature of rhetoric tends to lead people to be very un-objective and perhaps to delude themselves at times into believing their own rhetoric. At least if you are an academic you don't allow yourself to be fooled by your own rhetoric, or other people's.

Stern: Yes, but if you are seeing two sides of the question and your opponent is only seeing one side of the question, doesn't that put you at a disadvantage?

GF: It does. If, however, you have an argumentative disposition and enjoy selecting and presenting facts to prove a case without distorting it, or making false statements, then I think that extra bit of qualification helps. And I think that I have always had that quality.

Stern: You grew up in an intensely political household. Your parents had both been revolutionaries and your father had even gone to jail for his anti-British activities. Later on, after Ireland was partitioned, your father held important ministries in the newly independent Irish administration. What was it like to grow up in that kind of environment?

GF: Well, first of all, by the time I reached what's called the age of reason, my father was out of office because the government he was a member of lost office in 1932. My father was very clear that what he had done was right and he didn't have much time for people who didn't share that view. My mother eventually came round to his view, though they had been on opposite sides during the Civil War in 1922- 23 – my mother having sympathised with and supported the Republicans, while my father was a member of the government.

Stern: Did you go through a revolutionary phase like your parents?

GF: No, there was no reason to do so. I was brought up in a stable state.

Stern: Yes, but Northern Ireland was still part of Britain. Did you not feel that it was worth taking to arms to alter that state of affairs?

GF: No, certainly not. I have changed views on many things over the years. But in terms of the relations with Northern Ireland I have always held very consistently to the importance of trying to create the conditions in which a majority in Northern Ireland would wish of their own free will to join this state. There is no other way ahead towards Irish unity that is possible or worthwhile or justifiable.

Stern: What did you take with you from those heady days?

GF: Oh, an interest in politics and in international affairs, very early on, and quite deeply felt. But my father was very concerned that none of us should go into politics on the strength of his name, as sometimes happens, and therefore the idea of entering politics young was ruled out on that account. In any event, I wanted to get married and there's no money in politics in terms of earning a living at that age. You can turn to politics later in life having taken up another profession.

Stern: Did you always intend eventually to go into politics?

GF: Oh yes. At about 15 at school, a priest who was head of the debating society encouraged my interest in politics and international affairs. I recall him encouraging me to think of politics at some stage. And I recall his suggestion that I should aim at being Taoiseach (Prime Minister).

Stern: But what did you want to go into politics for?

GF: We were brought up with a sense that one is in life to serve people in some way and if you have a few developed talents which would enable you to serve the community then you should deploy them. It was never a determination to go into politics at all costs. It was a feeling that it was something to do if I could qualify myself for it and if the opportunity arose.

Stern: You said that the object was service, but service to whom, to Ireland, to Europe, to the world?

GF: To people. Obviously the people you serve in politics most directly are the ones in your own countries. But, of course, horizons widened during my lifetime and so as the European ideal developed in the 1950s it became possible to think in wider terms and I developed a loyalty to Europe as well. I have never understood why people should only have one loyalty. I have no difficulty in having loyalty to this state of which I have been Prime Minister, a sense of loyalty to Northern Ireland from which my mother came, and loyalty to Europe. And, obviously, we all have a common interest in the survival of the globe. I don't think these conflict with each other. I have never understood this idea that loyalty should be exclusive.

Stern: You have clearly been a political animal since you were a child. Was it your ambition to get to the top of the political ladder which you had joined in 1969 when you became a member of parliament?

GF: Yes, that was the logical thing to aim at. Most politicians, or many, must think in those terms.

Stern: They don't always say so.

GF: You never say so until you get there. It was something I had always thought of but without being too upset, or disappointed, if it didn't work out. But because I wanted to give a new direction to our policy on Northern Ireland and on Europe, and because I had beliefs about the social conditions and the social policies to be pursued at home, in terms of greater social justice, my chance of achieving them was obviously greater if I became Prime Minister.

Stern: Now, before becoming Prime Minister you became Minister of Foreign Affairs in 1973. Did you model yourself on your father who had had the same position?

GF: Not consciously, no. Obviously I was very proud of my father having been Ireland's first Minister of Foreign Affairs. And, to find myself, very unexpectedly in fact, in that job was a source of pride and pleasure to me. But the tasks to be undertaken at that time were quite different from the ones he had to undertake. Because I became Minister of Foreign Affairs about ten weeks after we joined the Community and before we had been able to take up any particular position, I was able to shape our policy in that area.

Stern: So how did you give definition to that elusive concept 'the national interest'.

GF: In terms of Europe, we have a problem in that we are not a member of the North Atlantic Alliance. We are militarily neutral. That and the fact that we were the largest single beneficiary of membership in terms of the scale of transfers of resources from the Community made it necessary for us to be as constructive as possible lest the fact that we were getting so much from it, and in defence terms giving nothing in return, could become a source of irritation to other people.

Stern: In 1977 you became leader of the opposition Fine Gael, and in 1981 you formed your first administration. What are the qualities you need for an awesome job like that and do you think you had them?

GF: I had some of them and lacked others. I think nobody would become Prime Minister without some of the qualities and nobody has all of them. I had a very clear view of what I wanted to do in regard to Northern Ireland, on our European policy and on domestic policy in terms of changing our society and creating greater equity and social justice. Unhappily, by the time I became Prime Minister the opportunity and possibility of doing that was, to say the least, diminished by the fact that the previous government had spent so freely that my entire time in government was spent trying to get our finances under control, to cut spending, to raise taxes, reduce borrowing. As a result very few of the things that I went into politics to do in the domestic forum were within my compass. In that respect it was a disappointing experience.

Stern: But isn't the art of leadership being able to turn disadvantages into advantages?

GF: Well, it is if you can do it, if you have the ability and the possibility. Sometimes you either haven't the ability or you haven't the possibility.

Stern: What did you then and subsequently discover about the art of leadership?

GF: Well, you are there because there are certain things you want to do and your job is to persuade other people to go along with your view as far as possible. I suppose there are two different styles of leadership: one, authoritative, relatively aggressive, forcing people to do what you want by frightening them; the other is a slightly less aggressive form in which you try to bring people with you.

Stern: Consultative leadership?

GF: No, 'consultative' is too weak a word, because you argue with people and jolly them along to come with you in a particular direction. You are not consulting them as such. Now, if you are not going to give the kind of dominant leadership, which is not my style, you have to select which policies are important and what came out of my selection was basically that Northern Ireland was the area in which I insisted that my policy and tactics would be pursued. I was also insistent that my view would stand in regard to the increase in development aid to the Third World but I was willing to pay the price – that other matters would then be collective decisions of government in which I would play my part more as chairman than as chief.

Stern: Do you think differences of perspective in cabinet are a help, or are they a hindrance to good policy-making?

GF: Differences in perspective are a help. If you don't have them, you will make mistakes. If you are all of one mind as to how to tackle a subject and don't discuss and debate it, you will do silly and stupid things, which is a very easy thing to do in government. You are locked up together in a room and you lose touch with the world outside.

Stern: Do you feel, though, that you controlled the cabinet, or that the cabinet controlled you?

GF: I controlled the cabinet in those areas where I chose to control it and the cabinet took collective decisions in other areas, very often against my view. But, as a democrat, I felt that if I were in a minority I would accept the majority view in those areas. But not in the crucial area of Northern Ireland policy.

Stern: What are the special problems in governing a country like Ireland, or is being Taoiseach much the same as being Prime Minister of any other state?

GF: Well, I think there are the problems arising from Irish nationalism and the division of the country, and the tensions that creates. There is the problem, because of the extreme sensitivity of issues in Northern Ireland, of avoiding situations where emotions are aroused in relation to Britain or British action that can be counter-productive. In the domestic government of the country there are problems which many countries have of giving effect to the decisions you take. Our people have a mind of their own. They had a long period of being governed by people they didn't want to have govern them, and they haven't entirely got used to the idea that government is now their own.

Stern: You're talking about the British here.

GF: Yes.

Stern: What about the role of the Church? Can't it have a significant, even decisive, impact on politics?

GF: Only in very limited areas. In Ireland the areas in which the Church seeks to have and has determining influence relate to aspects of sexual morality. I don't think outside that the Church has exercised significant influence, and when it has attempted to do so, for good or for ill, it has often been ignored.

Stern: Yet would it not be true to say though that you, in a sense, took on the role of the Church and lost?

GF: Well let's distinguish. On contraception I introduced a law and passed it through Parliament in five weeks, despite some protests from some churchmen.

Stern: So you can now get contraceptives in Ireland?

GF: Oh yes. That was settled without difficulty by decisive and quick action. In the case of abortion, the issue was nothing to do with introducing abortion. It was an issue that arose because of pressure from some people to introduce additional safeguards into the constitution to prevent abortion, and there was an argument about the wording proposed by my predecessors when I was in opposition. I accepted it without sufficient thought, then discovered that there were dangers in the wording, which our government then chose to amend. Unfortunately the Church did not see the wisdom of what we were doing and opposed it, and we were defeated on that particular issue. It was a silly issue to get involved in and collectively government, opposition and the Church made a mess of the whole thing. On the issue of divorce, yes, I took that on and we lost that, because of the opposition of the Catholic Church and because right wing Catholics raised a totally phoney scare about the possible loss of property rights by the first wife. Once the issue of property as well as religion was raised, we were lost.

Stern: But why did you take on these issues? Were you trying, in a sense, to show for the Protestants of Northern Ireland what your Protestant mother had shown for the Catholics of the south, namely, understanding?

GF: Yes, we couldn't seriously suggest to northern Unionists that they should join a state in which there was no right to divorce, and no right to contraceptives.

Stern: Now another, and related, object of yours was to achieve an understanding with Britain about Northern Irish affairs and in the end you secured the Anglo-Irish agreement, which for the first time gave the Irish Republic a formal advisory role in Northern Irish affairs. You had presumably to persuade Mrs Thatcher that you were a man that she could do business with. How did you manage that?

GF: Well, that's a question that should be addressed to her rather than to me, obviously...

Stern: Yes, but you got around her somehow, didn't you?

GF: Well, I can only guess, but for one thing I, and indeed the party I represent, have a very strong record of opposition to terrorism in all its forms and an unwillingness to have any dealings of any kind with terrorists, and I think that the firmness of my position and that of my government on these issues must have influenced her to some degree. And secondly, I did seek over a long period of time to present the problems of Northern Ireland in terms that would help her to see the importance of minimising the alienation of the minority, because it is out of that alienation that the IRA have been able to draw such small support as they have. And I sought to persuade her that it was necessary to tackle the problems of the nationalist minority, in order to weaken the IRA's hold. I did persuade her intellectually of that, though I'm not sure that I ever persuaded her emotionally.

Stern: You got to know her quite well during those talks. What sort of a leader is she?

GF: Well, as we all know, she's very decisive, very sure that she knows what is right in all the different areas of policy, and pushes issues through. She is not in the normal mould of Prime Minister in a Parliamentary system, she is more of a presidential figure and has indeed modified the British constitution in its operation in a way that perhaps people don't fully realise. She is a very different person from me, obviously.

Stern: Now this Anglo-Irish Agreement, what do you think it has achieved? Is it perhaps your most important and enduring legacy?

GF: It would be presumptuous to say what its long-term significance is because it was intended to have effects over time not to produce quick results. But the fact the Agreement was signed, recognising that the Northern Nationalist population looked to us in the same way that the Unionist population looked to Britain, has, I think, had a profound effect on Unionist thinking, in the first instance leading to a very negative reaction but beneath the surface to a rethinking of their position because there is, I think, a growing recognition that the idea of the relationship with Britain they had in the past was a fictitious one, and that they really have to look again at how Northern Ireland should be governed. I think what's also very important is that the Agreement established something which nobody had realised, that the division between Ireland and Britain, (the Irish seeking reunification of the island, Britain apparently seeking to retain Northern Ireland) has imperceptibly over 20 years been modified into a common policy, because the objective of both governments now is not to hang on to, or get hold of, a piece of territory, it is to restore peace in Northern Ireland. What the IRA have done is quite an extraordinary thing – they have brought the Irish and British governments and peoples together in a common cause, and the significance of the Agreement lies in the fact that it is a formalisation of a total reversal of the relationship between Ireland and Britain on this issue as existed over so many decades previously.

Stern: Looking back over your political career, you have held a great deal of power. Despite your widespread reputation for probity, do you think you were ever corrupted by it?

GF: I hope not and I don't think so, because I never wanted power for its own sake. I wanted to get in a position to achieve certain things, and so, when I had gone as far as I could do, it was with relief that I moved off the scene rather than with regret.

Stern: Was the historian, Lord Acton, wrong when he said that power tends to corrupt?

GF: Oh, I think it does tend to corrupt, but it does not need to do so. And in any event the checks and balances of the democratic system as we know it here are such that the opportunities to abuse power are fortunately few, and not everybody has the instinct to want to abuse power anyway. I have always been basically anti-establishment, even when I was in government, and often my sympathies were with people who were challenging us on issues. If you never become emotionally part of the establishment, I don't think you can be that easily corrupted.

Stern: But politics can be a very dirty game, can't it?

GF: It can be, but it doesn't have to be. And I think in Ireland on the whole it isn't.

Stern: Did you enjoy the trappings of high office?

GF: Not particularly. There were occasions I enjoyed – formal occasions.

Stern: The dinners, the banquets...

GF: Oh yes, I enjoyed some of that, I must say. But not the fuss that goes with it. And what I found most difficult really is the politics of performing to large crowds, the adulation of supporters, things of that kind. I was never very comfortable or happy with that.

Stern: What other sacrifices does having power involve?

GF: I'd say sacrifices of family and finance. It is not a particularly well-paid profession compared with what many of the people who practice it might earn elsewhere, and most people lose rather than gain by going into politics and sometimes find themselves under a lot of financial pressure. When I became Minister of Foreign Affairs my income fell by 40 percent immediately and I had to sell my house and move to a much smaller house further out of town, so there are sacrifices of that kind which one makes happily enough.

Stern: And when you became Taoiseach did it ever occur to you that you would probably need police protection for the rest of your life?

GF: Well, I never really thought that many people would want to kill me, though there was one period in the 1970s when there was reason to believe that a particular group were seeking to kidnap a minister or a member of a minister's family. That was a worrying period and we had to resolve that if anything happened to any of us or our families, the government must never, under any circumstances, give in, no matter what the threats were. And indeed the officials in my department in Foreign Affairs, when they went to Northern Ireland, asked that if anything happened to them their families should be adequately compensated, but that if they were kidnapped no-one should ever give in.

Stern: Were you ever afraid?

GF: No, not particularly. On the whole I don't think I felt under threat.

Stern: I imagine that one of the disagreeable things about being in office is the way in which you can be so easily removed from it, as you were twice after losing an election. How did you feel the day after?

GF: The first time, I was alone in my party in feeling exhilarated.

Stern: Feeling exhilarated after you had lost?

GF: Yes, because I knew what none of them seemed to understand, that if the election had occurred a couple of months later when the budget we brought in started to bite we would have possibly lost 20 seats. Because the defeat came when it did we lost two seats, and nine months later we were back in government again, as I'd anticipated.

Stern: Well, what about the next election which you lost by a greater margin?

GF: Well, I expected to lose that. We knew that the things we would have to do were unpopular, that we had lost ground with public opinion because of the cuts in spending and increases in taxation forced on us by the extravagance of the previous government. We knew that the blame for that would fall on us and not on our predecessors who were responsible for it, and what I wanted to do was to ensure that we lost with minimum damage and that the election would be fought on economic issues so that the incoming government would have no choice but to continue the economic policy we were pursuing. And I also wanted to ensure that, as far as possible, the new government, though it had denounced the Anglo-Irish Agreement when it was signed, would in fact support it and implement it, and I sought to have an election that would, in its timing, and in the direction it took, achieve that result. And those results were achieved.

Stern: You say you expected to lose, but how did you feel that second time? Were you distressed by it?

GF: No, not particularly. I knew that it faced me with a decision as to whether I left politics at that point, and on thinking it through I was able to satisfy myself that I wasn't just being self-indulgent in retiring from leadership of the party, that it was the best thing for the party and for the country. I then went on to America lecturing for ten days and came back to help organise the election of my successor.

Stern: Would you like to be back in charge again?

GF: No.

Stern: Why not?

GF: Because I am past that stage in my career. It was a great physical and mental strain. I don't think that it would be good for me or for the country to attempt that again. It is for younger people to get on with it now. I have had enough of the exercise of responsibility over 14 years as Minister of Foreign Affairs, leader of my party in opposition and Prime Minister. That has exhausted my enthusiasm for the exercise of responsibility. Before I was minister, I did pursue four different careers simultaneously, not just politics but economic consultancy, journalism and also an academic life. I am a natural pluralist. For 14 years I had to do one job only – I have had enough of that, and I want to get back to doing lots of different things.

Stern: When the historians come to look back on your career, what do you think they will say?

CHAPTER 7

GF: I think and hope that what I have done in regard to Northern Ireland and Europe will stand up. I think I shall probably get a bit more credit than I now get at this stage for what we achieved in government in terms of reducing borrowing and preparing the way for getting back to solvency again; but I think people may feel that as a Prime Minister, in terms of domestic policy, I didn't give as strong a lead as perhaps I should have, because temperamentally, outside particular areas where I am very clear on what needs to be done, I am by nature too much of a democrat to be a very strong leader.

Michael **MANLEY**

CHAPTER 8

Stern: Prime Minister, a decade ago, when your party was ignominiously defeated at the polls people said you were finished as a politician. Yet, here you are back in power after an election landslide equally as impressive as the one that seemed to bury you in 1980. What does it mean to you to be back in charge?

MM: Well, more than anything it means the resumption of responsibility and dealing with pressure.

Stern: I notice that even on a hot day like this you are wearing a well-tailored business suit in place of the informal open-necked long-shirt and slacks you used to wear, and that nowadays you recognise the importance of the private sector in Jamaica and good relations with Washington. Are you still the same Michael Manley that worked closely with Fidel Castro and spoke of the need to 'dismantle capitalism brick by brick'?

MM: I should have known that you would bring that up. Basically of course, I am the same person, with the same ideals, the same hopes, the same commitments to a better ordered society but, I think, what happens to people if they get the opportunity of defeat, is that you re-examine, go back to the drawing board about what can work. And, that means coming to terms with the nature of the productive process, coming to realise the real limitations on the capacity of the State to intervene as a producer. And finally, coming to understand the value and the dynamism of entrepreneurship. It's that I think that I have come to terms with.

CHAPTER 8

Stern: Well, that's where you are now. What I'd like to do is to take you back to a much earlier period. Your father, Norman, was a successful politician and eventually became Prime Minister. Your mother, Edna, was a noted artist and sculptor. Did they have much time for their children?

MM: Yes, you know, amazingly they both did. I suppose they were both very disciplined people. They were both very strong family people. And I must say that I never, ever, had a sense of parental deprivation. I would never claim that in defence of my many sins. However, I had a peculiar problem in a small society, that of coming to terms with a father figure who was obviously larger than life. He was a man of enormous ability, drive and energy.

Stern: Well he and your mother were in attention-seeking professions. Did you, in a sense, have to compete with them to be noticed?

MM: No, in fact I think I was the reverse. I was extremely shy actually.

Stern: You merged into the wallpaper did you?

MM: As much as I could, yes. But particularly if I went to anybody's dance. You know, I was terrified about asking a girl to dance when I was a teenager.

Stern: You are obviously not terrified nowadays and I wonder if you still woo the crowds with the phrase 'love, the word is love'. You clearly have been much loved by the masses who still flock to hear you speak and I take it by the women you married, all four of them. Is this affection that people shower on you something that just happens or is it something that you actively seek and need?

MM: Well, I think that if anybody had the effrontery to say that they didn't appreciate affection they would be warped or a liar. I hope I am not warped. Of course, one appreciates any kind of affection and, as you grow older, you become increasingly grateful for it. And as you grow older you learn more and more how little you deserve it perhaps or how lucky you are to get it.

Stern: After graduating from the LSE you were a broadcaster. And then you went back to Jamaica and were a brilliantly successful trade union organiser before entering politics. Who were the major influences on your political thinking at the time?

MM: From my father I would have gained several things. First of all, a deep commitment to nationalism and the process of working towards independence. Secondly, the tremendous sense he gave us of the relationship between organisation and action. And, thirdly, a deep commitment to democratic process. The other influence was Laski because what Laski did was to create a theoretical framework within which you could reconcile rather doctrinaire socialist ideas with rather Millsian liberal democratic ideas. His lectures were the greatest of all the intellectual stimuli at the LSE at that time.

Stern: Now, do you think a politician is a better politician for having that kind of academic background, having studied politics and economics?

MM: In some senses, yes because I think to the extent that you do study political theory and political history you get a handle on political process, but I think that it can also have great weaknesses. That if you succumb to an over-theoretical view of political process that is not sufficiently rooted in an understanding of your own culture I think you can make tremendous mistakes. I think I made tremendous mistakes in the 1970s. And, when I look back at them, a lot of them were the product of a theoretical concept, and although I had been a trade unionist I had not enough appreciation of the dynamic of the culture around me.

Stern: That's a very interesting point – that you can be over-theoretical and that this can distort to some extent your political perspective.

MM: I think it really can.

Stern: You've talked about making certain mistakes when you were first in power in the 1970s but what positive qualities do you think you were able to bring to the premiership?

MM: Well, I would hope energy. I would hope within any given context a certain sense of idealistic purpose. They say that that period left a sort of permanently elevated political consciousness in the country, that people thought more seriously in political categories than before. This I can't judge but other people say that.

Stern: So what is leadership? Is it an art? Is it a craft?

MM: It may be a chemistry.

Stern: You speak there as someone often described as a charismatic leader.

MM: I don't know what the word means.

Stern: You have a relationship to a crowd. You can turn crowds on and off as it were.

MM: I think there are certain types of people – you find this among lawyers and their relations with juries, actors in relation with their audiences, etc – who are very conscious of an audience and what an audience is feeling. And, I think if you have that ability to come out of yourself and enter into what you imagine is in the mind of an audience it just helps you to communicate. But whether this is charisma, I don't know. I do know that I am very audience conscious. I can even in a huge crowd tell if a little section is losing me, or losing interest, I sort of pick it up and try to adjust because if you have something you want to get across to them then you ought to be concerned with communication.

Stern: Before we look at the policies you pursued in your first two administrations, I'd like you to elaborate your often expressed view that the developing countries are in a kind of economic and political straitjacket imposed on them by the structure of the international economy. Does this mean that a country such as Jamaica is at the mercy of international events and has virtually no power of independent decision-making?

MM: Where you have come to your independence with a very fragile and, of necessity, dependent economy and then are caught in very acute problems to do with foreign exchange and things of that sort, those things impose severe limitations on what you can do, and whether you are in what you might call the IMF mould of countries or outside of it you still would face enormous constraints on action which are imposed by circumstances, your lack of resources, your lack of means. But, that does not mean that you have no power of independent decision. I don't accept that.

Stern: So the international economy conditions but doesn't determine what a small state can do.

MM: There is that, but you are increasingly dealing with an international economy with production globally organised, and therefore I think that anybody trying to elaborate national policy has got to see where are the avenues of opportunity in that global economy.

Stern: How do you think that countries like Taiwan and South Korea and Singapore, the newly industrialising countries, which had many of the post-colonial problems of a country like Jamaica, have been able to make such rapid economic progress?

MM: If you take South Korea, it started with the huge advantage of its strategic significance, after the North-South war. Its importance to the United States made it the recipient of huge and unprecedented levels of aid and support, added to which they were very smart in putting a lot of those resources to work on education. They invested years in massive training of their population. Thirdly, like the Japanese, they succeeded in developing a very clever model of government-private sector collaboration. I suppose the culture factor is there too, having a population used to discipline. But I myself put that as fourth down the list.

Stern: I would like now to look at the period when you were about to take up office for the first time. How did you arrive at your political programme? Did you seek advice in drawing up a political agenda?

MM: In our party we have never had a sort of personalised decision-making, not in my father's time, not in mine. We work through structures, through committees and through synthesising but obviously whoever is leader has perhaps a disproportionate influence on what comes out.

Stern: When you came to choosing a Cabinet did you appoint people of like mind or people likely to check you if they thought some of your policies were a bit over the top?

MM: No, I have always tried to construct Cabinets that balance what I think are strengths and tendencies within the party. Actually, it is of inestimable value to have people in the group around you who stand up to you, particularly for a person like me who is very enthusiastic and emphatic and will for some time scare people off what they think. And thank God for the ones who say, 'But, Prime Minister don't you think...'

Stern: OK, people stand up to you now. Did they stand up to you in your first administration, 1972-76?

MM: Not enough.

Stern: Ah. You got away with things you shouldn't have got away with?

MM: I think so, in retrospect.

Stern: At the time you conveyed contradictory impressions to the critics. Some accused you of personalism, of one-manism, of wanting everything done your way. Others said that you were of much less substance and that you'd tend to agree with the last person you happened to talk to. Which was the real Michael Manley?

MM: The one in front of you.

Stern: Early in your first premiership you claimed that, "Socialism was the Christian way of life in action. Socialism," you said, "is love." Now was that strictly for the birds, was it a piece of theatre, was it a bit of rhetoric designed to appeal to religious Jamaicans or was there some substance behind it?

MM: Well, I have always thought, if nothing else, that Socialism is about the use of political action to create social justice. As distinct from those who think that if you leave the forces of the market untended they will create social justice as an inevitable by-product. And to the extent that I have always been a person who interprets the significance of the New Testament as very much in the realm of the Good Samaritan, of concern, of God and Justice in action as distinct from just my salvation in heaven, I have always thought that there was a link between Christianity and what I think are the moral imperatives of Socialism.

Stern: You use quite a lot of religious imagery. Are you religious yourself?

MM: I am afraid I am not very strong on organised religion. I think my country is rather patient with me since they are very strong on organised religion. But I am a personally religious person in the sense of feeling there is some larger destiny and purpose.

Stern: Yet, despite the rhetoric of Socialism and Love there was a good deal of violence about your movement. I mean, various gun-toting fanatics attached themselves to the PNP.

MM: No. No. Political violence had been introduced from outside into Jamaican political life. And one of the tragedies of our country is that we had many elements who'd respond to that, and then you'd got this terrible thing between elements in both parties. But, it would be totally unjust to say that our party *ever* was the prime mover in that.

Stern: And you were, of course, the victim of political violence weren't you?

MM: Many times a victim. I do not complain. But I really can't allow that remark to pass.

Stern: I think that's a fair observation. Let's now look at a few of your policies in those first two administrations. You said you were trying to create a more socially just society. But do you think you were wise to rely so heavily on state intervention, on nationalisation, on heavy taxation and so on, which had the effect of frightening off the businessmen didn't it?

MM: No, I think that was unwise. I think the objectives we had were entirely laudable. But, there is no question that we over-estimated how fast we could move. And, there was no question that mixed signals did go out to the private sector, which one has very much regretted in retrospect. We over-reached ourselves, that was the truth.

Stern: How did Jamaica benefit from your rather high profile foreign policy, in particular, your close association with Castro's Cuba and your growing hostility to the United States.

MM: The fact that we were involved in trying to talk about the world economy, that we were very active in the Anti-Apartheid struggle, active in the support of the Freedom Fighters of Zimbabwe and so on and so forth, I think that all that definitely moved the level of Jamaican political consciousness and I think that was positive. But we paid a very great price in the upset of our private sector, the misunderstanding in our private sector and, of course, the souring of relations with Washington, we paid a very high price for that. That will never be allowed to happen again.

Stern: Right. At the time of your fall you tended to blame your fate on perhaps everybody but your own administration. I mean, the United States government, the CIA, the IMF, big business, the domestic bourgeoisie and so on. But, weren't your failures at least as much due to bad management as to bad luck?

MM: It is extraordinary that you find it necessary to say that. I believe that I can say that there's probably been no defeated politician, certainly in Caribbean history, who has been as self-critical, more quick to accept blame. In the first bruise of defeat there were obviously deeply hurt feelings because there were tremendous acts of aggression against us, Jamaica was massively de-stabilised. The violence that was let loose in our tourist areas was calculated and vicious and deliberate and had an effect. There were periods when Washington was unnecessarily harsh with us. So, of course, in the first flush of that defeat one tended to remember the viciousness that was let loose in our country, 750 people were killed – that's more per capita than the US lost in the Vietnam war – and, I tell you this, there was nothing that justified what was let loose on Jamaica. But in the maturity of reflection, I have had the time and the humility to look at our mistakes.

Stern: You asked me why I asked the question, I asked it because of some of the things that you said at the time, for example you said that you would remain, 'unrepentant and unreconstructed'.

MM: I am unrepentantly committed to the struggle against apartheid and nobody will reconstruct me about that. And I am unrepentant about the feeling that the poor have had a rough deal, because it's even tougher today than then. I am not repentant about those things. Nor am I reconstructed about the hope that a world will come one day that can deal with them.

Stern: Well, it's also true that you are reconstructed in other respects, isn't it?

MM: That is true, in terms of method.

Stern: While you were working on your new methods, you had nine years, or thereabouts, in the political wilderness. Did you ever think of giving politics up for a more congenial profession?

MM: I got myself a more congenial job, as a lecturer and as a writer, and I had a very nice time, thank you very much.

Stern: And you wrote a jolly good book on cricket.

MM: Well, you are very kind to say so.

Stern: Did you think you would be back in office one day? A lot of people wrote you off.

MM: I thought to myself that in the nature of the political party that I am a part of there is just no way that you are going to keep that party out of office for more than two terms. And also I think that as long as you feel you can make a difference, and as long as you retain an inner self-confidence you will always assume that it will work out that way.

Stern: You said that you never doubted your confidence. Did you ever doubt your fitness for office?

MM: I have always questioned that. You should always retain a large amount of scepticism about yourself, if you don't you're lost.

Stern: After your fall from power you said that you thought you'd find leading an opposition rather boring, did you?

MM: Truthfully, yes. I think that if you have any creativity in you it is the chance to make a new set of mistakes, perhaps, that's really challenging.

Stern: Meanwhile, in the nine years or so you were out of office rethinking your ideas, many of your former radical Socialist colleagues, both inside and outside the country, were rethinking their views as well. Why do you think radical Socialism is no longer quite as fashionable among Third World leaders today?

MM: Because it has proved to be ineffective. It completely over-rates state capacity and under-rates popular culture.

Stern: So now that you're back in power with a different image and a different set of policies to some extent, what are your objectives this time?

MM: I think that the most important thing that we can try to do is to really get our economy to grow in a manner which has internal structure, internal linkage, and a self-sustaining dynamic. If we don't do that, nothing else is going to happen. Secondly, I think we have as a very strong objective how to develop a powerful and increasingly integrated regional economy in the Caribbean. Without the economies of scale through regional integration none of us have a chance. And, thirdly, to see if we can put into effect more enduringly that programme of tremendous human-resource development in education without which we had better forget the 21st century or it will run over us. And, finally, you know, to have the resources to be able to support decent health services and look after our children well, and good nutrition and so on and so forth. It is really a very simple agenda.

Stern: But in the end how much power does a Jamaican Prime Minister have to achieve his agenda?

MM: The big thing to learn is that you don't have much. If you learn that you have a chance.

Stern: So what are the special problems that a Jamaican Prime Minister has?

MM: Well, he has the enormous problem of the highest per capita debt in the world. Let's start with that. We are paying 51 cents out of everything we earn to service debts. So we are running a 49 cent country. You ought to try that some time, it's quite a trick! Another of the things you have to wrestle with is the tremendous effect of the cultural penetration of the canned TV show – The Dallas, and the Falcon Crest – which promote an idea of what the society can achieve which has no relationship to your economic realities and tends, I think, to direct people away from a concern with savings and investment and sacrifice to make the economy grow. So you have serious social-psychological problems of that sort. But, you have to wrestle with them.

Stern: Do you and did you find running the country a lonely profession?

MM: As time passes increasingly so, yes. You tend to get absorbed into the whole pattern of problems and the demands on time are, of course, fierce whether in a big country or small. And also, you just get tired. After a long period in it you are more or less at the edge of exhaustion after the long 18 hour days. And those hours are not conducive to maintaining friendships.

Stern: Yet, you have chosen to take it up for the third time. Can power go to one's head? Can one become corrupted by it?

MM: So very easily. That is the constant peril that you have to guard against. That's why I made the earlier comment that if you can't retain a scepticism about the question, you can very easily succumb. It's a heady business – power.

Stern: Have you ever succumbed to that?

MM: I have tried not to. It's hard to judge that from outside yourself. I have never been accused of that by people that are close to me.

Stern: I wonder if there's anything you dislike about being in office?

MM: I hate protocol. I like a very relaxed lifestyle. I hate security around me and as a very private person who likes to live his own private life with my music and things like that with very, very few friends, I do not like the aspect of politics that demands the constant meeting of this and the social round.

Stern: Looking back over your long career in politics, what has been your proudest achievement so far?

MM: I would have to say, being a part of watching a party shattered in 1980 and slowly picking itself up off the ground, dealing with the problems in a mature way, being a very responsible opposition, playing our part in letting Jamaica heal after the terrible experience of the late 70s.

Stern: And, what about your greatest folly, something that you are perhaps a little ashamed of.

MM: I am genuinely ashamed of the fact that I allowed myself to be provoked by tensions that developed, say with Washington and with the private sector, into a sort of retaliatory rhetoric. That was not a thing I am proud of.

Stern: What are future historians going to make of Michael Manley? What do you think they are going to say about you?

MM: Well they will say that I came back from the abyss. What else is there to say? I am just another of the people who has tried to struggle with all the enormously complex problems of the Third World development. They'll have to say I tried. But I have no way of saying whether they think there was any success. That remains to be seen.

LEE KUAN YEW

CHAPTER 9

Stern: Prime Minister, although you've been in public life for 25 years or more you seem to have been remarkably reticent about certain aspects of your past and especially your early years. Is that because you think it's nobody's business, or are people afraid to ask you?

LKY: Well, nobody's interested. We are Asians and there's a certain form about not being too inquisitive. But my own people do know my past, they know who my parents were, who my grandparents were, and have a vague idea of what they did.

Stern: But they don't know quite where you were born. Some people say Singapore, some people say Java.

LKY: I was born in Singapore in Kumpung Java Road in what was then an upper-middle class Chinese home – a large compound house. It then became in the Japanese occupation a saki brewers factory, and might have been converted into something else now. But I come from I would say one of the more successful Chinese emigrant families – one of the few that hit the jackpot; but then they lost the jackpot with the great depression in the 1930s when rubber and properties went down, so we nearly had to start all over again. So I've known a silver spoon when I was born, fairly modest middle-class life and very harsh times for three and a half years of the Japanese occupation.

Stern: I was going to ask you about the Japanese occupation because for a time you were working for the Japanese news agency, and yet you hated the Japanese.

LKY: Oh, it was not the news agency, they called it the Hodobu. It was the propaganda department and my job, and I needed a job to make a living, was to do a kind of crossword puzzle. They intercepted without royalties all the allied news agencies during the war (it was very secret work because the general people were not supposed to know what was happening in the world besides what they published and broadcast), but because reception was never very good especially during daylight hours, there would be blanks in the transcription and my job was to guess what the words were and classify them into Eastern Front, Western Front, Pacific and so on. We were at the top floor where reception was best, and on the floor below us they would cook it up for propaganda broadcasts.

Stern: How were you able to work for these people?

LKY: When you are in enemy occupied territory you've got to live and some become collaborators, Quislings, others become good black market operators, or...

Stern: Does that mean you were a collaborator, you were a Quisling?

LKY: No, I did a job which marginally may have made their war effort a little bit easier in the propaganda field but I would have thought it was very marginal. I couldn't have cooked it up for them, that would have been distasteful.

Stern: What about the suggestion I've heard from some quarters that you were perhaps an agent for the British?

LKY: No, I was in Raffles College, the precursor of the University of Singapore, in my second year when the war came, and I was a stretcher bearer in the medical auxiliary services when the Japanese came in. All I had done by then was to carry injured persons on to ambulances and that was that.

Stern: But if you weren't working for the British, how did you manage to get passage to Britain on a British troopship shortly after the war? That was completely against the rules, wasn't it?

LKY: No, not quite. It was unusual, it showed a certain stroke of luck, also a certain seizing of opportunities. I started off being stand-offish and just living off the family for about a year, brushing up on my Chinese and refusing to learn Japanese. That became unproductive because resources ran out and you've got to make a living, so I got a job, after the first year, with a Japanese textile company called Shimoda & Company. Shimoda was my grandfather's friend and my father knew him and I became his clerk as a copy typist for a year and a half. It was very boring, dull and tedious.

Stern: Yes, but that doesn't explain how you got on that British troopship.

LKY: Well, then I took on this job as cable-editor. I could see the British returning; they were coming down the coast and going for Rangoon, while the Japanese were fighting every inch of the way, digging tunnels all over Singapore. I advised my parents we'd best move up to Malaya, preferably the Cameron Highlands, and grow the equivalent of rice there, and other things like that, but when I resigned from this Hodobu, the lift boy who was Chinese and very friendly told me "Your file has been given to the Kampetei" – their military police. They felt that I had some links or prior signals to get out of the place. I subsequently discovered that one of my fellow cable-editors who didn't like me had passed on to the Japanese chief editor that my loyalties were suspect, and they decided that I was up to no good. So I found myself tailed, which was a devastating discovery.

Stern: So you skipped the country?

LKY: No I did not! That could have been the end. I would have landed up in a military police headquarters and have been beaten up for no rhyme or reason to disclose who my 'links' were or what 'directions' I was getting and so on. But once I had discovered that I was being tailed, I decided that I couldn't go, because if I had attempted to leave Singapore I am sure that they would have arrested me. So my family also decided not to go rather than leave me behind, and we stayed put. Then after two or three months when they found nothing was happening I went into the business of selling gum arabic with a friend, a Raffles College science graduate. We used tapioca as a base and added carbolic acid and it became the product.

Stern: You made it yourself and sold it.

LKY: Yes I sold it. My family helped make it.

Stern: But at some stage you went to the Cameron Highlands.

LKY: No, I did not. That would have been a disaster.

Stern: The books say that you did.

LKY: I had gone on an exploratory trip before my resignation.

Stern: But you weren't hiding there?

LKY: No, once I discovered that I was being tailed and suspected, my best course was to stay put and be under their control and their surveillance.

Stern: So you were in Singapore at the end of the war?

LKY: Oh yes, I was.

Stern: And then you got on this ship in '46. How did that come about?

LKY: Well, from selling gum I went on to selling paint and all sorts of other things which were getting scarcer and scarcer and passed through hands in the black market, and from there I went on to building contracting – repairing homes and so on; and when the British came back they needed labour and I got in touch with them. I produced workers, got work done and I got to know the Colonel in charge, and through the Colonel I got a passage on board 'The Britannic'.

Stern: But what did you do for the Colonel?

LKY: Repaired his godowns, moved his goods.

Stern: And in return for that they gave you passage to Britain?

LKY: Well yes, I made friends with them; I was English speaking, and well-mannered. So I must have been an unusual contractor.

Stern: So you find yourself on this ship, you come to Britain to do law. Why Britain? Did you see it as the 'Open Sesame' to fame and fortune?

LKY: No, because for a bright student in Singapore the only two professions which would give you a certain independence of the government were law and medicine. Medicine didn't appeal to me because it took more years and it was a harder life. I could see that the lawyers had a more congenial life – there was more leisure time, less of the urgent calls, and the consensus in the family was that I would be better off as a lawyer.

Stern: I wonder whether in taking law you envisaged that one day you'd help to mould and shape the destiny of a nation. Was politics really at the back of your mind?

LKY: My entry into politics was fortuitous because the furthest thing from my mind was having anything to do with government. I mean the British Raj was secure as it had been for nearly 150 years and looked like going on for another 1000 years.

Stern: But by 1947 that was no longer the case, was it? Churchill was out, India was getting its independence.

LKY: No, I'm talking now of pre-war...

Stern: But when you got to Britain in 1946, when you started your career first at the LSE, then at Cambridge, didn't you think "One day, I'm going to run a nation"?

LKY: No, it's much simpler than that. We settled on law because it was easier than medicine, it was more congenial and politics was not in my mind.

Stern: When did you start getting political ideas?

LKY: When the Japanese came in I got my first lesson in politics, because the first thing I discovered was they were brutal. I was personally assaulted by them, just because I didn't bow to a sentry. They, by force of arms, became the ruling class in substitution of the British and I saw no reason why my life should be determined this way.

Stern: So what did this give you? A hatred of foreign occupation? A hatred of authority, or what?

LKY: No, a desire that we should at least be in control of our destiny and not be subject to the vagaries of other people's policies.

Stern: Is that why you joined the Labour Society at Cambridge and got involved in socialist politics?

LKY: The Labour Club...

Stern: Yes, the Labour Club. Did you see socialism as the answer?

LKY: Students from the colonies could not find any empathy with the Conservatives, with the Conservative Club, because they were for the maintenance of empire. We wanted to run our own lives.

Stern: So socialism was really for you to do with the national struggle.

LKY: Yes, and also because Britain at that time under Attlee and the first Labour government after the war was undergoing a social transformation – a period of great excitement. For me it was the formative years of my life. I was in my early twenties, mature enough to understand poverty, hardship and what it meant to be a 'have-not'. And here was a tremendous experiment, an adventure in recreating or building something more just, more equal, more fair – a utopia come true. I mean, a great war had been fought, everybody had made sacrifices and now it was fair shares for all.

Stern: But what remains of that flirtation of yours with socialism?

LKY: Well, a great belief in equal opportunities.

Stern: But do you still describe yourself as a socialist?

LKY: To use British, or continental European nomenclature, I would be classified as a Social Democrat. But I believed then that you must have an equal society if you're going to have everybody producing, giving of their best, and that anything less than that must stultify the potential of a society.

Stern: And that's not incompatible with the kind of capitalist utopia which you've established here?

LKY: No, it's not a capitalist utopia. It's very much a free er...

Stern: Free enterprise?

LKY: Free enterprise and...

Stern: Isn't that capitalism?

LKY: No, a freely socially mobile society. I mean, in my cabinet, amongst my panel of secretaries, are people born from the poorest of families. We have a panel of secretaries whose fathers were taxi drivers. I have a cabinet minister whose father was a tailor. We are the exact antithesis of Britain. It was a completely unstructured society. There were the British on top, then there were the governed colonials – the Chinese, Malays, Indians and between us we were all 'untouchables'. Equally 'untouchables'. Some made money and others didn't, but there was no class distinction, and we have retained that advantage. So a Singaporean's ability to rise depends upon his innate gifts and his application.

Stern: So when in 1954 you helped to found the People's Action Party and in 1955 joined the Legislative Assembly, were you in politics to bring about first of all independence and then social democracy in Singapore?

LKY: More than that. It was first of all to get the British out, to take over control, join Malaysia and on a bigger base build a socialist society.

Stern: Now why was joining Malaysia so important for you? What role did you see for yourself in Malaysia?

LKY: Well if it were only Singapore we couldn't have a secure base and a socialist society. It was too commercial a centre: there wasn't the hinterland to provide the ballast for a redistribution of wealth.

Stern: But you have got a secure base, so were you wrong in your earlier enthusiasm for this great federation?

LKY: No no, I don't think I was wrong. I still think it's one of the great pities that it didn't come off. Had it come off it would have been a better solution both for Singapore and for Malaysia.

Stern: Yet did you really give of your utmost to make the thing work?

LKY: Absolutely – no question about it, though the Tunku [Abdul Rahman, Prime Minister of Malaya/Malaysia 1957-1970] thinks otherwise. He sent me a book of his writings a few years ago and inscribed it 'To Lee Kuan Yew who worked so very hard for Malaysia, and worked equally hard to destroy it'.

Stern: But didn't you in a sense? I mean you clung to the title of Prime Minister, which you'd first acquired in 1959, instead of calling yourself Chief Minister. You pursued a high profile foreign policy of your own and you spent a lot of time attacking the new federal government. Would you yourself tolerate that kind of behaviour in an opposition leader?

LKY: I don't know how much of the history of Singapore you've read, but first, how did Singapore have a Prime Minister? Because the British, who helped us in the negotiations to rejoin Malaysia, knew of the difficulties of Singapore being subsumed as just another state because I would have had to take a vote in Singapore and they knew that I would be accused of selling out. So certain sectors, like labour and education, were reserved for the state government which wasn't the case for other states. And they thought the Northern Ireland model would be ideal, where you are really a part of the United Kingdom but at the same time not quite the same as Scotland or Wales; hence this was a British formula and I went along with it because it seemed eminently reasonable.

Stern: So you would maintain that you did your utmost to merge Singapore into the new federation?

LKY: I think that would stand up to any scrutiny by any Ph.D student.

Stern: Well that may be, but quite a lot of people weren't convinced. I think the suggestion is that your intention all along was that Singapore, and yourself, should lead the Federation and that if you weren't going to lead it you were less interested in it. Now, is that fair or not?

LKY: That's a very simplistic and distorted view of what happened...

Stern: Is there any truth in it?

LKY: No, I couldn't lead it, because to lead it I would first have had to make the voting non-communal, and voting was communal in Malaysia. We had attempted and succeeded to a marginal extent in making the voting across ethnic or racial lines, but it was not possible to change Malaysia for at least 10, 15 or 20 years and we would have had to wait that long. So any expectation of high office in Malaysia, to become the Prime Minister would mean a gap, a time lag. We were prepared for that, but what we could not conceive was that within Malaysia the Chinese and the Indians, who were the non-indigenous peoples regardless of how long they had been in the country, would be second-class citizens. That was the challenge. And we could see that if we didn't challenge it immediately, it would be too late. If you went to Malaysia now, it's openly talked about that Malay is the Bumi Putra, which means the prince of the soil, and the others are...

Stern: But isn't that what you'd expect? I mean, it wasn't called Malaysia for nothing, was it?

LKY: But the terms of the contract in the constitution were very unequivocal: that we were all equal regardless of our race, regardless of our religion and regardless of our being either indigenous or non-indigenous in our origins, and we had to assert that right.

Stern: But given the tensions which existed you can't have been surprised, can you, when in August 1965 came the official, possibly inevitable divorce? When the Tunku more or less told you to go, weren't you expecting it?

LKY: Only towards the very end, in the last few weeks. He had two choices: you either have a Malay Malaysia, or a Malaysian Malaysia, and we campaigned hard and strenuously for a Malaysian Malaysia.

Stern: But after 1965 wasn't it obvious that the thing wasn't going to work and that you'd have to fashion Singapore on its own?

LKY: No, I don't think so. There were several other alternatives, one of which I urged right up to the end was a confederation in which greater power should be given to Singapore, after which we would disengage from federal politics for 10, 15, 20 years and then recouple. The Tunku wasn't prepared for that. We were prepared to let things cool off, have more powers transferred to the State, disengage from federal politics, have a committee in which we would be represented for defence, foreign affairs and finance. That was also unacceptable to him. If only he'd been a younger man, and stronger, physically... He was tired and the pressures from his 'ultras' were too much for him. He was very much a cosmopolitan, but was trapped in a situation that made compromise impossible.

Stern: But in those days you were a young, dynamic, thrusting person of ideas. Didn't you really want to run the show?

LKY: But it wasn't on.

Stern: Yes, but wouldn't you have liked to have done?

LKY: It just wasn't on. I couldn't get the votes, and we had to be realistic.

Stern: Did you already have in mind, though, what you would do if you were forced to go it alone?

LKY: No! It was one of the big traumas of my life. We had started off on the assumption that an independent Singapore made no sense, and we campaigned in 1961 and '62 convincing the people of Singapore that the bigger whole was the way to the future.

Stern: But by '65 you had to start again.

LKY: Yes, it was a terrible blow, a shock, and an enormous challenge which we just had to surmount.

Stern: Well, how did you surmount this challenge? Was the creation of the new Singapore your own idea or was it a collective decision?

LKY: No, no, it was the Tunku's idea. He said 'go it alone'.

Stern: But what was fashioned is something unique isn't it – an efficient and prosperous, clean and puritanical society. Was this your own, or a collective idea?

LKY: Why do you toss out these words without having tested them against reality?

Stern: I will test them by asking you is it not clean? Is it not efficient? Is it not prosperous?

LKY: Is it puritanical? You can belong to any promiscuous sect you like so long as you're not a nuisance to others. We've got heroin addicts, not many but we've had our fair share.

Stern: And the death penalty for them.

LKY: In spite of the death penalty, we are the biggest trans-shipment point in South East Asia and people risk other people's lives to get trans-shipments through Singapore. Because they know that we are strict, any airline that has taken a passenger through from Singapore is less rigorously checked in Europe. So they come in from

Hong Kong, from Bangkok, trying to get on a Singapore plane.

Stern: But it is efficient, it is prosperous, and clean; and it is also, I think, highly regulated.

LKY: No, clean by comparison with London, but not if you compare this to Zurich or Geneva.

Stern: But it's a highly regulated society, isn't it? I think you once called the Singaporeans 'digits'. Was the creation of this rather paternalistic society your own idea?

LKY: I don't think it was an idea, it was a problem to be solved and the only way to solve a problem is to divorce ourselves of any emotions and say 'what can be done?'. We had to make a nation out of something which wasn't intended to be one and didn't have the basic elements of nationhood.

Stern: I'm interested in who the 'we' is there. Is that you?

LKY: 'We' means my Cabinet and I (no, I'm not Mrs Thatcher), who suddenly found ourselves flung out and responsible for the livelihood of then just under two million people. From this building where we're talking now, Government House in Singapore, the British ran the whole of peninsula Malaya, large chunks of Borneo, parts of islands in the Indian Ocean, Christmas Island and so forth, and it made its livelihood importing products from the neighbourhood and exporting them to Europe and later America and Japan, bringing back manufactured goods, breaking up and distributing them in the region, and we knew that after separation all that was going to stop. They were going to have their own harbours, their own import and export houses, and we were going to have to make a new way of life.

Stern: Yes, but there could have been different approaches to this and I'm just wondering how much the approach to Singapore was your own, how much that of the Cabinet and incidentally how influential your own wife was in fashioning the new Singapore, because the wives of Prime Ministers are often very influential, aren't they?

LKY: She runs my family, she runs my domestic affairs, she doesn't run my office.

Stern: But do you consult her when you have to make a difficult decision?

LKY: No, I don't consult her on major political decisions. I may consult her on, say, an education matter, but in going off on our own, when the Tunku said 'out with thee' I only consulted my cabinet. We had a problem thrust upon us and we had to find a solution. How do we provide a livelihood for two million people without the hinterland?

Stern: So did you have a model in mind?

LKY: No, none whatsoever.

Stern: Not Switzerland? Not Israel? Not Monaco? Not Luxembourg?

LKY: No, we borrowed, in an eclectic fashion, elements of what Hong Kong was doing, what Switzerland was doing, what Israel was doing, and we improvised. I also went down to Malta to see how they ran the dry docks. They had the British navy there, and when we were ousted in 1965 from Malaysia the British navy was still in Singapore. I wanted to see what I could do with the dry docks at a later stage if and when the British left, which they did a few years later.

Stern: And did you use advisers from these countries to help?

LKY: Some, yes.

Stern: What have been the special problems in governing a small city state like Singapore?

LKY: There's a Chinese proverb which says: 'A sparrow although small has got all its five organs complete', and to be a nation, we had to have all these organs complete, and that was an enormous problem. Our total Gross Domestic Product in 1965 could not equal say even that of the Sony Corporation, and yet out of that we had to run a defence ministry and build up an army, navy, air force, and a foreign office, and out of a population of two million, have missions in all the key capitals of the world for trade and security. I would not recommend it as a way of life for other than those in dire circumstances.

Stern: Have you found running Singapore a lonely occupation? Do you feel isolated in some way?

LKY: From time to time, when at the end of the day I've discussed a problem with all my colleagues and taken opinion and advice and things are evenly divided, I have to toss the coin in my mind, that's the lonely part. But it's not very often; in most cases the decision is quite obvious or fairly clear. It is only occasionally, I would say one out of 30 or 40 decisions, where opinions are evenly divided and when if I chose the wrong one we could all come to grief.

Stern: 'If I chose the wrong one' you said. Now I'm interested to know how decisions are made in your cabinet; I mean, do you play the Chief, or are you the Chairman? Do you tell people what the decision is going to be, or do you lead from behind as it were? What is your style of leadership?

LKY: Where it's not an important item, and there's a long agenda I would state my view straight away and say 'look, I feel that this is the solution, and if a minister feels differently, let's hear him'. I would say on about half of the usual cabinet agenda everybody's more or less agreed. I don't waste time taking opinion all the way round and then proffer my own at the end of it, but come out and say 'this is where I believe we ought to go'. But where it's a tricky decision and it's come up for a tentative position first, I would state the problem as I see it from the political angle – 'if we take this decision, this will be the cost, if we take that decision, that will be the cost'. For instance, we had to decide what to do about a Chinese language university we inherited from the Chinese Chamber of Commerce. It was creating enormous problems, producing graduates difficult to place in jobs as we had to move towards the English language. It was also a political hot potato. It was a kind of hotbed of Communist revolution. It was the apex of the recruits into the Communist general staff. First, should we leave it, in which case every year x number of graduates come out who are misfits and have to be slotted into jobs they're not going to be happy with? Shall we let it die a natural death because parents will know that if you send your son or daughter there, the chances of a good job are poorer? So at first we said 'this is too tricky' and left it to time to bring the message home to parents. By the 1970s, the message was sinking in. Students were switching over, but we facilitated the switch by running special classes for Chinese school students, to help them master the English language and go on to the University of Singapore (or the University of Malaya as it then was called) and do their degree in English so as to get a job more easily. The University authorities reacted by taking in students of lower calibre who would not have been admitted to the University of Singapore/University of Malaya before, and that created a deeper problem. Now not only were they not properly educated for the economic system, they were not properly qualified to be. So that then forced our hand – we had to do something.

Stern: Are such decisions basically your decisions with endorsement from the Cabinet, or are these genuinely collective decisions?

LKY: In this particular case it was a collective decision because we all knew what dynamite it was. The more important it is, the more I must commit all the others to the decision, because if it goes wrong then we all carry the can. That's my principle.

Stern: Are some of your Cabinet colleagues afraid of you, because quite a lot of people in the country are? In other words, do they do what the boss says?

LKY: Maybe the weaker or the younger ones, but my old colleagues – some of them actually older than I am – they're my seniors...

Stern: They can still be terrified of you...

LKY: They're not, I can tell you. And probably I benefited because they were not terrified of me. I have never had a compliant Cabinet. You see Rajaratnam, he's still around, or you see Goh Keng Swee or Toh Chin Chye...

Stern: But a lot of people are not around. They're either in exile or in jail or you're about to take action against them...

LKY: Nobody in the Cabinet is either exiled or jailed, or have I taken action against them.

Stern: No, not in the current Cabinet, by definition.

LKY: No, not even in any Cabinet. We have always had a cohesive group.

Stern: But as a lawyer, you resort quite easily to law, don't you? I mean if people in your view fall foul of certain principles, you sue them and you generally win. Now isn't that enough to terrify quite a lot of people who work with you?

LKY: No, I fail to terrify them because they keep on making defamatory remarks; they keep on alleging corruption; they keep on alleging things which are completely untrue

– that I've sold out the country and things like that, and if you don't take action and subject yourself to cross-examination like any plaintiff, from doubts will come convictions that you are what they said you are responsible for having done, and it's because I challenge it each time that nobody doubts that this government, and I in particular, have not put our hands in the till. If you say I have – and it was said even in the last election – I go into the witness box, I'm open to cross-examination, you can bring evidence of unjust, unlawful gains, of my style of life, and demolish me. And if you can't then you pay damages which I then contribute to charity so that it is quite clear that I have made a political point.

Stern: When was the last time you lost a case?

LKY: I have not lost a case because I have never been my own lawyer. It is always my counsel, my lawyers, who advise me whether or not to proceed.

Stern: When you were at Cambridge, you learnt all about checks and balances on power. Are there checks and balances on power in Singapore?

LKY: If you compare this to, say, the United States of America, it's a totally different constitution; if you compare this to Britain it's also a totally different situation because there you have an ordered, established old society where the checks and balances are not just constitutional in the sense that you have an upper house that can send back non-money bills and so on but there are constraints on the exercise of power as a result of independent civic institutions. We don't have those civic institutions. It's a raw, young, plastic society. Therefore checks and balances are less, but the final checks are the values and attitudes of the population.

Stern: You've had the premiership now for 30 years. What qualities did you bring to office?

LKY: I'm not the best judge, but I would think that the main reason why my colleagues and I have lasted so long is because we were prepared to face unpleasant truths, presented them to the people when the situation was so dire that they said 'Yes, we'll go along with you and work out the solution with you'.

Stern: But how did the people do that?

LKY: I'll take a very simple graphic instance. We spent two years in Malaysia – 1963 merger, 1965 separation. We had two nasty race riots, one on Prophet Mohammed's birthday and the other three months after in 1964 where Muslims ran amok and slaughtered Chinese and the Chinese hit back and hundreds were injured, two dozen died. And the population could see that a largely Malay police force and a Malay army were inert and didn't stamp trouble out. So when we were ousted from Malaysia they said 'even if life is hard, at least we'll be in charge of the army and the police and we're going to have fair play'. So as a result of that painful experience they were prepared for the very severe measures which we had to take to make Singapore viable.

Stern: So one of your qualities of leadership is being prepared to take severe decisions?

LKY: Yes, so I seized that moment and told them that to make a go of Singapore on its own we had to change our way of life. No more going on strike for almost no reason at all other than just to twist the tails of the bosses, which became a Communist habit (you know the Communists were in charge of our trade unions). I got through a new Employment Act which spelt it out that the employer shall have the right to hire and fire, promote and to do many other things which the unions had encroached upon, and made it part of annual negotiations. So there was no subterfuge about it. They were told 'if you are not going to do this, we are not going to get the investment and if we don't work hard and concentrate on productivity and skills then we will perish'.

Stern: But doesn't this give rise to a problem, that there's a lot of telling going on? You tell them, the government tells them, you exhort them and so on, and you change their lives for them, and I wonder whether young people...

LKY: What was the choice?

Stern: Well, maybe there was no choice before, but there may be a choice now.

LKY: Well, that's up to them. They think they have all the freedom of choice now of a mature developed society but I do not believe them and they will discover it to be so.

Stern: But aren't you worried that what's happening in Russia, in China and South Korea, will happen here?

LKY: You are talking in stereotypical words and phrases. We are as far removed from China or South Korea or the Soviet Union as any other country can be.

Stern: Yes, but what you have in common is that these were disciplined societies, as yours is, and in those societies discipline is collapsing, and it's collapsing because you've got a conflict between the younger generation and the older. Can't that happen here too?

LKY: You have thrown in such a hotch potch of contradictory ideas that I am at some difficulty where to begin. First, we were a most disorganised and disorderly society. We were not like a Communist party that takes over and runs the administration and says 'right, now, party discipline and the party ethos will prevail'. We took over a colonial administration in which the British officers left within five to seven years, and a nascent domestic Singaporean civil service had to be nurtured into the job of being neutral administrators. The problem was that it was an undisciplined society.

Stern: But it isn't any longer, is it?

LKY: Ah, but it was done by regular popular vote. On the average we went to the polls about every four and a quarter years. The difference between the Soviet Union, China and Vietnam on the one hand and Singapore on the other is this. Whether it's anti-litter, cutting out disorderly traffic, keeping down the noise from the neighbours or from big dogs in high-rise flats, it had to be done by proper legislation, or subsidiary legislation which then had to be enforced properly in the courts which implied first and foremost a majority in parliament, which meant an election within five years. Now if the people didn't agree with orderly traffic or unlittered streets, they just toss us out.

Stern: Not necessarily, not if they were afraid of you, they couldn't.

LKY: Are you saying that we have hypnotic powers to make them fear us when they know that they can go to that ballot box and toss us out?

Stern: Well I'm saying that it's not always easy for opponents of yours to make their views known.

LKY: If they had an alternative, there's nothing to prevent them from putting that alternative.

Stern: Well how many opposition newspapers are there, for example?

LKY: I don't have any newspapers. The newspapers are owned by private citizens, private corporations. But I run a party newspaper, and so do the other parties.

Stern: Yes, but some newspapers which opposed you have been closed down, haven't they?

LKY: No no. We have closed down only papers which have been or proved to have been owned by people who are not Singaporeans. Or where they had been in receipt of Communist funds from Hong Kong – Chinese Communist funds.

Stern: Are you worried about what's going to happen to Singapore after you retire? You were going to retire when you were 65, and you are 65, and you haven't retired yet.

LKY: I was ready to go after the last elections. I think my successor, Goh Chok Tong, is ready to take over.

Stern: And when will that be?

LKY: He wants two years.

Stern: And what will happen to you?

LKY: Chances are I will stay in the Cabinet. That's what he said.

Stern: And is that what you'd like?

LKY: I would like to see them succeed, and if I can help them from within the Cabinet, I will.

Stern: How much does Singapore depend on you, though? I mean, some people think that this is a one-man band, a one-man show.

LKY: They do my colleagues a grave injustice. I mean, if you've met Rajaratnam or Goh Keng Swee or Toh Chin Chye, you'd know that isn't so. They are big minds, very strong. No one man could have had such a polyfaceted mind.

Stern: Are you happy with what you've created here? It is all these things that we've talked about, efficient, clean and prosperous, but I also think it is very regulated. I wonder whether it hasn't perhaps lost its soul.

LKY: What does that mean?

Stern: Well, it was a vibrant society.

LKY: Was it? Have you been here before?

Stern: No I haven't.

LKY: Well, your colleague there was born and brought up part of his life in Singapore. You ask him whether it was vibrant then or is vibrant now. That's my answer.

Stern: One final question: what do you see as your place in history?

LKY: It's such a small place. It would not even get a footnote in the history of the world. My place in history is negligible. All I have proved is that if you are determined enough and you've got a cohesive leadership and a people willing to work with that leadership you can make a country work with almost all the factors against it, provided everybody knows we are going against the tide and willing to row that way. That's all I have proved. My problem is the tide is still against us and a younger generation believes it isn't, but I know it is. All we have succeeded in is in putting a motor onto the canoe. It's got some power of its own but it is still going against the stream.

Junius JAYAWARDENE

CHAPTER 10

Stern: Junius Jayawardene you've been in politics for more than half a century, and like Churchill and de Gaulle and Adenauer and Franco and Mao, you remained active in politics until you were well into your eighties. Why? Was politics a kind of narcotic you couldn't give up?

JJ: Firstly, I was healthy and health is a very important factor in most human ventures, certainly in politics. I have always said that a politician should be like a trained racehorse, ready at any time to run the Derby!

Stern: But I wonder whether somebody in his eighties can take stock of and react to situations as quickly as a younger man?

JJ: Well, I didn't find any difficulty. I find the brain working as actively and as quickly, as efficiently and as usefully as before.

Stern: It was said of Churchill and de Gaulle and Adenauer and Mao, by their friends as well as by their foes, that perhaps they stayed on a bit too long in politics. Some people have also said that of you. Were the critics right about them, were they right about you?

JJ: I don't know the reasons given. Churchill, as you know, had physical problems at one time – he had a stroke. But in my case I had none like that. Naturally there is a slowing down, not mentally but physically – walking and running must be slower. Fortunately I've had no organic illness through my life. Not one single organ has shown waste or erosion or rust. I've had a lot of illnesses caused by foreign bodies, like pneumonia but no organic problems like diabetes, heart trouble or something like that. So that's really the main cause of my being able to last.

Stern: Let's go back to September 17th 1906 when you were born into rather a prosperous, Anglophile Sinhalese family in Colombo. Your father was a Supreme Court judge and you had what is sometimes called a British colonial upbringing. Can you explain what that amounted to?

JJ: Well, the families that could afford it would want their children brought up in the English way. We had a British governess living with us looking after us for several years. My mother was more Sinhalese in her attitude, in her customs, way of living and speaking. Although she talked a little English she preferred to speak to us in her mother tongue. But my father thought his boys – and I was the eldest in a family of eleven – should know their English well and so got us an English governess.

Stern: Did that mean that you were a kind of race apart, a privileged elite who did not really mix with the lower orders?

JJ: We did mix with everybody. My father and family were politicians so they faced elections. As a matter of fact my grandfather came forward for the first municipal election in Asia in 1865, though he was disqualified on some objection. After that the eldest son came in 1897 and he won a municipal seat. After he died in 1913, his brother, who was my father, came and after my father went on the bench, his brother came, and after him I came. So we were all elected people.

Stern: What kinds of people did you mix with? As a child, for instance, did you have many friends who were Tamils?

JJ: A large number of friends. At our school, Royal College – one of the premier schools in Sri Lanka – we all spoke English. The English language was a bond at that school. We didn't think of one another as Tamil or Burgers or Muslim or Sinhalese.

Stern: As a child, were you loving, agreeable, dutiful, or were you arrogant, aloof and rather self-centred?

JJ: None in our family were arrogant, again I would say because of the electoral process which permeated our household. People used to come here from all grades of society, all types of people. Electoral politics is a good mixer.

Stern: You're the first person I've ever met who's called Junius. Why did your parents give you that name?

JJ: My father was a Christian, my mother was a Buddhist, but even the Buddhists use Christian names. My father's younger brother, who was Junius Quintus – Quintus because he was the fifth brother – had just died at a very young age, so they wanted to perpetuate his name. Why he was called Junius I don't know.

Stern: Aren't there political overtones to that name?

JJ: That I don't know.

Stern: You said your parents were involved in politics. Did they expect you to have a political career as well?

JJ: No. My father died when I'd just joined the Bar. We never talked about a political career with him.

Stern: So did he expect you be a lawyer?

JJ: Yes, definitely.

Stern: So when did you decide to enter politics?

JJ: Politics came naturally to me and to my brothers also and when our cousins, girls and boys, gathered we used to have mock elections at home!

Stern: Who won?

JJ: Well, I think I generally won.

Stern: I guessed you might! When you did go into formal politics, as distinct from the kind of politics you had at home, what was it all about? Was it to make a name for yourself? Was it to throw your weight around?

JJ: It was all about the Indian movement. By the time I left school for university in the 1920s, I was about 18 or 19 at the time, a young man's fancy lightly turns to public affairs. What drew me was the Indian political situation. Nehru, Gandhi and all the leading lights of the Congress Movement were in jail. But the movement wasn't violent, it wasn't killing, it was trying to uplift not only the Indian people but the British people to show what was wrong, and it had a tremendous influence on the younger generation of the subject peoples throughout the world. So Nehru and Gandhi were really the people who led me, as it were, into politics.

Stern: Did your family connections help further your political career in any way?

JJ: Yes, because the political parties accepted me as a man who had to come in, and my first venture in elections was in the seat that my father had held. When I sought election in 1940, I had the support of my father and uncles, and I came uncontested. But my main interest was not so much in municipal politics as in the freedom movement, which was in the doldrums in our country, since the original enthusiasts like our first Prime Minister, Mr D S Senanayake, forgot about that once they got into the legislature, the state council, and co-operated with the British. So younger people like myself and D S Senanayake's own son rejoined the Congress, which in 1918 had been the first political party, and formed an organisation with the Indian Congress to ask for complete freedom.

Stern: Did you do some of the things that Gandhi was doing? Did you go on fasts?

JJ: No, we didn't come to that stage but we went to the Indian Congress sessions in 1940 and a few of us accepted Nehru's invitation to come and stay with him. Then we went to the Congress Executive Committee meeting in Bombay. I was there sitting behind Gandhi's chair when he moved the 'Quit India' resolution, and he said "We don't stop at this. It's do or die!" Well, that had a tremendous impression on young people, especially when on the way back our train was stormed and Gandhi and the whole lot were arrested. Remember it was wartime. I am sure if it were not for Mr D S Senanayake we younger people would all have been put in jail too. Marxist people were put in jail but D S Senanayake prevented myself and his son from being put in jail by saying "well, I'll keep them".

Stern: How was he able to do that? Did he have especial influence with the British?

JJ: He did. While we, like the Indians, wanted direct action against the British, he said "don't do that because the British are going to win the war and when the war is won, the British will give freedom, so co-operate with them".

Stern: When you first set foot on the political ladder, as you have described, were you determined to get to the top of it?

JJ: No, it never struck me. I didn't know that we were even going to be free – to have a constitution with our prime minister. I just wanted to be free.

Stern: But when you got freedom in 1948, did you then start thinking that you might become one day the Prime Minister of the country and, indeed, its President?

JJ: No, I didn't think like that because though Dudley, D S Senanayake's son, who was a very dear friend of mine, wanted me to succeed his father I had always thought that he should be the successor.

Stern: What did you think you lacked?

JJ: Political clout. Because his father had been in the freedom movement, had been very influential and had become the first Prime Minister, and for me to challenge him when we had similar ideas about democracy was out of the question.

Stern: When did you start thinking that you would, and you should, make it to the top?

JJ: When Dudley died. After several years in power he'd lost the 1970 election, and before his death (in 1973) he wanted me to be leader of the opposition and I said "certainly I'll take it".

Stern: In the end you became Prime Minister in 1977 and then President in 1978. So what are the kinds of qualities which are required for leadership in general, whether you are a Prime Minister or a President?

JJ: Our presidential system secures a president from certain opposition tendencies which a prime minister cannot hide from. The president can only be removed after very strict conditions have been met – a two-thirds majority in the House and a Supreme Court investigation, but with a prime minister you can vote a certain resolution against him and he is out. So there are two different systems.

tern: Would it be true to say that you invented the Sri Lankan Presidency as it has become?

J: In 1960 we had had two elections in one year. Your countries can afford it but Sri Lanka can't afford two or three elections in a year. In a developing economy you want stability, so I thought you must have a secure executive. They have it in America, they have had it in France since the de Gaulle system, so I thought let's have it here also.

tern: What kinds of qualities does a president of Sri Lanka require?

J: Firstly, he must be able to come to decisions. Second, he must take those decisions to help the people of that country without thinking of himself or his party. Thirdly, he must be able to say "no". When Mrs Kirkpatrick, Mr Reagan's representative in the UNO, came to Sri Lanka I said "you know, Madam, a lady must know two words". So she said "what are the two words, Mr President?" and I said "'yes' and 'no'". So she said "I'll go and tell Mr Reagan!"

tern: But is this a collective 'yes' and a collective 'no' or an individual one? Did you consult your Cabinet or tell them, "it is 'yes' or 'no' whether you to like it or not"?

J: I never did that. I was too friendly with my Cabinet. Even in the signing of the Indo-Sri Lanka Agreement, I specially summoned the Cabinet two days before Rajiv Gandhi came. Some people didn't like this part of the agreement, some didn't like that part, but that I should sign it they all agreed, because that would end that war in the north and the east. Then I put it to my parliamentary group, they agreed; I put it to the working committee of the party, they agreed. I didn't put it to parliament because I am not in parliament. As an executive act it wasn't necessary for parliament to sanction it. When your country went to war with Germany, you didn't summon parliament. On a certain day, at a certain time, on a certain hour, England was at war with Germany, in 1914 and 1939.

ern: And yet there are reports that when it came to the Treaty with India, a good deal of your Cabinet objected and you overrode those objections.

J: That's all wrong.

ern: Was it unanimous?

J: Unanimous that I should sign it, though they said "let us consider the details later".

ern: Was it unanimous because they agreed with it or because they were worried about their jobs if they didn't agree with it?

J: Well, my Cabinet didn't consist of a single fool. What fool would say "you should not sign an agreement when the war is over?". The only person who had some doubt was the present leader of the Tamil Tigers, Mr Prabhakaran. But just before I signed Rajiv Gandhi showed me a telegram. "I am bringing Prabhakaran in an Indian plane

121

to Jaffna. He has agreed to join the democratic process. He has agreed to give up arms." And he did, and that was the end of the war.

Stern: But it wasn't the end of the war, was it?

JJ: No, no, that was a month later. A month later he broke it, but at that time he came and did it.

Stern: But that agreement of yours stirred up a hornet's nest within Sri Lanka itself.

JJ: It didn't, my dear friend, it didn't.

Stern: But didn't a lot of the Sinhalese regard this as a sell-out, either to the Indians, or to the Tamils?

JJ: Some thought so. You can't help that in a democracy. Some pacifists in Britain in 1914 and 1939 thought that you should not fight Germany.

Stern: But it didn't bring peace to the North did it?

JJ: That's the point, my dear man. It didn't bring peace when one person broke it.

Stern: But there was also trouble in the South with the JVP (People's Liberation Front).

JJ: The JVP at the beginning were supporting the Indians. Then when this treaty was signed they were against the Indians. They are a totally untrustworthy organisation and nobody believes them. Now they have been found and killed. But when the agreement was signed there was peace for a month and everybody was happy. But after a month because certain of the Tiger's leaders were caught for criminal acts and were to be brought to Colombo for investigation by the police, Prabhakaran said "No, keep them in Jaffna". When they were being put on the plane they took cyanide and died, and with that Prabhakaran re-started the war a month afterwards.

Stern: The present President Premadasa wants the Indian troops out. Do you agree with him? Is that the right thing to do?

JJ: I wouldn't say that it is the right thing to do. But I would that say if he wants them out, it must be done. If a President says "go", you have to go, that's the agreement.

Stern: So, is it your view therefore that it was the right thing to have the troops there in the first place in 1987 and that it is the right thing also to get rid of them in 1989?

JJ: The troops were invited by me because of trouble during the signing of the agreement. I had no people to guard our police stations so the Inspector General didn't know what to do. Rajiv had come to sign the agreement and he saw this trouble – some crowds a few yards away from the President's house – and said "can I help you?" I said "yes, you can help me. Can you help me get some of my troops from Jaffna?" He asked "what do you want?" and when I told him he gave me helicopters and planes in a few hours, and to fill the vacuum he sent some of his troops from India and also arms – a very small number, a few hundred, I think. So for a month it was so, then when Prabhakaran broke the agreement, we found him fighting with the Indians, not with me! And that's how it happened. India didn't come here to fight him at all. India came here as a peace-keeping force. I think Rajiv thought that he would deal easily with this man but he couldn't, though he didn't give up. He could have said "this isn't our job" and gone away, but he didn't, he kept there.

Stern: So what have those peace-keeping forces achieved in two years?

JJ: If Prabhakaran is now talking to the present President (and really he's a finished force as far as violence is concerned), it's been achieved by the Indian peace-keeping force. They lost over a thousand men, with two thousand injured; they spent about ten million rupees a day without our asking for anything and they brought Prabhakaran to his knees.

Stern: So there's hope?

JJ: Well, the Tigers' are talking to the present government and I think it will end in something. They can't start again now. My real worry was that when the Indians go, we would send our troops to the South and deplete our forces here. But now with the collapse of the JVP movement, the capture of their leaders and their deaths, I think we need have no such fear and the present President will be able to tackle both situations.

Stern: What do you say to those people who criticise you for not having realised the depth of Tamil emotions in the early '80s? They say that you were busy with the economy and that you took insufficient notice of what was happening with the Tamils.

JJ: No, we had a new constitution of district development councils written after a commissioner was appointed, and at that time the terrorist Tamils were not very evident. The TULF it was called – the Tamil United Liberation Front – fully co-operated and we had elections to those councils, which some of them won. From that we went on to another All Party conference that met for about two years and they evolved the provincial council system which was incorporated in the agreement. But I was not ready for any violence. That was something new.

Stern: But shouldn't you have been?

JJ: I am against violence, I do not know why people take to violence and I didn't think that they had all that support for violence.

Stern: But in your second Presidency, upwards of 8,000 Sri Lankans were killed. Do you not feel in any sense responsible?

JJ: Certainly as President I should be responsible for that, though not fully, but how I could stop it I do not know.

Stern: If you had had elections earlier...

JJ: Without a referendum? But the people wanted the referendum and to postpone the election – that was not my decision. The referendum means that you ask the people.

Stern: You say it was not your decision, and yet you've observed that one of the qualities of a Sri Lankan president is to be able to say 'yes' or 'no'. Could you not have said "yes" or "no" as you thought the situation demanded?

JJ: No. Because under the Constitution if you want to extend the life of Parliament, you have to go to the people. Because Mrs Bandaranaike had extended the life of parliament for two years by just a vote in parliament we put in the Constitution that even a hundred per cent vote could not extend the life of parliament by one day. So having put that in I thought that we should give a chance to the people to decide whether this parliament should continue or whether they should have a parliament elected by proportional representation. That was the Constitution. Proportional representation would have meant that the opposition would come almost 50:50, as they are today. But the SLFP (Sri Lankan Freedom Party) was in a very difficult situation at that time in 1982/83. A group had captured SLFP who were very Naxalite.

Stern: Could you explain that?

JJ: The Naxalites are a movement in India where, like the JVP, they are killing people, they are cutting their necks. They are called the Naxalite Movement because they came from a village called Naxalgari. They are assassins really and are spreading throughout India. Well, they had captured the SLFP. They were ousting Bandaranaike and if we had had an election at that time they would have either formed a government, even though I was the President, or they would have had 50:50, and I'd have found the country very unstable to deal with, especially with the situation in the North. So I said "I will ask the people" and I put it to the people – "Do you want the Naxalites to govern this country?" By 52% they said "no".

Stern: But the situation in fact went from bad to worse. Did you ever feel like resigning? Did you ever say to yourself "I can't handle this, I had better leave it to somebody else"?

JJ: No, I handled it. It would have been worse if not for the way we handled it. They would have overthrown the government.

Stern: So you are saying that there would have been more than 8,000 deaths if you had not done what you did?

JJ: They would have overthrown the government. There would have been deaths and there would have been a dictatorship. Mrs Bandaranaike and her son, whom I took to be democrats, would not have been given the chance to run the SLFP. This group of Naxalites would have been in power. We would have been overthrown and there would be an end to democracy in our country.

Stern: Do you think you made any mistakes during that period?

JJ: I may have, but history will decide that, I would have thought. Some say that the signing of the agreement was a mistake, but you can argue that if not for that the government would have been overthrown. Some said that the referendum was a mistake, but if not for that you may have had a completely unstable government. So those have to be judged by others, not by me.

Stern: Do you think it is one of the marks of leadership to be able to admit mistakes when you think you have made them, or is it one of the marks of leadership to cover them up?

JJ: I think it is a mark of strength of character to admit a mistake, but the point is you must be sure that it is a mistake. It is too early to say that the Indo-Sri Lanka Agreement was a mistake.

Stern: Would you admit to anything else you may have done as being a mistake?

JJ: Sometimes I seem to think that having the referendum to postpone the election. But the decision was not mine. It was that of the people. But perhaps I should have avoided going to them for that decision, because now I realise that the JVP who had contested the Presidential election in October/November 1982 were looking forward to coming in the General election and when they were forbidden that they were preaching violence. I knew from the police they were preaching violence, that's why I proscribed them. But why they were doing that I couldn't understand then, but now I think they may have done so reasoning "we have no chance of being in office; we lost the presidency, we lost all the local bodies and we lost the chance of contesting parliament. Therefore our only refuge is in violence". I don't think like that. I don't think any violence is justified for any reason.

Stern: But you've had to use it sometimes yourself?

JJ: The government has to. All violence must be concentrated in the hands of the government, all weapons of destruction.

Stern: But you give the orders if you are President.

JJ: Well, if it's a democracy you give orders only against people who are breaking the law, not against others.

Stern: You are a Buddhist, you say you believe in non-violence and yet you have had to give orders for violence to be used, for people to be killed. Does that cause you a special pain?

JJ: Well, Gandhi answered that question himself. In his own ashram there was a calf that was very ill and in pain, and he gave orders that the calf should be killed and as he said, "that doesn't violate the non-violent principle".

Stern: Hold on, though. Some of the people that you have had to order into battlefield were not dealing with sick calves, they were dealing with perfectly healthy individuals who had views different from theirs.

JJ: Sick men. Mentally sick. They are psychopathic cases. They would not cut your neck off and hang it outside on a spike if they were not sick. They wouldn't go to a policeman's house and kill his mother, his brother, his sister-in-law, her children, who are absolutely innocent, and burn the house with them alive.

Stern: So is it your view that anyone who belongs to the JVP or to the Tamil Eelam Movement is mentally sick?

JJ: I wouldn't say all, but there are people who are mentally sick. I don't say "catch them and kill them", but in a shoot out, if you had to shoot and kill, then, yes, certainly. Otherwise you can't run a country. Individuals have no right to use violence, only organised, disciplined people where it's relevant, and if they exceed those powers, they should be punished; but within the rights of an army they have to kill. If I disagree with that, I must resign. You can always avoid killing people by resigning.

Stern: Did you have any sleepless nights about this?

JJ: I've never had sleepless nights. Because it's a democratic state, and the state must govern. If the people think I am wrong they can turn me out. I am not a dictator. They could talk against me in parliament, they could talk against me in public, they could publish criticisms in the press.

Stern: Is this presidential skill, which I think you would by implication say that you had acquired, something which you are born with or is it something that is learnt?

JJ: I think one is born with it because at a time of decision a leader instinctively takes certain positions. He has no time to think too much or study books or consult people. There was one factor in the Indo-Sri Lankan Agreement which needed a quick decision. All the measures in the Agreement concerning provincial councils and devolution were tabled in parliament, but one decision, the temporary merger of the North and East parts (temporary because by referendum the Eastern province could opt out), was something new and our people got very agitated about that. I took that decision because without that we couldn't have got these people to sign. I took it because the signing of the Agreement was a signing for peace, for ending the war, and I thought I should take the decision, risk my future, hoping to convince the people that if the peace continued – this is in July – by August we'd have provincial elections and three months later the referendum. I took that decision, though I consulted my Cabinet and others.

Stern: Would you have bowed out of politics if that hadn't gone wrong?

JJ: Oh yes, certainly. That was nothing to do with the Agreement. We had completed our part of the Agreement, there was nothing more for us to do.

Stern: Now, in your long career you have met most of the world's leading statesmen. Who has impressed you most and why?

JJ: Well I was very much enamoured of Jawaharlal Nehru. Gandhi is a different type, he's not a politician, he is a reformer.

Stern: Can't politicians be reformers?

JJ: Reformation and politics go ill together, especially if you are for non-violence like Gandhi was. I draw a distinction between individual non-violence, as Gandhi and Tolstoy preached, and the non-violence which I'm talking about. You will find that 99% of people in the world are in fact non- violent. They don't hate each other, they don't kill each other. In my country in 1988 the notifiable offences were 50,003. This includes all this terrorist violence – 50,003 out of 16 million. In your country, England and Wales, 50 million people, the notifiable offences are 4 million, but most of them are property matters, and 90% are settled. So if you look into that in that way, again, less than 1%.

Stern: And yet in Sri Lanka, Northern Ireland, the Punjab, the Middle East, almost wherever you look people are killing other people in groups, in droves, in clans, in tribes and so on. How do you explain that?

JJ: I explain it by the possession of modern sophisticated weapons.

Stern: But the weapons don't kill people, it's people who decide to use weapons to kill people. It's the people who make the decision to use the weapons.

JJ: I agree. But the percentage is less than 1%.

Stern: But if you didn't have the arms and people wanted to fight, then they would fight with sticks and stones and bottles and knives...

JJ: But the state can control them. The state must have the arms. But just as human beings gradually gave up arms to a central authority, so nations should give them to a central authority and then war would disappear. You must not allow people to make arms. To make arms, nuclear bombs and other weapons and distribute them is all wrong. The leaders of the world should get together and say "we mustn't do this", and gradually even terrorism will disappear. Otherwise, I agree, it might get more and more.

Stern: You are clearly a person of very strong views on a whole lot of different subjects. I'm interested to know how you chose your Cabinet. Did you want people of independent mind or did you want people who would agree with you?

JJ: Well, I chose my Cabinet from my Party firstly. It had to be from the Party and I had freedom to choose because we were a majority. And into the Party I inducted through elections young men who were educated in their own language and in English, who knew the political system, and I felt were loyal to me and could control a country. I didn't think of people opposing me. They have the right to oppose within the limits of the Constitution.

Stern: And did you listen to them?

127

JJ: Oh yes. Very much.

Stern: Are you a good listener?

JJ: Yes, a very good listener. I listen too much!

Stern: So you would consult, you would listen. But when you look back on you presidential career, did you regard yourself as a chairman or a chief?

JJ: Chief. And one of the great attributes of a chief is that he listens.

Stern: In the end, how much power does a Sri Lankan president have?

JJ: Well, unfortunately, we haven't got a press as powerful as the press in India or in the USA or in France, which is very vital when you have an executive president. Secondly you must have independent judiciary. We have that, I think. I can admire our judiciary. Public opinion is very nascent in Sri Lanka and the political opposition is almost dead. We were much more active when we were in opposition, but that can't be helped.

Stern: What were your guiding principles in the Presidency?

JJ: My guiding principles were political freedom, political democracy and the welfare of the masses.

Stern: If circumstances demand it, do you have to compromise on principle?

JJ: On certain principles, yes. Times change, situations change, environments change but never would I compromise on violence. I would never say that a person is justified in trying to achieve his objects no matter how good by violence.

Stern: You've been in politics for more than half a century. You've held almost every post in the government, not simply Prime Minister and President, you have also been Minister of Finance, of Defence, of Food, of Information, of Local Housing and so on. It's a very long list. Now, you know the British historian Lord Acton said that "power tends to corrupt". Were you ever corrupted by power?

JJ: I wasn't corruptible, but I agree with that.

Stern: So you think other people were, but not you?

JJ: I wouldn't say all of them, but there are people who are corrupted by it. It's like drink. You take a glass today and after some time it influences you, it affects you, it affects you mentally. Or drugs. Power is also like that, it is a drug.

Stern: So how did you manage to avoid this narcotic, yourself?

JJ: I avoid liquor, I avoid drugs.

Stern: What about the corruption of power though?

JJ: Well, if you keep yourself alert and know it is so, then it is easy to avoid, it doesn't come your way at all.

Stern: Did it never go to your head?

JJ: No.

Stern: But you had the state issue portraits and busts of your likeness and didn't you re-introduce ceremonials outside the presidential palace that hadn't been there for some time?

JJ: But that's not power, that is part of the system.

Stern: But you changed the system to introduce that.

JJ: I introduced that part of the system so that the President should have certain ceremonies attached to his office.

Stern: Are you saying that this wasn't personal vainglory, this was for the glory of the state?

JJ: Yes. Of Sri Lanka.

Stern: Did you enjoy the trappings of office?

JJ: No. I didn't enjoy it, but it was necessary.

Stern: But some people would then say that if you didn't enjoy the trappings of office and you remained in politics for 52 years, you must be a masochist?

JJ: But I was not in office for 52 years, I was in politics.

Stern: OK, but you were in office right at the top from 1977 until 1988.

JJ: By election.

Stern: But you could always get out of the political process if you wanted to?

JJ: Why should I when I was elected?

Stern: Yes, but you didn't have to put yourself up for election.

JJ: Whether I was in office or opposition, I was very attached to the political system and to political behaviour.

Stern: So are you saying that you remained in politics as long as you did because it was your duty?

JJ: The question you should ask is 'why did you remain in politics for so long'?

Stern: Yes, why?

JJ: You might ask 'why you are playing rugger', you won't ask 'why are you playing forward the whole time'? 'Why are you back the whole time, why are you the scrum half the whole time?'

Stern: Well you play rugger because you enjoy it.

JJ: That's what I'm saying.

Stern: So you did enjoy politics?

JJ: If you ask me ,'why are you playing rugger for so long?' I'd say I enjoyed rugger – and I enjoyed politics.

Stern: But when it came to the top job it was more a matter of duty. Is that your view?

JJ: It was a duty, yes.

Stern: When you handed over the reins of power to your successor Premadasa, was it difficult to let go?

JJ: No.

Stern: Have you let go? There are some people who say that rather like General Ne Win in Burma you probably still exercise a certain amount of power behind the scenes. Is that true?

JJ: No.

Stern: You really have let go of power?

JJ: Completely.

Stern: Looking back on your career, would you say it has been a successful one?

JJ: Well, that is a matter for history. But if history always reports accurately, it would not be unfavourable. Maybe on some matters they would criticise me but it would not be an unfavourable report. But mind you, it should review the whole 52 years. You can't just take the Indo-Sri Lanka Agreement or the constitutional changes and say "this is good" or "this is bad". You have to take the whole 52 years and decide.

Stern: What's the thing you have done that you are most proud of?

JJ: I think my most brilliant achievement was bringing the United National Party into power, and keeping it active after 1956 – the first defeat of a democratic party in a developing country. Because people thought this is the end of democracy, no Party can lose like that and come back. I brought it back and created the two-party system, the democratic system in this country alone, almost single-handed. Others did help me but none of them could take the leadership as I did and I fought until we won the next election. I would say it was entirely due to my thinking and my work and I am proudest of that and I wish to be remembered for that.

Stern: And what do you think is your greatest folly?

JJ: Greatest folly? I haven't thought of that. I will have to think of that.

Stern: Is there any unfinished business? Are there things that you would still like to have done that have not yet been achieved?

JJ: I don't think so. One couldn't do more than what I did. But one thing more, about instinct, I feel a leader takes certain decisions by instinct. When your instincts begin to fail as it began to fail in Napoleon's Waterloo, then you must give up. Fortunately my instincts haven't failed. I gave up in spite of that. But a leader by instinct takes correct decisions and when he is not taking correct decisions I think he should go.

Stern: So you went before you started making wrong decisions?

JJ: Yes. I might have, I don't know.

Meiczyslaw **RAKOWSKI**

CHAPTER 11

Stern: Mieczyslaw Rakowski, you were born into a country which had just reappeared on the map after 130 years of partition. As a boy growing up in the late 20s and 30s, did you have any inkling that Poland might again be under sentence of death?

MR: No, not at all. I was born in 1926 into a peasant family, and though my father was politically active, nobody in my family expected that war was coming.

Stern: You said your father had been politically active. Was he a Communist?

MR: In no way. He belonged to a party which was on the right. I don't know why he chose this party, and never had the chance to find out because he was arrested after the Germans invaded the western part of Poland, and then was sent somewhere. We didn't know what had happened to him, and it wasn't till '43 or '44 that we got the information that he had been killed.

Stern: Your family was split up during the war?

MR: Yes, after the Germans invaded I left our village and went to Poznan. There I worked in a factory until February '45, when as a volunteer I became a soldier of the Polish army.

Stern: What happened to the rest of your family?

MR: It was rather a small family, and during the occupation my mother was working in a factory in Poznan, and my only sister stayed in the village with our relatives.

Stern: So when did you decide to become a Communist? Was it the experience of war?

MR: Partly. I hated the Germans and it was my belief that my place was in the army to fight the Germans. Sent to the officers' school, I finished as a Lieutenant, and in the army, in 1946, I became a member of the Communist Party of Poland, but I should say with no knowledge about Marxism or Leninism. Just 19 years old, coming from a peasant family, for me this new system was not only an adventure but the only means of fulfilling my dreams of getting a position in society, since the schools were now open to the sons of workers and peasants.

Stern: But you'd come from a rather conventional, Catholic, right wing family. Did your joining the Communist Party bring about a rift between you and the rest of your family?

MR: No. Because in this period the level of political thinking in such a family was very low. They hadn't any idea what the new party or system meant, or the significance of '45 when the Red Army came to Poland fighting the Germans.

Stern: Ah, but the Red Army which had liberated Poland had also invaded it in the first place after the Stalin/Hitler Pact. You had grown up in the part occupied by the Germans. Other people grew up in the part occupied by the Russians.

MR: Yes, but the eastern part was very far from us. The western part of Poland in 1918 had belonged to Prussia, and technically this part of Poland was much more developed than the East. Where I was born and grew up there was no anti-Russian feeling.

Stern: But did people not know about the execution of thousands of Polish officers in 1940, about the mass deportation of civilians, or of the failure of the Red Army in the vicinity to honour its pledge to relieve Warsaw in 1944 until after the Germans had mopped up the Polish Home Army?

MR: Well we knew, but in Poznan the circumstances were very different from Warsaw and other parts of Poland. No one from my family was involved in the underground movement, and the sources of information concerning this part of Europe were one-sided. As a matter of fact there was no Polish paper in Poznan. We were somewhat cut off.

Stern: You say you joined the Communist Party in 1946, and in 1949 you worked for the Party Central Committee drafting documents and propaganda material. Now by this time, as in the Soviet Union and the other Communist countries, there were political purges; there was central planning with priority to heavy industry, strict censorship, curbs on religious practice, the cult of Stalin and so on. Working in the Central Committee when Poland seemed to be a kind of carbon copy of the Soviet Union, did you never question these policies?

MR: Yes, of course, but until 1948 in Poland the leading person was Gomulka with his concept of a specifically Polish road to socialism. Then came the Yugoslavian events...

Stern: When Yugoslavia was expelled from the Cominform...

MR: Yes, and from this time Poland really became a Stalinist system or country. But these were the years when Poland built a huge industry, hundreds and thousands of young people left the villages and came to the new towns. This was for our generation totally new. It was an adventure.

Stern: But are you saying that all these developments could not have happened without Stalinist socialism?

MR: Well I think so.

Stern: On the other hand, of course, plenty of western democracies were also developing very rapidly at that time. So did you need Stalinist socialism?

MR: Well wait a minute. There was a huge difference between west Europe and eastern Europe. Eastern Europe was the undeveloped part of Europe and the goals we achieved in the industrialisation of Poland had been achieved in the western countries 50 or 100 years before.

Stern: So you would still now defend the Stalinist policies of that period.

MR: As a historian, I think that in every such undeveloped country a strong government based on dictatorship may be useful, though only for a limited period.

Stern: But would you justify everything that was done in that period?

MR: No, of course not. But remember, people like Garaudy or Brecht or Zweig believed at this time that we had really started to build a new society, a new system. And this Stalin cult was accepted by people much more intellectual than I. For us the Soviet Union was the first country of socialism.

Stern: From being a Stalinist you later became an apostle of reformist communism, and *Polityka*, the journal you helped to found in the 1950s, developed a reputation for outspokenness. What brought about this change of heart?

MR: Well, I started to be critical towards the practice of this system after the celebrated twentieth party congress of the Soviet Union...

Stern: When Khrushchev attacked Stalin and called for de-Stalinisation...

MR: Exactly. And then came this so-called 'Polish October' in 1956 when Gomulka returned to power. I was quite sure that Gomulka would reopen the Polish road to socialism, but after three or four years he started to evolve a dogmatic policy opposed to his concept, and I started to be critical. Publicly. In Gomulka's opinion Rakowski was "a guy who has crazy ideas, a bit of a revisionist and a liberal, even if loyal".

Stern: Were you?

MR: Yes. This is in fact one of my weaknesses, because I was usually very loyal to the leader. Maybe I am one of those people who need someone over him.

Stern: That's very interesting. You were loyal to Bierut, the first Communist leader, you were loyal to Gomulka, who was a different kind of Communist, and then later on for a while you were loyal to Gierek, the man who took Gomulka's place. What does this say about you?

MR: Well, this is a psychological problem, maybe. I wanted to be loyal but began to criticise them when I felt they were failing to fulfil their programme.

Stern: You were saying earlier on that you had lost your father when you were 12. Would it be fanciful to suggest that in these politicians you were looking for a father figure, and that in the end they disappointed you?

MR: I can't exclude this. It's possible.

Stern: That's one way of looking at it. Another way is to say that what kept you apparently loyal to these people was not so much conviction as political ambition. Perhaps one day you might succeed them. Was that ever on your mind?

MR: No. When I started to be a political person, and later editor in chief of *Polityka*, I never thought that I would ever be Vice Prime Minister or Prime Minister.

Stern: But you accepted a role under Jaruzelski, and as Deputy Prime Minister your job was to negotiate with Lech Walesa and with the trade union Solidarity. Did you have any qualms about accepting the post then? Was it on your terms or was it on his terms?

MR: I think on my terms. I had just written a celebrated article in Poland advocating partnership between us and Solidarity.

Stern: When you were talking about partnership did you have the idea that perhaps Solidarity should share power in government with the Communist party?

MR: Well, not at this time. At this time I thought that the main task was for the party to accept the independent trade movement as an historical and political fact.

Stern: So in January 1981 you found yourself Deputy Prime Minister. Later on in September 1988 you were Prime Minister. What qualities did these offices require, and do you think you had them?

MR: Well, I think that I was intellectually and politically prepared for the post of Deputy Prime Minister. I was part of a team, but responsible for the negotiations with Solidarity, and relations with artists, intellectuals and so on. For such a post I was prepared because for the last 20 years I had been editor-in-chief of *Polityka*, and politics was something in which I was well trained. I was, during these 20 years, a member of different round tables and travelling from one place to another giving hundreds of lectures.

Stern: So is persuasiveness one of the chief qualities of leadership?

MR: Yes, but of course as Prime Minister you have to know not only politics but also the economy, about things connected with everyday life, and in the period between 1985 and 1988, when I was Deputy Speaker in Parliament, I acquired knowledge about the economy. Funnily enough, when I became Prime Minister a famous Polish political writer wrote to tell me that I was the right man for the job because I wasn't a professor of Economics. In Poland, economists are politically strong, but often have no experience in practice. They have built their concepts in higher schools of learning to an audience comprising only students.

Stern: I'd like you to look closely at two prominent Polish leaders you've had to deal with. First of all Lech Walesa, the shipyard electrician who became head of Solidarity, and survived internment under martial law to become head of state. Do you think that he has what it takes to be president?

MR: Walesa is a 'political animal'. He knows what politics means, but I don't share the opinion that he is prepared for the role which he has now.

Stern: Why?

MR: I think a lack of education. He could be a good president but is not intellectually prepared. He was for the whole of his life a worker. Even if he had stayed as leader of the trade union movement he should have added to this knowledge something more: the knowledge about the work, of the position of leader, about the possibilities of leadership. If you take for instance his speeches, every second sentence is 'I'. 'I Walesa', 'I am doing this', 'I have given you freedom', 'I have given you this and this'. So this man seems too self-important.

Stern: Is this why you described his rule as 'the dictatorship of the proletarian'?

MR: I was joking of course, but there is an element of truth, because at the time we were trying to build up 'the dictatorship of the proletariat'. We built up as a matter of fact the dictatorship of the First Secretary of the Politburo. Now the workers have chosen Walesa for his post in a very democratic way, but I think that Walesa psychologically is prepared to be a dictator.

Stern: What about the leadership qualities of General Jaruzelski?

MR: I am critical of him also, but when I compare Jaruzelski intellectually with Gierek or with Gomulka then I should say that for the first time in the post World War II period we had a properly qualified leadership, with an impressive intellectual background, a knowledge of politics – a modest man, a bit shy, but a master tactician.

Stern: You said that you also had criticisms of him.

MR: Well when he became Prime Minister his knowledge about civilian life was very limited because he had spent the last 40 years in the army. Every army is based on discipline, and Jaruzelski in these years was often unhappy because as he said, "when in the army I gave an order, everyone obeyed. When I give an order as Prime Minister, nobody pays attention". I had to explain to him that there's a huge difference between the army and civilian life. And then, though I think that generally his policies were right, from time to time he made unsuitable appointments.

Stern: You said that Jaruzelski didn't always get his way. Does that mean that his Cabinet was a little more collective than it appeared from the outside?

MR: It was very democratic. He accepted that everyone could come with proposals and every proposal was discussed, but of course, like every leader, Jaruzelski wanted his view to prevail.

Stern: Did you ever manage to get him to change his mind on something?

MR: Yes of course. Jaruzelski is a politician psychologically and intellectually prepared to say 'I was wrong'. For a leader this is rather rare.

Stern: You have also encountered a number of Soviet leaders. What was your impression of Leonid Brezhnev?

MR: When we speak about such people as Brezhnev we have to take into account that his generation of leaders grew up in the Stalinist period and that he was a prisoner of this Stalinist system. Secondly, this generation of Brezhnev had produced leaders very limited intellectually, believing their way of thinking the only right way. Such things as democracy were not in their vision.

Stern: Yet you'd been a Stalinist too, at one time. How was it that democracy could be in your vision and not in his?

MR: Because I was growing up in a climate in which democracy was not an empty word. Though Poland in the period between the two wars had established a kind of dictatorship, it remained nonetheless a qualified democratic system, and after all in previous centuries Poland had been a democratic country. It was one of the very few countries in Europe in which the kings were elected (not always with very good results, but that is another problem). By contrast, in the whole history of Russia there was only a six month period in which there was democracy, and very limited. I mean from the February revolution of 1917 till the coup d'etat of General Kornilov in July. You couldn't say that Lenin, a very good journalist, was also a very good democrat. It is one of the problems of history that if an intellectual who gathers his knowledge from books takes power, it's a disaster for the nation.

Stern: Would you say that Brezhnev was a dictator?

MR: Of course he was, though not with such power as Stalin or even Khrushchev. You have to take into account the fact that in this system the General Secretary was surrounded by the people who every day told him 'you are right'. The circumstances and the people surrounding him were responsible for such a type of leader.

Stern: What about Gorbachev?

MR: He is totally different from all previous Soviet leaders. Firstly, he was born in 1931 – that means he was too young to be influenced by the system during those terrible years. Then I think as a student he was influenced by people like Mlynar (who was to become a leading reformer during the 'Prague Spring' of 1968), and after he finished university in Moscow he became a party worker, but far from the centre, which gave him an opportunity to observe the centre from a safe distance. As he observes, he learns. Having met Gorbachev seven times, it seems to me that from year to year, even since perestroika, he discovers more about the stupidity of this system, and now, in 1991, Gorbachev is a totally different politician from that of 1985.

Stern: Is he still a Communist?

MR: It's difficult to find a clear answer to this question. He knows that the system created by Lenin, Stalin and other leaders should be totally changed. But I think that he still believes that it is possible to change to democratic socialism.

Stern: In a Communist country there's the Party and there's the government. Now, in the government that you served, what was the relationship between the two? Who decided, for example, who should be in the cabinet?

MR: Usually the Politburo, but I was the first Prime Minister who didn't ask the Politburo whom I could take into my cabinet.

Stern: Did General Jaruzelski not have any say?

MR: Well it was a condition of my taking this post that I would decide who would be members of staff.

Stern: If you had wanted non-Communists, possibly even anti-Communists, in your cabinet would that have been feasible?

MR: Yes. I proposed at that time to include four people from the opposition. Though none accepted my nomination I was able to take for the post of Minister of Industry Mr Wilczak, a private entrepreneur. For the party at this time, in 1988, this was something nobody had expected.

Stern: Was this in effect the first coalition government since 1947?

MR: Yes.

Stern: But what about the martial law government. There were non-Communists in that, weren't there?

MR: Well, there were people from the Peasant party and from the Democratic party, but at this time these parties were still satellite parties. However, in the following years these parties became more and more independent, so when I chose someone from the Peasant party for my government, he was very different from someone in the Jaruzelski government.

Stern: I'd like to focus on a few of the key decisions with which you've been associated. First your negotiations with Solidarity in 1981. For a time they seemed to be going well, but by August you were calling Solidarity's leaders 'blockheads' and 'peasants'. (By the way, what's wrong with being a 'peasant'?) And you more or less called off the discussions. Why were you so angry?

MR: I was under the pressure of fear that the Soviets would intervene in our internal affairs, because Brezhnev and his crew couldn't accept the fact that a movement in our system could want to be accepted as an opposition, or as maybe an independent force. If Walesa had been ready to accept in practice the leading role of the Party, then of course there would have been a very different situation. But Brezhnev and his people knew this Polish internal situation very well, based on the information from their own 'good comrades' in this country. And after his first attempt to intervene in Poland at the beginning of December 1980 we were under constant pressure – the more so because the Czechs and the DDR were even more critical towards us.

Stern: So why didn't you tell them 'look I can't accept your demands because the Russians, the Czechs...'

MR: We told the Solidarity people every second day, but when I think about 1981, I come to the conclusion that neither side was ready to accept a kind of partnership. We believed at this time that the leading role of the Party was the mainstay of this system. Solidarity wouldn't accept this, but was not prepared to accept that the way to change the system was through compromise.

Stern: But there were people who said that all along you'd been looking for a pretext for a crackdown on Solidarity, that you'd never been negotiating in good faith.

MR: It's not true. For me it was quite clear that Solidarity was something new in our system, and I was ready to accept, for example, the workers' main demand that they were an independent trade union movement. On the other hand Solidarity was in part formed by intellectuals – people not practised in the art of compromise.

Stern: On 13th December 1981 there was this crackdown, when General Jaruzelski imposed martial law and you played a leading role in administering it. So were you one of those who took the decision to impose martial law?

MR: No, I was informed later.

Stern: Yet you were the Deputy Prime Minister.

MR: Yes, but in this government the main role was played by Jaruzelski and his colleagues in the army, and the whole apparatus of martial law was prepared by the army and by the security forces. I was informed just two days before 13th December.

Stern: So when was the decision taken?

MR: In the first week of December. After the session of Solidarity in Radom on 5th December, during which Walesa made a very hostile speech, which we knew about the day after. This was because among the participants was our spy, a double agent, a member of Solidarity, even one of their leaders, who was working for not only us but also the Americans. In addition Mazowsze, the Warsaw region of Solidarity, announced that on 17th December they would organise a huge meeting in Constitution Square, and with tensions growing and growing in the country at the end of November, one strike after another, demonstrations and so on, the signs of anarchy were visible. We were afraid that even if there were no danger from the Soviet Union the situation could lead to civil war.

Stern: So the decision to impose martial law was made in Warsaw, not in Moscow?

MR: Of course.

Stern: When you heard the news that there was going to be martial law in a couple of days time, were you surprised?

MR: No, because in the last months of 1981 martial law was discussed at the top as a possibility, and I was among those politicians who accepted the need. For me the main task was to do all possible to prevent intervention from the Soviet Union. It was quite clear that if the Soviet Army together with the Czechoslovakian army and the DDR intervened in Poland, then the behaviour of the Poles would be not like the Czechs in 1968.

Stern: There'd be a war?

MR: There'd be a domestic war. And the tragedy of Budapest after the 20th Party congress in the Soviet Union, that was supposed to usher in a new era based on justice and so on, was something much on my mind.

Stern: So when had you been discussing the possibility of martial law?

MR: The end of October and in November – but only as a possibility.

Stern: But it would have involved, as it did, tight censorship, increased surveillance, widespread internment, possibly people being killed, to say nothing of the suppression of Solidarity. So did this not, as it were, go against all your reformist Communist beliefs?

MR: No, because, as I mentioned, for me the main task was to remain independent and hence avoid any action from the Brezhnev clique. The main thing was to avoid bloodshed.

Stern: But you didn't avoid it. There was bloodshed.

MR: Yes but, you know, we really paid a very small price.

Stern: How many people were killed?

MR: Well when soldiers opened fire at the Wujek mine on 16th December eight or nine people were killed, but I should add that someone from the Catholic camp said that two thousand people or more would lose their lives.

Stern: Well it was less than two thousand, but it was more than eight or nine, wasn't it?

MR: Yes, but in the following years I guess no more than 20 people lost their lives.

Stern: Plus thousands of people interned.

MR: Yes, but don't forget that after two weeks or so, many people were released from internment. I accept, though, that too many people were taken, but this was complicated by the fact that the lists of people to be interned were prepared in the localities. And of course often the reasons why this or that man was taken were far from politics.

Stern: Was it your intention that martial law should only last two or three years?

MR: From the beginning the intention was that if it were possible then we would end it, and as a matter of fact after two years we finished with martial law.

Stern: Had the danger from the Soviet Union gone? Had the danger of internal anarchy gone?

MR: Both.

Stern: Whatever the reason for martial law, at least a third of the journalists on *Polityka* resigned, and at least one of your two sons followed your first wife into exile, and I believe your second wife continued to support Solidarity. This must have been an awful time for you.

MR: Well, you know, that's part of the human tragedy. This was not the first time in the history of Poland in which families were divided, friends became enemies; if we go back to the 20s and Pilsudski's coup d'etat this too divided families, but if you have power, you have to pay a price. Sometimes the price is very high. I lost at this time many friends. Now some of them are coming back, but some of them are still far, far away from me.

Stern: Let's move on to another momentous event – this time in which you may have made a few friends: your decision as Prime Minister to hold elections in the middle of 1989. Now, what made you take that decision, because you must have known that the Communists wouldn't do terribly well in such an election?

MR: Well, at the beginning of 1989, when I proposed the election based on the first achievements of my government, nobody in Poland at this time expected such a result.

Stern: You expected the Communists to win the election?

MR: Yes, at the beginning of 1989. Then of course two weeks or a month before the election it was more or less quite clear that we would not be the winner.

Stern: Yet given that you had been associated with the Party and martial law, I am surprised that people should have thought the Communists would win an election.

MR: Well, when I was nominated Prime Minister and started with our early reform programme, all the opinion polls predicted our victory so there was a base for such a belief.

Stern: You accepted the result of the election, and your party was prepared to accept a minority place in the new government headed by Solidarity. Were you worried about what the Russians, the East Germans and the Czechs might think?

MR: No, by this time it was well known that Moscow, for instance, would make no attempt to change the situation.

Stern: Is it true that you actually received a phone call from Gorbachev urging you to share power with Solidarity?

MR: No, this was gossip which was first I think printed in the *Los Angeles Times*. In reality I'd become Party leader and wanted to go to the Soviet Union just to see Gorbachev. Gorbachev replied that he would like to avoid a meeting because this might be construed as an attempt to intervene in Polish internal affairs. Then he asked me "Mieczyslaw, since you have changed so much in the last few years, tell me why the Party fared so badly in the elections?" I replied "The key is the economy, the whole development of Poland in the last decade". After my explanation he said "Of course, you have to take into account the new conditions", and that was all.

Stern: And when was this phone call?

MR: This was on the 22nd August.

Stern: I see. But by your own decision to have what was effectively a Solidarity government you actually ushered in the post Communist age, not only in Poland but in almost the whole of Eastern Europe. How did you feel the day after you handed over power?

MR: Well, I think that no politician is very happy to resign his powers. But for me it was at this time very clear that the kind of Communist movement which was growing up in the 20s, and had propounded the concept of socialism in the following decades, had no future, and that there was no way other than just to accept the results of this election. And, moreover, to accept the historical fact that the Communist parties in Europe had ceased to be a politically influential force in society, and that the only task now was to make place for a New Left – a New Left which would be totally separated from the past, from all the traditions of the Third International, and the generation of Stalin, of Khrushchev and so on.

Stern: Yet you'd repeatedly warned about the dangers of turning Poland into a western style democracy. Well it is moving in that direction now. Do you still fear the outcome?

MR: It seems to me that democracy without a strong economic base can degenerate into a dictatorship. In my opinion Poland and Eastern Europe have entered into a period of enormous conflict, a period of de-stabilisation. If you observe the developments of the last two years you notice the rise of nationalism and anti-semitism, and though I am quite sure that this is the inevitable price we must pay for this transition from one system to another, it is an open question what system will in the end prevail.

Stern: Well you served the Communist system for well over 40 years. What did socialism achieve in Poland?

MR: Firstly, Poland was an undeveloped country before the war, and now it is a partly industrialised country. My generation of the left changed totally the social and economic conditions in Poland. In 1945 there were 80,000 people with higher education; now it is over 1,700,000. New classes, new forces are coming up. I mean the peasants and workers. The position of Poland as a nation has vastly improved in the last 40 years. For the first time in the last 300 years we have no quarrel on any border. Furthermore, if you are on the bridge of the Odra in Frankfurt then Berlin is only 90km away. The irony of history is that we have got this part of Poland thanks to Stalin, who fought at Yalta and Potsdam for this.

Stern: But you also lost a lot of territory.

MR: But these lost territories were totally undeveloped and in any case the Poles there were in a minority. Yes, we paid a price for the Odra-Neisse territories, but historically we as a nation were pushed to the west – a part of Europe more highly developed than the eastern part of Poland – something Stalin hadn't taken into account. Maybe this westward shift explains why Solidarity – with its western overtones – was born and grew up in the 70s.

Kenneth **KAUNDA**

CHAPTER **12**

Stern: Mr President, like most prominent people you inspire mixed emotions. Different people tend to see you in different ways. To your friends and admirers you are gentle, generous minded, and god-fearing. To your critics you appear inflexible, self-righteous and sometimes autocratic. How do you see yourself?

KK: I believe I am trying to do an honest job, and this stems from the fact that I can see no force on earth that would help contribute to the growth of mankind in the right direction apart from the force of love. Love for God our creator, love for man he has made in his image. Whatever others say about me is really immaterial. I care about my fellow human beings.

Stern: You probably remember that the poet William Wordsworth talked about the child being 'father to the man'. As you were growing up in your father's Church of Scotland mission station, in what was then Northern Rhodesia, was there anything that marked you out as someone who'd one day determine the destiny of the nation?

KK: Nothing at all, except that the teaching of the priests, including my own father, at Sunday Schools helped me I think to show some modest leadership qualities. For example, when we had, say, nativity plays, I always played quite prominent roles. I also remember that when I came to the age of about 14 or 15 or 16 I began quarrelling with my missionaries. I argued that there were high seats and low seats in the church. High seats for white missionaries, lower seats for the rest of us. I didn't like that. So when it came to matters I considered to be of principle, I argued. In other respects I was rather shy.

Stern: What was the effect of your being the youngest of eight children. As the baby of the family were you rather spoilt?

KK: I think I was fortunate that my father didn't spare the rod. One time I remember I quarrelled and fought with the headmaster's son and I paid the price, for my father whipped me very hard. And while he was doing that he was imparting to me the philosophy of 'non-violence'.

Stern: So you can beat people into non-violence, can you? You were talking earlier about the way you objected to the division of seats in church. Was that your first politically conscious act?

KK: Yes, without hesitation.

Stern: And when you took your first step on the political ladder, which was I suppose when you became founder Secretary of the Lubwa Branch of the African National Congress, were you determined to get to the top of it?

KK: I wouldn't say that at all, Geoff. First of all it was not so much the African National Congress as the African Welfare Society that brought me into active politics. It had branches dotted all over the country, and I was its Secretary in my home district.

Stern: Was it like a trade union?

KK: Not really. We got together to get the ear of the District Commissioner, so he would listen to us. I was working because I thought there was something wrong with society.

Stern: But you did work for the ANC, and then you split away from it to form your own Zambian ANC? Was this on a point of principle or did you want to lead your own movement?

KK: Well when the veteran politician, whom we all loved and respected, Harry Nkumbula, came back from Britain, from the LSE, he gave us young men a grounding in nationalism, and I was one of those who canvassed for him to become our President, and in 1951 he won. He was really the founder of modern Zambian nationalism, and we worked together. In 1951 I was ANC Provincial Secretary for two huge provinces, and after that, 1951, '52, '53, I was elected Secretary General of the African National Congress of Northern Rhodesia, and I moved over to headquarters here in Lusaka. But there was a clever colonial man called Harry Franklin who got hold of our own Harry, and the two Harrys became very close. We believed that this Harry Franklin had over-influenced our own leader, and that instead of the dynamism with which he started he was beginning to falter a bit. We argued about this, but his friendship continued and it worried us a lot, especially when it led to his acceptance of a new constitution, which we youngsters couldn't accept.

Stern: Why not?

KK: It wasn't giving us anything. We thought we were just being used by the Colonial government, and so we rejected it.

Stern: So are you saying that Harry Nkumbula had become a kind of stooge?

KK: I wouldn't say a stooge, but he'd become a bit soft. So a group of us decided to leave and I was immediately elected leader of that group. Non-violent non-cooperation was our policy. We wouldn't cooperate with the Colonial government. When those elections came, he was elected, and we went into detention camp, as guests of Her Majesty's Government.

Stern: Well you know from history that going to jail is often a prerequisite for becoming President later on. Did you have presidential ambitions when you were in jail?

KK: I was just waiting to help gain the independence of Rhodesia, and had no ambitions at all until my colleagues asked me to become Secretary General of the African National Congress, and then the President of the Zambia African National Congress.

Stern: Was it then a surprise that you in fact got on the ladder to power, and ended up as President of Zambia?

KK: Geoff, the thought of becoming President of Zambia never occurred to me at any point. We'd been involved in a bitter struggle, and then of course when we came out of prison in the early '60s, we began to plan for independence.

Stern: And then in four short years you became President of the United National Independence Party (UNIP), Minister of Local Government and Housing, Prime Minister and then, in 1964, President of a newly independent Zambia. Do you think your parents would have seen in your path to power the fulfilment of their hopes in some sense, or a rejection of their religious aspirations?

KK: No I wouldn't say rejection of their aspirations, Geoff, because I think my mother, who died in my arms here at State House, was inwardly quite proud of me.

Stern: But you'd given up teaching to go into politics. Was she pleased?

KK: Well, she was a very strong believer in her children and she always taught me to pray for guidance from God in everything that I thought and did, and I've tried to stick to that. So I wouldn't say that my parents would be sorry to see me where I am. I think that even though they lie now in their graves, they're happy with what I am trying to do for my country.

Stern: And yet politics can be a very dirty game, and Zambia really isn't an exception. So how do you reconcile your religious with your political aspirations. Politics is about partisan interests, and principle often has to be sacrificed for expediency, doesn't it?

KK: Quite right. But regardless of what bothers you, regardless of who insults you, you are still head of the nation, elected by the majority of the people. You have no choice but to accept the job, to try and guide even those who are against you. It's not easy. Sometimes you 're bound to have them prosecuted, and they go to prison. But that's the law of the land. In every society there are always bad elements, but you as a parent must remember that they are still your children.

Stern: But I can't quite see how politics and religion really mix. I mean, you can't tell a whole nation to turn the other cheek, can you?

KK: I don't believe that you can separate religion from politics. That would be dead politics, in my opinion. We are dealing with man, and man is made in God's image.

Stern: But people are sometimes very rude to and about you, and sometimes you strike back. You don't turn the other cheek. You lock them up or impose some other kind of penalty.

KK: I don't lock them up, Geoff. The law locks them up.

Stern: But you and the law are not wholly distant from one another. You are the boss.

KK: I think you've got to look at society as a developing entity. I firmly believe that man is developing from the primitive to something better. And on the back of science and technology man is always riding to something higher. But the fear I have is loss of spiritual development. Without that, man would become an animal, no different from a hyena in his thoughts and his words and deeds. But if you add a spiritual tinge to, as we say in 'humanism', the five main areas of human endeavour – political, economic, social and cultural, scientific and technological, defence and security matters – you are on the right course.

Stern: As somebody who believes in the Ten Commandments, you believe 'thou shalt not kill', and yet you've also supported the guerilla struggle in various white minority regimes. How do you reconcile those two ideas?

KK: I have had no difficulty. Man is central in the whole of creation. Nothing can be worse for this earth than the oppression of man by man. Whether it occurs in East, West, North or South, where it exists it must be fought. Now we in Zambia were fortunate to be under British colonial rule – fortunate in that though the British might imprison you several times and check on you, if they saw that you were strong enough they would eventually say 'perhaps this fellow is strong enough to continue now on his own'. This I think was the experience in the latter part of the empire, when the empire was dying. Not so with the Portuguese. If you argued, they shot you on the spot in those days. Happily there was a revolution in Portugal itself in '74 and so things changed. But in those days because the Portuguese could not allow imprisonment as the only punishment, the alternative was to kill. I had no spiritual right to say to the Angolans and Mozambiquans who wanted to fight to gain their independence, "don't use force because we used non-violent methods here".

Stern: But on the other hand in a guerilla struggle innocent people get killed, don't they? So what do you feel about that?

KK: Very sad, but that doesn't empower me spiritually or politically to say to FRELIMO, to ZANU, to ZAPU, to the ANC, to SWAPO: "don't fight for your rights using the gun". Admittedly, when people have to fight like that it's very difficult to stabilise the country when they get their independence, as has been shown around us, but then even that is better than being under colonial rule, colonial power.

Stern: I'd like to come to the question of the qualities of leadership you think you've been able to display. What have you brought to the leadership?

KK: I'm not sure I have ever said to myself I am the best example. But if you ask what would be the type of leader I would like to follow, I would say one who loves God, one who loves man. My prayer is 'God, please teach me how to know you', because I don't believe I know him yet. And I ask God to teach me how to know man, because I don't know him yet.

Stern: But I can't quite see how that keeps a country or a Cabinet together, or enables you to choose the right kind of Cabinet and so on. What is the political implication of what you are saying?

KK: I'm giving you the right measurement. I'm not asking for angels because I'm not one and can never hope to be. But I am looking for men and women who at least shy away from deliberately doing things that harm the interests of their fellow men.

Stern: But have you done that in practice, and chosen around you people who are like that – God fearing, just and upright?

KK: I'm glad to say that in my Cabinet or the Party Central Committee very few people drink their heads off. Very few.

Stern: There are other sins, though, aren't there?

KK: Oh, plenty. What about myself?

Stern: Yes, what about yourself?

KK: I agree with my friend Jimmy Carter who says that the very fact that you look at a girl's buttocks and begin to imagine things is sinful. You are committing a sin already. I've sinned many times, but that does not stop me from trying, falling and getting up again, to try to develop from the animal type of life to something nearer to God. And in politics in all the five areas of human endeavour I've spoken about, one must struggle to become and do something better.

Stern: That's interesting. I asked you about leadership and you say well, it's about understanding God better, or getting closer to God...

KK: ...And man.

Stern: And man. I ask other people about leadership and they say , "it's about inspiring trust", or "it's about inspiring confidence", or "it's about having a political agenda that works". Now isn't it also about those things?

KK: I agree entirely, but if you don't have spiritual help, if you don't love God and you don't love man, whatever you plan would be useless. Yesterday I sent messages of congratulations to Gorbachev and Bush and to De Klerk and the African National Congress in South Africa. Now these are two different subjects, but they are about man's struggle towards something better in both societies.

Stern: Do you see yourself as a kind of reconciler between people of different outlooks?

KK: Well, I don't know whether I see myself as such, Geoff. But in times when it was taboo to meet South African leaders, I did go to meet them because I knew I would not cheat. I did not meet Vorster because I wanted money. I wanted to tell him "apartheid is wrong". I met Botha when I thought he needed to be told by independent leaders about how bad apartheid was. I met De Klerk to try and find out what he stood for. You probably know my strong statement to him, "I've come to size you up, find out whether you are just another Boer or something better".

Stern: What do you feel like as an African leader meeting people that at one time you would have dismissed as white racists?

KK: I'm trying to get racism out of their blood. I'm trying to show them sense.

Stern: Do you think you've had an effect on their thinking?

KK: I can't boast, but I think I've helped.

Stern: In Zambia, as in many African and indeed Third World countries, there seems to be a special style of leadership – one which puts great stress on the leader and on the party which he leads. Why is that? Do you think its necessary for the development of a national consciousness perhaps?

KK: There have been great civilisations on this continent, but those were smashed by first of all the slave trade, and then colonisation, and all we had to hang on to was tribal identity, and to keep the tribe together you had to have a strong leader. And in a leadership contest if one leader stood out, the others had to either go away or completely surrender to the one who had assumed leadership. So in a tribal context there was always a search for strong leadership. We are coming from there now, but we've had to unite a number of tribes in our systems and we're looking for strong leadership. And since the advent of parties, parties assume the role of an all embracing organ of the nation and so you have to have strong parties with strong leadership.

Stern: So you see this as a stage which an African country has to go through. There has to be a strong leader. Does there have to be a one-party system as well?

KK: Well, we started out as a multi-party system. But, you know, in every general election, or bye-election, we had dead bodies, maimed bodies and houses burnt down across the political divide. The late Harry Nkumbula and I remained friends, but our followers were killing each other. So in the end we had to agree to come together and form one party.

Stern: So when you established this one party state in 1972, were you in effect saying that Zambia isn't yet ready for democracy?

KK: The situation was saying so. And since then indeed there was peace lasting and continuous. There has been no killing over political problems.

Stern: But certain other things have gone wrong and I'm wondering where are the checks and balances in such a system. I mean, if there are political or economic errors, how can they be rectified?

KK: Well that's a real problem, I agree. But it's better than people killing each other, much better.

Stern: So you would say that there's really a dilemma here, that on the one hand you can have pluralistic democracy, but it may be violent, on the other hand you can have a one party system, but there are no very good checks and balances on power.

KK: That's true.

Stern: Well, you're now about to end one-party rule. Do you do so reluctantly and with apprehension?

KK: Not really. I am very happy to contribute to this coming of multi-party politics. Today we have 7 million young men and women who were born either in 1960 or thereafter, and they did not experience this killing across the political divide. And I am hoping and praying that they will be more sensible than their parents, and that they can make this system work. Certainly it's better to have checks and balances and that's why I proposed this new system of having four pillars of democracy: the national assembly, chamber of representatives, the judiciary and Cabinet. Each one is a pillar standing on its own, and having a constitutional court as adjudicator in the event of a quarrel, but this was misunderstood and when I realised we were not yet ready for this type of democracy I said to my colleagues, "let us do only that which we can understand".

Stern: But for some time you had argued against a multi-party system. Do you feel that in a sense you've been defeated over that issue?

KK: Certainly not. What this is about, Geoff, is listening to the voice of the people and I believe in that. The majority of them have been saying "Let's go back to the multi-party system". And I agreed.

Stern: You have been subject recently to a great deal of what I'd imagine was very hurtful criticism, and many apparently rejoiced when they thought a year or so ago that you'd been overthrown. Is being Mr President a very lonely occupation?

KK: You've hit the nail on the head. Being leader of a nation is certainly a very lonely job, because in the end after serious discussion you have to decide on very difficult matters. I have what I hope is a very democratic approach to the issues. We discuss matters at various levels- the National Council, Congress, the Central Committee of UNIP and the Cabinet, and I'm presiding over these institutions; but in the end I've got to analyse what people are saying, and from Cabinet to parliament law is made after a long process. In the end I take full responsibility for what comes out of this. It is a lonely job.

Stern: I'm sure it is. But when people criticise you, what do you do? How do you cope?

KK: I have no problem with that one. I listen carefully, Geoff. If I think that what they're saying makes sense I go along. If I think that they're misguided I stand my ground and explain what vision I'm seeing in such a situation, and in all this I pray very hard for guidance.

Stern: You were talking a moment ago about your Cabinet, and I'm interested to know how you set about choosing one. Do you like a team which reflects your own views, or do you like a group of independent minded souls who check you if they think you are going over the top?

KK: Well I like to think I am a very free man, and I want others to be free also to think as they like. We spend hours on end discussing in various committees. Quite often I take copious notes and assess in the end what they are talking about. So really I want a Cabinet of men and women, old and young, who contribute freely to any given subject.

Stern: Can they persuade you to change your mind?

KK: Certainly. I have just given you an example of what happened to my proposal for the four different pillars of the constitution. I met church leaders here, young people from the university, teachers, judges of the high court, the Justice of the Supreme Court, Chief Justice, Deputy Chief Justice – all came and spoke to me about these matters. I listened carefully and I realised that perhaps I was moving too fast, and I joked about this and said "some people say that the late Nkrumah used to be so much ahead of his people that when they looked down they didn't see his footprints. Other leaders remain so much behind that when their people make dust, they can't see the footprints of their people". I am saying that UNIP is not like either – UNIP is with the people.

Stern: And yet you seem to reshuffle your Cabinet very frequently, and often those who lose out are those whose views are known to differ from yours. Doesn't this really suggest you really do like to have a pretty compliant Cabinet?

KK: Who doesn't reshuffle the Cabinet? I think there have been more reshuffles in some other countries than in Zambia.

Stern: Ok, so why do you do it?

KK: You haven't given me examples of those I have reshuffled, but I will tell you. A number failed in their posts. Others have gone out because I felt they were dishonest, though I did not disclose why I released them of their responsibilities. I just released them quietly. But they've gone around and published false stories about "tribalism" and what have you. I can never be tribal.

Stern: In view of the fact that you have had to relieve a number of people of their posts do you think that you've made some pretty unwise appointments?

KK: I think I can defend almost every appointment I have made to Cabinet. You see, in a new country like Zambia, though you must of course look at the ability of the person, there are also times when you must appoint some people because you want the nation to stand as one Zambia, one nation. This isn't new. I remember the late Kennedy had to appoint Johnson from the south so as to have a balanced leadership in the USA.

Stern: And that's what you try to do, to have a balanced Cabinet.

KK: I have to.

Stern: So can you take me through a Cabinet meeting. First of all, who draws up the agenda?

KK: The agenda is drawn up by the Cabinet Office, but in the light of a five year programme drawn up by UNIP's congress which meets once in five years. The National Council which meets once or twice a year tries to carry out the programme. Its resolutions are taken to the Central Committee, which in turn passes them on to Cabinet ministers. Ministers then prepare agenda papers, which go to Cabinet Office for processing. They then come to Cabinet meeting, over which I preside.

Stern: Right, now, how do you preside? Are you the chairman or are you the chief? Do you say 'make up your own minds', or do you say 'this is the policy, take it or leave it'?

KK: I am the chairman, not the chief. I say to my colleagues, "this is what we are told by the congress, this is what we are told by the National Council; the Central Committee says this, how are we going to go about this?" Every minister who draws up a paper, defends it, having had it circulated to all ministers to be returned with their comments and their reasons why they agree or disagree. Quite often I read the papers long before Cabinet meets, and I see the comments and then am able to bring different views to bear on a decision.

Stern: So how are decisions taken? By consensus, by majority vote, or what?

KK: No, we have no vote in the Cabinet. Decisions are by consensus.

Stern: Is there always a consensus?

KK: Not always. Sometimes there are bitter arguments and I've got to crack jokes to try to reconcile both sides.

Stern: Is that when there's likely to be a government reshuffle.

KK: No, it doesn't come that way.

Stern: What about delegating power? Are you good at that or do you, as some of your critics complain, tend to concentrate too much in your own hands?

KK: No, I'm a democrat through and through, and I'm proud of it. If you believe in God and man, you must give people a chance to do what they think is best. I believe in de-centralisation.

Stern: In the end how much power does a President of Zambia really have?

KK: Plenty of it. When you are chairman of all these different organs of the state you have power. I don't think it's abused. It's sensibly used. But you must know how to use it in the interests of the people, not in your own interest. You don't go around parading with a placard, 'Don't you know I'm the President'. You go around saying 'I am the servant of the people'.

Stern: What are the special problems in governing a country like Zambia?

KK: Many. The foremost problem is economic development. Around that hangs many other problems. Because your economy is weak you can't build schools, you can't build health centres. On the other hand, one thing that we in Zambia do know how to do very well is to reproduce – and by the end of the century we may be 15 million if we are not careful, and with that you need a lot of development. But I'm glad to say we are creating an environment now which is going to, I think, speed up economic development. Many businessmen, local and foreign, ask for copies of our proposals for an investment code, and I am very optimistic. I think our economy can turn round, and once we do that then I think that other problems will be on the way to being solved.

Stern: But the economy of Zambia wasn't always weak, and some people think you may have made a mistake by putting so much emphasis on nationalisation and on centralisation of industry and to some extent of agriculture. Do you think it was a mistake? Has that contributed to the country's economic problems?

KK: No, I don't accept that. The reason is that at independence we only had 100 university graduates, and not all that many young men and women who had done senior secondary school. At independence all command posts were manned by foreigners – in the civil service, the army, the air force, the police force. The highest ranking policeman at independence was a sub-Inspector. In the army, Regimental Sergeant Major. In the church, very few Zambian priests – you could count them on one hand. In agriculture, maize produced by black men was paid very little. So everything was along colour lines, and in that situation I had no choice but to take controlling interests in major industries.

Stern: But you also subsidised consumption rather than production.

KK: I agree, that is one major error. We should long have begun to subsidise production, which we are trying to do now. But then it's not been easy at all, because our people are used to being subsidised.

Stern: Were you frightened of removing those subsidies because of the political effect it might have?

KK: Not quite that. It was the security problem. We tried it in 1986. We had 17 people dead on our hands. We tried it in 1990. We had 24 dead, and so we have to do this very carefully. We have taken the first steps to de- regulate administratively, and slowly we are allowing so-called market forces to take control. But many people are very poor indeed, and we have to do these things gradually.

Stern: But weren't they made even poorer by policies which you pursued? After all, for your high principles, such as support for guerilla groups operating in Rhodesia and Mozambique, as well as sanctions against Rhodesia and of South Africa, there was a high price to pay, wasn't there?

KK: I agree. But I am unrepentant, Geoff. Because it was a matter of deep rooted principle, I could not compromise.

Stern: I would like to ask you about one other controversial policy. I'm wondering why, towards the end of the 1980s, you broke from the International Monetary Fund and pursued an economic austerity programme of your own, and then rejoined the IMF. Was that a wise thing to do?

KK: Very wise indeed. As a result the IMF, World Bank and other relevant agencies have begun to behave better. Zambia led the way, I am proud to say. All those who are opposing us have benefited from our policies of free education and free health services. I remember the school which my own father founded chased me away three days after he was buried. Hardly had the tears dried up when I was told I had to bring half a crown, which my mother in those days could not raise. I knew most of my countrymen were in the same position . So my colleagues and I who had suffered that kind of humiliation decided in favour of free education. We invested wisely in education, wisely in health. People today are healthy, when they used to be dying of malnutrition, and so on. We are proud of our policies. All those now opposing me and the party I am privileged to lead, benefited not only in terms of education and health, but also from the fact that we put them in charge of the commanding heights of the economy. They were the general managers, managing directors. And they learnt by running government institutions, and now they have to learn how to start private enterprise.

Stern: For over a quarter of a century you've held, on your own admission, enormous power. Indeed, you've had the power of life and death over people; you've had the power to incarcerate and to release. Above all you've had the power to influence people in their daily lives. Now bearing in mind what Lord Acton once said about power tending to corrupt, Mr President have you ever been corrupted by power?

KK: Geoff, I thank God that I can tell you, proudly and frankly, that I don't believe that I have been corrupted by power in any shape or form.

Stern: But it's very heady stuff, isn't it, power. Has it never gone to your head?

KK: I'm too balanced I think. It hasn't corrupted me at all.

Stern: Do you enjoy it?

KK: Only in the sense that it helps me to help my fellow men, to help my country. But I don't enjoy power for its own sake. Humility is something that I treasure and I believe that I am genuinely a servant of God my creator, and genuinely a servant of his people in Zambia.

Stern: But some people around you have been accused of corruption or even worse, and one of your sons is even on a charge of murder. I just wonder whether you sometimes feel that perhaps your judgment or even your parenting might have been deficient in some respect.

KK: I can't speak about my boy, who is now on trial. It's *sub judice*, as you know, but the truth will come out in the end. In terms of my own children I should pay tribute to Mrs Kaunda because I don't have enough time to be with my children. I remember, one time I was away in the north of the country for three months, and I brought back a very big beard. My first-born couldn't recognise me. He ran away and went to his mother and said "Mum, there's a strange human being outside".

Stern: So you can't really be a good President and a good parent at the same time. Yet you are clearly anxious to continue in office. Is that because you feel you're doing a good job and your presence is vital, or because you enjoy it?

KK: At no time have I thought that I was perfect because I'm not, and I'll never be, either politically or as a human being. But one of my principle tasks has been to prepare some of my own men and women for leadership. Sometimes I send them elsewhere, exposing them not only to Zambians but also to the international community. Some of them have gone out as Ambassadors only to return as Vice Presidents, or even Prime Ministers. I move people around to expose them. I want to go having prepared the ground for leadership.

Stern: Do you think you'll be forced to go in October when you have the multi-party elections?

KK: I am glad to tell you that going by what's taking place now, UNIP is fully assured of genuine and handsome victory.

Stern: But supposing you are wrong. Supposing you actually lose. What will you do then? Will you try to fight back, or would you retire?

KK: Fight back? If you believe in the ballot box you hand over. You say to your fellows "I'm going home now. Goodbye, God bless you".

Stern: Well there are two ways of responding to that. One is Edward Heath's way, which is staying on in politics. The other one is Margaret Thatcher's way, which is getting out of politics. Now, if you lose the election, do you stay in politics or do you get out?

KK: I would go by what my colleagues say. We would talk about it. They would decide. But I said several times that if I should lose the elections, I would go back home and participate in the politics of the local branch of my party. And I would fight the chairman of the branch there for the leadership. And if I defeat him, become chairman of the branch and continue to serve my party and my country.

Stern: So if you lose you'll stay on in Zambia, but go home.

KK: I would go home. But you've touched on a fine point. "You'd stay on in Zambia", you said. Only four days ago I received a report that some embassy is spreading a rumour that the reason why I'm giving in on some of these points in the new constitution I'd proposed is that I'm planning to go away to Belgium, if I lose.

Stern: I won't say I haven't heard that rumour.

KK: Nothing is further from the truth. That embassy is being mischievous, and as for the envoy concerned, I'm going to speak to his government after this election. It's a stupid rumour designed to demoralise our party's new recruits. I want clean politics here, not lies.

Stern: Have you made provision for a successor as head of UNIP in case you lose the election?

KK: I have not been making preparations of that type because I am quite sure that we will win. But I have been identifying some young men, quite brilliant, quite committed, with similar principles as I, and I shall be putting someone up later.

Stern: You are very confident of winning.

KK: Very confident.

Stern: A lot of people say that you are "a great survivor", and that while a lot of your fellow leaders have lost out, you're still there. How have you managed to hold on for so long?

KK: Geoff, perhaps it sounds too simplistic, but I have seen many things happen in Zambia which I cannot attribute to anything else except God's good hand. I pray that God will allow me to write my memoirs, for I hope to reveal the good hand of the Lord at work in Zambia. Really it is an amazing story. Some people say "God revealed himself to the Israelis, and he is the God of Israel". I look at that story in the Bible as saying to us that, any nation can be Israel, if only they see God revealing himself to all human beings. He is not just the God of Israel. He is God of the world. God has been guiding, defending, and protecting us in many complicated situations.

Stern: And yet some of your fellow African leaders who also believed in God didn't last as long. Some lasted hardly at all.

KK: I can't answer that. God's work is at hand, and I believe that he has given us his love, and sinful as I am, I have made a total surrender to him.

Stern: What has been your proudest achievement?

KK: Without hesitation, the independence of Zambia. Secondly, maintaining the peace within our nation when others have gone to pieces. Even though there have been many attempted coups, thank God they haven't succeeded. I have now been able to release those who went to prison for treason last year, because I want to start afresh. Those charged with looting have also been released so that I could have a clean start for the third republic which I was preparing for. That is a record second to none, and I am proud of the fact that there isn't a single Zambian in political exile.

Stern: Are you prepared to say what you think was your greatest folly?

KK: I have said it. I think it was subsidising consumption for far too long, because I admit we didn't understand economics. We did this on the advice of other people, but we didn't understand what they were talking about. We have learned the hard way. That I think is our greatest folly. If we had tried to subsidise agriculture instead of consumption we would be in a stronger position today.

Stern: You've often expressed the hope that you would leave Zambia better off than when you found it. Do you think the history books will say that is precisely what you did?

KK: I believe that historians will say that I played honest politics in the name of God and his people.

Benazir **BHUTTO**

CHAPTER 13

Stern: Ms Bhutto, you are of course one of the few women who have made it to the top. Could anyone have predicted when you were young that you'd not only get into politics, but go all the way to the top?

BB: I wouldn't have predicted it myself, because I'd seen how time consuming politics was for my father and it wasn't the life I wanted for myself. But many people tell me that my father very much wanted me to go into politics and believed that if I did I would get to the top. He used to admire Nehru's idealism and he felt that if Nehru's daughter Indira could become Prime Minister he would like his daughter to become Prime Minister. He never said it to me. I'm just saying what I picked up.

Stern: But if you'd known he wanted you to go into politics would that be a reason for entering the profession? I mean, did you usually do what your father told you to do?

BB: I usually did. I think I was a good and obedient girl generally. I was always trying in a way to please authority figures. But I didn't want to go into politics, and don't think I would have gone into it if it hadn't been for the circumstances in Pakistan, when military rule was declared and I found myself propelled onto the path that I myself had thought to avoid.

Stern: What, then, were you hoping to do?

BB: Well, when I was a very young girl I used to say I'm going to be a barrister, and then when I was a little older I wanted to join the foreign service and serve my country in a

159

way which I felt was less threatening to family life and yet in accordance with the traditions I'd been brought up with – the duty to society, to one's community, to one's people and country. And I used to think that when I retire I'd like to run a newspaper because it is a forum from where one can argue a certain set of policies.

Stern: You grew up in a very political household. What was it like growing up in such an environment?

BB: I was the eldest child and I think that eldest children in every home are treated as mini-adults. From the time that they are born they are given greater responsibility, even care of the other children, so in that sense I was treated differently from the others. I had to take care of them, take care of the house, and in terms of attention I remember my parents, particularly my father, always listening to everything I said as though they were pearls of wisdom.

Stern: Were they?

BB: No, they certainly weren't. I once took sweetpeas from the flower and thought they were peas and cooked them for my father, and he ate them as though they were the most delicious gourmet dish ever served, and I think that helped give me confidence.

Stern: So you were a dutiful daughter, somebody with responsibility. Were you also perhaps spoilt? After all, you grew up in quite a wealthy household didn't you?

BB: Well, yes and no. Spoilt to the extent that when my parents used to go abroad, particularly my father, they'd come back with lots of pretty dresses and chocolates, but at the same time my father was very keen that we were treated like other children. We couldn't have our own way, there was discipline. We had to have what was laid on the lunch table whether we liked it or not. We had to have our meals on time, we had to go to bed on time, and when we were very young we had an allowance, and had to live on that allowance. We couldn't have just what we wanted. If we were going shopping with our parents, we were allowed to choose one gift, so there was a sense of trying to put a framework or a discipline in life.

Stern: When you went to Oxford University was that discipline still in evidence or did you find, as so many students do, that you socialised, you had a good time.

BB: I think that university for all students is a marvelous time because for the first time in your life you're on your own, you make your own decisions, you come in at the time that you want to come in, and you do what you want to do, you set your own priorities and your own agenda. At the same time I was always a little cautious because my father was Prime Minister at the time I was at Oxford, so I didn't want to let him down in any way.

Stern: Were you a scholar?

BB: I can't say I was a scholar. But while I did go to many social events, took part in a whole series of organised meetings, nonetheless I did work, I did my essays even if it meant staying up all night.

Stern: Are you going to tell me what sort of degree you got?

BB: I got a second.

Stern: Upper or lower?

BB: Upper.

Stern: What did Oxford do to you in terms of your attitude to the outside world. Did it change it in any way?

BB: I think Oxford teaches one to live in a pressure cooker. Oxford taught me how to cope with crises, to meet one's deadlines; one had to get the essays on time and, on the last eight to ten days you enter an examination room, pick up a pen, don't stop for a breath, just write, write, write. So at Oxford one really has to have nerve, and I think if it changed my view it gave me an ability to put up with pressure (which came in very handy subsequently) and it taught me not to lose my calm if there was a storm around.

Stern: Oxford prides itself, on creating leaders. Do you think whatever leadership skills you have were instilled then, or before, or acquired in office?

BB: Oxford I suppose does take people which it feels have leadership qualities. It's not, however, that one is born a leader. I would say leadership comes as an evolutionary process. I think the environment, the parental attention, the teachers' attention, the opportunities of education at a higher level, learning how to cope with crisis and so forth are among the many different factors that go into it.

Stern: You've spoken a lot of your father, who clearly had a great influence on you. Were you 'daddy's little girl', or were your relations with your mother just as good?

BB: My relations with my mother and father were very different. My mother would scold or criticise us if things went wrong. I don't remember ever being slapped or even getting a scolding from my father. I think the role of a mother is more difficult because she is around more often, and the duty of disciplinarian is given normally to mothers, whereas the fathers go away to their jobs in the day, and are not around that much. My father put a lot of time in for the children, gave attention to small details, and was very loving and affectionate. I did have a different relationship with my father. Conversely my brothers had a much closer relationship with my mother, and I'm told that it often happens that mothers are closer to sons, and daughters are closer to fathers. I make an effort now to be especially close to both my children, but I find that my son gravitates to me. He is loving, always trying to please me, whereas my daughter, is a little devil. She's always saying 'no' to me. She won't listen to a thing I say, and I find myself saying 'wait a minute, was I like that? Is that why my mother had to discipline me?'

Stern: I just wonder whether you were disturbed when your father married again?

BB: No, because my mother was his second wife. My father first got married very young when he was about 12 and his first wife didn't have any children. My mother was the second wife, and when I was growing up so many of my relatives had first and second wives, but in that particular environment one just took it as a normal state of affairs. Later, however, my father was a firm believer that these double marriages were unfair, particularly to the first wife who is married for convenience. In large feudal families where there were large land holdings and properties at stake, the women of the family were never allowed to marry outside the home, so that the property would be retained within the family, and women were only married to their male cousins. If there was no male cousin available they were never married. And my father changed that when he allowed my cousin to marry outside the family when there was no male member around. He felt that property should not be the criterion, but what is best for the young people themselves.

Stern: When you finished at Oxford were you anxious to go home to Pakistan as soon as possible, or did you want to stay on for a while?

BB: Well I loved being at Oxford and was a little hesitant about going back to Pakistan, because my father was so well known that I couldn't be myself in my own country. I was always watched and observed. I felt I was on show, whereas in England I had a greater degree of freedom. But Pakistan was my home and I wanted to serve my country, so it was with a mixture of emotions that I returned home.

Stern: You returned home and soon got into politics. Were your views identical or similar to those of your father? Or did you have some important differences with him on political questions?

BB: At that particular time I was a clone.

Stern: It's very courageous of you to admit it.

BB: I was. My father was not just my father, he was my leader, a charismatic leader who stirred the emotions of millions of people in the country, who would faint if they happened to touch him, who wouldn't wash their hands for days once he shook hands with them, who'd write letters to him dripped in their blood saying 'we love you'. He was such a larger than life figure that I completely duplicated his views. But as I went on in life I found that objective situations change and one has to respond by doing what's best for one's country, by doing what's best for one's people, and not just doing it because it was done by one's parents. What was right for the 70s need not be right for the 90s, and therefore I am no longer a clone.

Stern: Which brings us on to what is leadership. I mean, is it the art of persuading people to do what you think is right, or is it something else?

BB: There may be different types of leadership, but as far as I am concerned leadership is having a set of beliefs, of values, and then seeking to further those beliefs and values, gathering together a group of people who believe in those sets of values and then sitting together and arriving at consensus decisions. I know some leaders who say 'I know best, this is the way we are going to do it'. I am not one of them. I believe in group decisions. At certain times, perhaps 10% of all the decisions I have made, I may intervene and say 'no, I believe this is the way it should be done'. But on the whole as long as we're a set of people who have a common belief in certain principles I believe in consensus. And when I was Prime Minister, I changed the mode of seating at the Cabinet Room: I had the Prime Minister sit in the middle and I had everyone sit around so we were all one group, one team, and now the new Prime Minister has gone back to the old way where the Prime Minister sits alone at the top and all the others sit down. I believe in team work, and in delegation, but if there are certain tough decisions I think a leader has to own them.

Stern: So how do you decide on which kinds of decisions you as leader should take on your own responsibility, and which should be collective decisions?

BB: Supposing there is a very important decision and I have heard the arguments and am not convinced by what is looking to be the consensus, then I will go with what I think is the large interest. I'll give you an example: the Gulf crisis. It evoked a lot of emotion not only in Pakistan but in a lot of Muslim countries, because the picture that was coming across was Western bombs falling on Muslim masses. And there was a hue and cry within the party that we should come out with a clear pro-Iraq sentiment. I intervened, because I understood the longer strategic implications, international relations and what was best for Pakistan's democracy meant observing UN principles and that we couldn't deviate from those UN principles. The fact was that Kuwait had been occupied as Kashmir has been occupied. So that's one of the decisions where I felt I had to intervene.

Stern: You've shifted imperceptibly from talking about your father as a decision maker to talking about yourself as a decision maker, and we've left out some very important steps. It's usual for males to run the affairs of Pakistan; it's extremely unusual for a woman to get to the top. How were you able to do it? Would you have got there if tragedy hadn't befallen your father?

BB: I wouldn't have entered politics if this tragedy hadn't befallen my father. But in South Asia we have a tradition of women leaders: Mrs Gandhi in India, Mrs Bandaranaike in Sri Lanka and of course Miss Jinnah, sister of the founder of Pakistan. She ran for presidential elections and actually won them, but they were rigged, so unfortunately she wasn't able to take over. It was difficult being a woman, there is no doubt there is prejudice at every level, and particularly in a society like Pakistan. But because the cause I symbolised was for so many millions of Pakistanis what my father stood for I was able to invoke in them a sense of dedication and a sense of mission to complete what had been left unfinished.

Stern: But how do people feel in Pakistan about taking orders from a woman? How, for that matter, does your husband feel, when in a way you're the boss?

BB: I don't give any orders to my husband. He is the master of his own life. I look after mine. We keep politics out of our family life, but as far as my colleagues are concerned I think they think we are all together as a team, and most people look upon me like a sister. But the clerics, they weren't happy at all. To some of the right wing elements of our society it was absolute gall to them to be told what to do by a woman and they could not reconcile to the fact that there was a woman Prime Minister. I think that even for the President of our country one of the major difficulties I had with him, even though I'd helped elect him to that post, was that I was a woman and I was young, and he couldn't cope with it. His own wife never went to public functions until I became Prime Minister. But amongst Pakistani society there is a strong liberal sentiment which finds its roots in our own freedom struggle, in the founder of Pakistan who had a theme of liberalism, to my own father who reinforced it.

Stern: It was said of your father that he had a western mind and an eastern soul, is that true of you?

BB: I don't see myself as either an eastern or western person. I see myself as a universal person. I believe the earth is one and all mankind is one, and that instead of having differences we should be working for greater harmony.

Stern: You have said that although quite a lot of people in your country were pleased to see a woman at the top, there were an awful lot of people who were not pleased, and I just wonder whether in a sense your government ever stood a chance.

BB: Originally we weren't given three months. And the fact that 20 months later the President had to take the undemocratic decision of dismissing the government proved that a government which has the support of the masses in normal democratic circumstances cannot be overthrown. After all, at the time I was dismissed I had the majority in parliament, and despite an austerity programme with the IMF, people refused to come out on the streets. And I think those 20 months showed that a country like Pakistan can have democracy and development, that it can have full freedoms – the freedom of the press, human rights – and still progress. I am very proud of our record in office in the social sectors. For instance we increased education by 70%; on women's development we increased expenditure; on population growth we increased expenditure. Health went up by 40%. And I mention these sectors because the new government has turned its back on the reforms I undertook and brought about drastic cuts of their expenditure. I am also proud of the economic report: investment quadrupled; inflation came down to less than half of what it was. Given the obstacles, given the opposition, it's a matter of satisfaction that we could build 1000 primary schools and electrify 5000 villages in 20 months, when normally 260 are electrified a year.

Stern: And yet isn't it also true that you disappointed some of your followers as well?

BB: There was a systematic campaign to destabilise the government by elements of the government itself. And this led to certain disappointment amongst people who don't go into details, who don't want to know what is actually being done in education or women's development, or health or the economy. But now with the passage of time I think those who were disappointed are looking at how things are today and are wondering whether they were really fair in not giving us more time.

Stern: Do you think you made some mistakes?

BB: Oh yes, I think everyone makes mistakes. But I think one learns as life goes on, and I and many of my own assistants and aides learned tremendously. I had never been a minister, leave alone Prime Minister, so one learns the functioning of the system, one learns about the responses of different institutions that are components of that whole area, and yes, I think that if I had the experience that I now have perhaps I would have done many things differently. I think that some of the relations with the military for instance wouldn't have been strained, given what we have learnt now.

Stern: What was the single most difficult decision that you had to take?

BB: When I came to know that the President was involved in trying to overthrow my government and I had to decide whether to dissolve the assembly myself or allow the President to dismiss me. And ultimately we decided that rather than dissolve ourselves it's better to be dismissed. So that was very difficult decision, because some people thought that 'if he's going to dismiss us let's dissolve the assembly, go to the people with a fresh mandate'. But if I took that step, then the President could under the constitution take all the powers upon himself and people might have turned around and said, 'serve her right, she dissolved the assembly'.

Stern: But in the end how much power did you really have?

BB: I had power, but there were certain areas where I took the decision to let things drift a bit. Afghanistan was one of those, because I felt that if I'd pushed for an early political settlement for Afghanistan it might strain my relations with the military and the President, so I took a conscious decision not to do so. Finally, about a year into my government I found that our constitution gave me certain powers, but the President was bent on not accepting them. I give you an example. The constitution gave the Prime Minister power to appoint the judges, but she had to send the advice to the President to sign, and he'd just sit on the files. What does one do? Create a constitutional crisis by saying the President and the Prime Minister are fighting at a time when in Afghanistan a civil war is raging, when relations with India are not perfect? So it was really the attitude of the President that made it more difficult for me to deal with problems. I would say that I could exercise power, but I felt exercising it in certain areas would bring about my downfall faster, so I preferred not to exercise it.

Stern: But is that why some people said of the early months of your administration, that it was pretty inactionary. It really wasn't doing very much.

BB: That's a perception that exists and it's really not fair. When we took over government there was no legislative action at all. We had to prepare our own agenda, and it takes time, you know, because to make something into law one has to first prepare it in the concerned ministry, bring it to the Cabinet, send it to the parliament, send it to the select committees. Democracy doesn't mean rubber stamping or issuing an ordinance. So obviously six to nine months is a gestation period.

Stern: During your administration there were plenty of suggestions of corruption, if not of yourself then of your family. How did you feel about these allegations?

BB: Extremely hurt. And one of the regrets I have is that I did not take formal action about it earlier. My own husband suffered a series of business setbacks, because when he became engaged to me, Zia cancelled all my husband's loans. When I was Prime Minister he said 'I am not now going to start a new project while you're Prime Minister. Most people will say it's not my own project, it's yours', so he lost out when I was in opposition and he lost out when I was Prime Minister. And yet the gossip and the innuendo – to the extent that people believed that my daughter was retarded. People believed that I had bought the BCCI bank. It hurt. It hurt tremendously. One just didn't know how to react to it. We had given freedom of the press. We thought that a libel action filing criminal suits against the journalists would be misinterpreted as trying to silence the press. And then by the time we got round to the libel action (my husband actually sued in May 1990), three months later our government was dismissed. But now both my husband and I are very pleased that the new government at least has filed these charges. They have filed only three charges of corruption against my husband. He's been acquitted in one of them, and only two remain. And we think the same principles will apply in the other two, and given the judgement he should be acquitted on all three. As far as the public is concerned they now know that there was no truth to such rumours, and that this was information done to 'get' the Bhutto government. We are pleased that the smoke is clearing, and that the truth is becoming known.

Stern: When you say the truth, does that mean there was no corruption in your administration?

BB: I am sure there's corruption in many governments but I do feel that there was less corruption in my government than in most Pakistani governments, including the present one.

Stern: I'm interested in how you as both a student and a practitioner of politics, respond to Lord Acton's famous phrase that 'power tends to corrupt'. Does it?

BB: I think that power does tend to corrupt. I have seen a lot of it around me. I have seen it go to people's heads. I have seen their attitudes suddenly change. I was lucky that I grew up in a political family, and from the time that I was five or six Lord Acton was quoted to me again and again and again. We were never allowed to bring requests. Our friends would say, 'my father's requested that your father get this done' or something. We weren't allowed to get into any of that. So coming up in such an environment I think that it had a salutary effect.

Stern: Are you saying you weren't corrupted by power?

BB: No, I don't think I was corrupted by power because if people are warned about it then I think they'll be careful. Of course many people say that power is a heady experience. For me power wasn't a heady experience, it was a responsibility, and my every effort was made into fulfilling that responsibility. I had no time for my children, I had no time for rest. I recently read a review of a book that's got a beautiful picture of me on the cover (I think to sell it), which says that 'she spent more time deciding menus than on running the government'. I wish it were true. Forget deciding menus; there were times when I couldn't even eat a meal. I'd be having sandwiches in my office; I was pregnant with my second child and going to public functions because a Prime Minister has so much to do.

Stern: How could you actually run the affairs of state when you were perhaps seven, eight, nine months pregnant?

BB: Well, I wanted to show that a woman could have a career and a baby, and I guess it was that determination to show it which helped me go a long way. I wanted to show that a woman is not half a man, as the mullahs in our country would like people to believe. And then the clerics spread a rumour saying that my child was deformed, trying to say that a working woman couldn't have a healthy child and that because I'd worked up to the right day my child wasn't healthy.

Stern: But when you were about to deliver your child were you still running the affairs of state or did you delegate them?

BB: I was running the affairs of state except for I think 24 hours when they were delegated according to the rules of business and the government of Pakistan. And then after 24 hours I was out of anaesthesia and we had a lot of problems with India and I was having Foreign Office files being brought to me right up there, nursing the baby with one hand and nursing the Foreign Office files with the other.

Stern: But how much did your motivation stem from vengeance – getting your own back on the people who'd killed your father and on all those men who said that women can't run the affairs of state?

BB: I wouldn't say that I went into politics for vengeance, but I must say it was a tremendous vindication and with a tremendous sense of joy when I took my oath and felt now my father must feel that the life that he gave had been redeemed. But there was so much more to the struggle. It really was for developing a democratic Pakistan. It was an attempt at alleviating the pressing social and economic problems.

Stern: Did you enjoy the trappings of office?

BB: Trappings meant nothing to me. I'd seen the trappings of office when my father'd been minister from the time I was four or five years old, and even when my father was not in office there were a lot of trappings, because we come from a family that's well known. In fact I felt the trappings were time consuming. For instance, every time I came back from a foreign visit all the ministers had to be lined up and the diplomats, and I just thought it's so time consuming for the secretaries who should have been in their offices working. But it was the done thing, so we did it. Some of the trappings I enjoyed. I enjoyed going to the military bases and I particularly enjoyed a session I had in Jhelum where there was an officers' meeting and a shooting competition and, suddenly they gave me a gun and said 'shoot'. Here was a lady who was scared of weapons and had never picked one up in her life, but how could I turn round and tell the officers 'your Prime Minister is scared of a gun'. I couldn't do that. So I picked up the gun and my advisor of Defence told me 'just keep the point slightly above the bullshead. Don't aim for the bullshead.' So I closed my eyes and then 'bang, bang, bang'. Luckily for me they all hit in the right place.

Stern: What did you dislike about office?

BB: Sometimes I'd see a lack of an organised approach and that I didn't like. I disliked the sort of social chit chat one has to often make. It's so time consuming when other things could be done. I disliked living in such an imposing mansion that it wasn't really a home, and didn't give the feeling of a home. I disliked the fact that one doesn't have time for friends or for relatives. One's time is simply not one's own. I couldn't just go out and shop for myself; I had to literally leave it to other people's personal taste.

Stern: Can you now?

BB: Well, not in Pakistan. But I do sometimes do a small shop.

Stern: I suppose one of the most disagreeable things about office is the way you can so easily be removed from it, as you were. How did you feel the day after?

BB: Well, we knew our government was being destabilised, but on the day it happened I suppose I was angry. I was angry that it had happened, I was angry that it had interrupted the work that I had started out to do and I was determined to fight back, and that's what I did. It wasn't easy. I had all these messages from the government, including a cabinet minister telling me that my husband wouldn't be spared and that I would be imprisoned if I didn't leave the country. And I had no intention of leaving the country and disappointing all the people who believed in us. And he was determined to stay on, so that was a very difficult period. Even after that, right up to March I was told, 'you know what happened to your father. Unless you compromise with the regime the same is going to happen to your husband'. I just sat down and told them, 'you know it's so shabby to tell a woman whose father has been killed, whose brother has been killed, that her husband's life is threatened. But I'm a believer, and I believe God has the power to give life and to take life, and that's why I won't be frightened of what you're saying to me'.

Stern: So you're not afraid for your own future or for that of your husband?

BB: Of course one can't say one is not afraid. But belief has to overcome fears. My recipe for my own personal survival, and I've had so many difficulties in my life, is hope for the best, keep working for the best. Don't dwell on the worst or it will get you down.

Stern: Do you think Pakistan still needs you?

BB: Very much so. I think Pakistan needs a government which has support in the four provinces of the country; Pakistan needs a government that can understand the changing international environment and make Pakistan relevant within that environment; I think Pakistan needs a liberal government which can act as a bridge between the Christian west and the Muslim east, and which can within the Muslim community help solve intra-Muslim disputes, because it acts not as a partisan but more as a mediator. And I think Pakistan needs a government like the Peoples Party offered, because it understands how to bring about investment in human resources and complement that with a privatisation or a deregulation which is an equaliser.

Stern: Do you think you'll ever be back in power again? Will the army let you come back?

BB: Well, obviously I am going to make sure that the Pakistan People's Party and I develop a good relationship with the army and seek to make it a good working relationship for the future. My colleagues and I have learned a lot from being in office, and I certainly think that we are fighting for something which many Pakistanis want, a liberal, democratic Pakistan, where democracy and development go hand in hand.

Stern: What, looking back on it all, do you think was your greatest achievement?

BB: It's difficult to say what was the peak, because there were so many different things that we were doing, at many different levels. For instance sustaining and increasing United States aid at the time the Soviets were leaving Afghanistan could itself be called an achievement. Managing to get international assistance from countries like England and France and many others could also be called one. But I think that the achievement which gave me the greatest degree of satisfaction would be the agreement to get a nuclear power plant from France, because power is a very important project for people in Pakistan. We have load shedding, our factories don't run because there isn't enough electricity, and this was supposed to be under all international safeguards. I was very proud of that achievement because it showed confidence in Pakistan not going nuclear. If one looks at it differently, not from satisfaction but from a challenge, I think the most challenging effort was averting war with India. We were very, very close to war, last spring.

Stern: And dare you talk about your greatest folly?

BB: There were lots of little follies, but the first major folly was the row we had over the retirement of a military officer. I felt some reservation about it, but nonetheless I take the responsibility because I was the leader. I think that was a major folly, because it started a new turn in the relationship with the military. From that moment on they didn't trust the government the same as they had before.

Stern: And what do you see as your place in history?

BB: I would like history to record that I showed that a Muslim woman could not only become Prime Minister, but a woman in any part of the world could combine home and power together and at the same time have a successful, happy home and meet the challenges of the career.

King **HUSSEIN**

CHAPTER 14

Stern: Your Majesty, You belong to a rare and endangered species – namely royalty. Now since there are comparatively few monarchs left around the world do you think the role of monarchy needs to be defended. I mean, what's the point of it?

KH: What's the point of it is beyond me at times, except that here in Jordan it really is an honour and a duty that we perform against a background of belonging to a family that is a member of the oldest tribe in Arabia. And we have gone on being the descendants of the Prophet Mohammed which, in any event, I believe is far more important than being a monarch. Nonetheless, I have always regarded myself as an ordinary person who has been placed in this position and have always tried my utmost not to let people down in terms of their hopes and expectations.

Stern: But there are people who attack monarchy as being un-Islamic, or say that Middle Eastern monarchies such as yours are the creations of imperialist powers. What do you say to people who argue that way?

KH: That is their view, though I believe it shortsighted and maybe inaccurate. But I think that the survival or otherwise of any system of government really depends on whether it has the backing and the trust and confidence of the people. I can't really categorise monarchy as a system in the same manner as one can speak of other governments.

Stern: Indeed, but I wonder whether it makes sense at the end of the 20th century to have rulers who are there merely because of who their parents or grandparents were. Isn't it a bit out of date?

171

KH: As far as it goes here, and as far as it has gone with me, my father, grandfather and great grandfather, who was the leader of the great Arab revolt for revival, unity and freedom...

Stern: ...That's the revolt against the Ottoman Empire. . .

KH: ...Yes, really it has not been anything more than an attempt to live up to the hopes and expectations of people. As far as I am concerned, I felt it my duty to carry on beyond what I received, to enable people to govern themselves, share in power and make of this country a democracy. Whether monarchy survives or it doesn't in the future is something that the people will decide, and no one else.

Stern: When you were growing up in Amman, and being educated in Alexandria did you understand you would be King one day?

KH: It was not absolutely clear to me at all, and certainly it wasn't something I looked forward to or anticipated might happen. But then there were some very tragic events in my life and some of them brought me to this responsibility at a very early age.

Stern: Indeed. But since there was always a possibility that you would be King one day, did you lead a rather unusual kind of childhood? Were you surrounded by protocol and by security and so on?

KH: Hardly at all. You would have found a rough and ready young boy at that time living the same life as everybody else.

Stern: You referred a moment ago to the fact that there had been a lot of sadness in your life, and of course there had been. Your baby sister died, your father was ill for much of the time and on 20 July 1951 as you accompanied your grandfather, King Abdullah, into the Al Aqsa Mosque, he was gunned down by an assassin and you too were shot but mercifully survived. Can you remember the emotions and thoughts that were going through your head when all that happened in a split second?

KH: It seemed to have taken much more than a split second. It seemed, first of all, as if time stopped, and then after that a feeling of anger and rage as I went, or tried to go, for the assassin who turned around and fired as he was himself gunned down. I received a bullet that bounced off the medal that my grandfather had honoured me with, as an honorary Captain in the Arab Legion of the day and as his Aide, but when I went to him I found that he'd already passed away. I looked around and suddenly the place was almost empty. Most of the people who were always around him and enjoyed his protection and tutelage had gone. And that was another shock that has lived with me.

Stern: Why was the place almost empty?

KH: I think everyone was looking after themselves and their safety in a dangerous situation.

Stern: But you weren't. Weren't you afraid?

KH: No, I wasn't. Not at that moment. Maybe, as has happened so many times afterwards in moments of real crisis or real danger, I seem to cope well. The shock comes considerably later. But it was a terrible loss and I didn't know what it meant. But I knew that he who was really a father to me, as nobody else was for a brief period in my life, and who was a mentor and inspiration had gone.

Stern: And he taught you how to be a King?

KH: Only by watching his love for his people and his commitment, despite all the setbacks throughout his life in the cause of Jordan and the Arab world.

Stern: You were still very young when this tragedy happened and following the assassination you were sent to Harrow school in Britain, weren't you? And in little over a year you received a telegram from Amman addressed to 'His Majesty King Hussein'. Your father had abdicated. And you were then only 17. Now, at 17, were you qualified to be a King?

KH: No, I wasn't, and there was a regency council. I returned to Jordan of course, and toured the country, and everyone was so warm to me. To the older generation I was like a younger son; to the younger people, I was one of them. And then I decided that until I became of age, which was going to be some time, the best thing for me was to go to receive some military training, and a special, fairly condensed course was arranged for me at the Royal Military Academy Sandhurst. I believe that was the turning point in my life, and it was one of the nicest periods I had spent till then. I changed, you could say, from a boy to a man both physically and mentally, and with a sense of responsibility. I enjoyed the atmosphere of friendship and the team spirit that existed there, and then I returned. I was to assume my constitutional responsibilities at the age of 18, but the constitution didn't specify whether it was 18 lunar years as we have them in terms of the Arabic calendar or the normal 18. However, people decided that it should be 18 Hedjira years, and therefore although I was almost six months younger than my late cousin the King of Iraq, King Faisal, on the 2nd May 1953, I assumed constitutional powers.

Stern: Can I just ask you about those six months spent at Sandhurst. You said that it was one of the happiest times of your life. Can you explain that a bit more. Were you one of the lads?

KH: Of course I was 'one of the lads'. I remember the Commandant asking me, did I 'want to be treated in any special way', and I said 'no'. But I suppose because of my background and because I couldn't spend the full time that was required, I had to work much harder. But beyond that I was just one of the cadets.

Stern: I'm just wondering whether you went to Sandhurst because you needed military training – that part of your royal duties would be to lead your people into battle if necessary.

KH: Not necessarily that. But my father had gone to Sandhurst, and my son Abdullah graduated from the Royal Military Academy and one of my daughters as well, and another son went to Cranwell after completing his university studies, so it's in our family, our tradition. The King in Jordan is the Supreme Commander of the armed forces, and I was always as proud of being one with the troops, as I was of being a cadet at Sandhurst.

Stern: Now you reminded us that in May 1953 you were crowned, and of course you have been in charge ever since.

KH: Crowned symbolically.

Stern: Symbolically, yes. But what does being a King mean to you. You say that you are really just an ordinary bloke. But you're an ordinary bloke doing an extraordinary job, aren't you?

KH: Sir, in my book you fear but two things in life: you fear God and you fear your conscience, and as far as I am concerned one of God's blessings has been that I care for people, for everybody. I feel more uncomfortable in this office or in this building than being out in the open with people. There is nothing exceptional about me at all. In fact I am just an "ordinary bloke" as you say, trying to do his best and trying to contribute towards a better future for people despite Jordan's very difficult location and its very difficult circumstances. I am a sort of a dynamo that tries to encourage, and if there is anything wrong tries to address it. It is also a happy country in the sense that no grudges are held. I have never believed that a difference between people should reach the point of no return. I believe in discussion, debate and argument, and in democracy here, not because it was demanded but because the leadership itself contributed what it could towards making it a reality. It's really one of the greatest delights of my life to be able to sit with people who might have been very much on the opposite side, talking things over, preparing for the future, preparing for pluralism.

Stern: Can I ask you then, what qualities you feel you bring to the leadership? Is being a conciliator one of them?

KH: Well, that may be one of them, and I feel that the experience of years, and the difficulties that we pass through have given me maybe the privilege of being able to suggest to people where we should go next. And regardless of my position, I believe there is a degree of credibility that has been established over these years that is enabling us to move forward even under very difficult circumstances.

Stern: Do you need the skills for your office that other people need for their kind of leadership, or do you have something special as being of a royal household?

KH: I don't believe I have anything particular or special. I am not seeking power for the sake of seeking it. I am not competing with anybody. I am trying to serve and to make my life worthwhile. But as a system of government you can't apply this everywhere, though I believe, by the way, that monarchy in certain parts of the world provides continuity and stability. For myself, I have always felt that if I ever was a hindrance to this country I wouldn't be there. And I'd move out myself without anybody suggesting it. There are those who are power hungry, who try to seek it at any expense. I am not one of them.

Stern: Have you ever thought at times that you would be better off out of this job than in it?

KH: It would be much more peaceful, I suppose, in terms of one's mind.

Stern: Of course, you're not just a King, you are an Arab ruler. Does running an Arab state require special qualities?

KH: A lot of tolerance and a belief in people, I suppose, as it does conceivably everywhere else. But I don't run the state. There is a government that runs it; there is a parliament that is freely elected that runs it now. In the fifties we started along this approach, because I believed in it. It didn't work then and when we had the disasters of 1967 having free elections seemed impossible; but as soon as it was possible we went back to it, and now it is our way of life and I hope it will remain so.

Stern: I don't know if I am alone in this but I detect a kind of contradiction in you. You are a very friendly, gregarious person, and yet you've got a job which I would have thought is a very lonely one. Is there a contradiction between what you want to do and what you have to do?

KH: There is a contradiction because there are limitations. It's not the kind of job as far as I am concerned which ends at a certain hour and that's it! It is a continuous struggle night and day to have to be ready to answer a phone or an appeal, or to act or react, and it's a very, very heavy burden. In that sense you are right, it is a very lonely position even though one is surrounded by love and care from so many people.

Stern: You have said that Jordan's been moving towards a democracy. Would you describe yourself as a constitutional monarch?

KH: Certainly, or if not so, we are on our way towards it.

Stern: So what are the checks and balances on power here? How are errors of policy rectified?

KH: By the clear divisions between the legislature, the government and the judiciary, and at the end the King or head of state is really the element that watches over everything, unites the people and at the same time somehow creates the balance to ensure this division is kept.

Stern: How do you keep this balance? I mean, do you have in your cabinet Palestinians and non-Palestinians. Do you have people from the right, from the left and so on?

KH: Everybody in Jordan, regardless of their origins, is equal in terms of their rights and their responsibilities, so there is no difference in that regard at all. And we have always been proud to be one family in the sense that there is no difference between people in terms of religion or faith. We are all believers in God, we are all followers of monotheistic religions and this is something I have never permitted anyone to tamper with.

Stern: But there could be disagreements within a family, and I am wondering whether, when you choose an advisory team you want people around you who are likely to agree with you, or whether you like people who are going to say 'Your Majesty, I think you've got it wrong'.

KH: I certainly like having people who would say, if they feel it, that I was wrong about something. I welcome that. And I can assure you, sir, that the day's work includes a lot of discussion – friendly and open. I believe one of the greatest tragedies of this region, and maybe some others in the world on occasion, is one where a leader or leadership elevates itself in its own eyes or is elevated by people to almost demi-god status. This is what brings about disasters. This is not our way. I believe in frankness, openness and cooperation.

Stern: Can I ask you about the relationship between your own team of advisors and the Prime Minister and his Cabinet?

KH: Before anything becomes official the Cabinet, elected by Parliament, makes its decisions. If there are laws enacted they go through Parliament, then through the Senate, which is an appointed body, and by the time they come to me there shouldn't be any difficulty, and I ratify them. On very rare occasions, I have had to return a 'no' for them to then jointly sit together and try to work out a compromise.

Stern: What is the role of your brother, Crown Prince Hassan?

KH: He has been to me the greatest help over the years. When I was considerably younger and, as always, under threat I was very worried regarding the future. My own children were then very young and I thought that if anything happened to me the future would be very bleak and uncertain, and so I did something rather unusual. After discussion, I made him the Crown Prince. To me he was like a son that seemed to have all the qualifications that would enable him to contribute much to the progress of Jordan. In fact, he is an academician and very involved in the political as well as the economic life of the country, and planning for the future. So again, another dynamo alongside.

Stern: Would it be fair to say that perhaps he looks after the domestic and you look after the foreign side of things?

KH: Not necessarily, sir. I think both of us do much of the same. We coordinate very closely together.

Stern: Some rulers are much influenced by their wives. Now you've been married four times. Have any of your wives played a political role? Do you discuss your affairs of state with them?

KH: I don't think to any great extent, sir. I have never felt the right to involve others, as close as they are, in everything I do. Of course, those who have been able to help have done so, and continue to do so. But you know, I feel there is no-one in this world that I can turn to and speak openly about everything that is of concern. It's too much of a burden. I am willing to take it on my own shoulders, but that is the way it is. That's the way I am.

Stern: That again emphasises the point about the loneliness of your position. In the end I just wonder how much power the King of Jordan has.

KH: As much as the people of Jordan care to give him through their trust and their confidence in him. But the power is mainly the power of persuasion, more than anything else. What we have achieved is this ability to talk together and face up to a situation together and to share responsibility, and I believe this is the only way by which Jordan can have a future. I believe Jordan is stronger this way than it could ever be under one leader or just a group sitting in positions of responsibility right at the top.

Stern: I'd like to ask you about the circumstances that Jordan finds itself in. It's a small, vulnerable country. What special problems are there in governing it?

KH: Meager resources, but the greatest asset has always been the human dimension that Jordan has been blessed with. An able people, a people who have suffered. If you take the Arab-Israeli problem for example, that is one area that has caused us to be on the receiving end of every negative development regarding the Arab perspective in the Palestinian issue. The problems that occurred in this region in the last year have also had their effects on us. But we have always tried to stand on principle, to uphold ideals, and that might cause us at times to feel isolated in a world where sometimes interests come first. However, our haul is the long haul and we believe that this is the best way, the best approach.

Stern: But don't you find yourself sometimes in a position where whatever you do, you're going to be criticised for it?

KH: Yes, there are occasions when, I believe, people pass judgments maybe prematurely. But if you have done the right thing, what is important is people's judgment, long after we are gone, of what we are and what we have done.

Stern: You were talking just now about the principles that guide you. Could you just elaborate what some of these principles are?

KH: That people should be treated equally, that issues should be addressed on the same level. So, for example, we had already accepted Security Council Resolution 242 in 1967 – its preamble being the inadmissability of occupation of territory by war. We had taken a similar position on the occupation of part of Cyprus and of the Falklands. We couldn't alter it in the case of Kuwait. We were against the military move against Kuwait and its occupation and annexation. But we tried to reverse it peacefully and we were misunderstood for a long period of time. But I believe that this will pass and that people will realise that we sought to protect lives, and to correct the situation peacefully if we could, rather than through means that put in jeopardy lives, resources and maybe even the environment, with which I am personally very concerned.

Stern: You've used two words: one is principles, the other one is interests. Now other leaders frequently sacrifice principle for expediency or for interest. Are you an exception?

KH: I don't know that I am an exception, but I'd rather be able to live with myself and with my conscience than do anything else. One has had to bend a few times, but at the same time one has tried to explain situations, and eventually we go back to a record of having stood on principle on almost every issue so far.

Stern: For the most part yours has been a staunchly pro-Western regime. Why? Isn't there a price to be paid for that? I mean, wasn't this bound to make you pretty unpopular with a lot of Arab nationalists?

KH: Arab nationalism in my blood, mind and heart meant Arab freedom – but in interaction with the rest of the world. So I came into conflict with those who wished to switch sides and place the Arab world under another domination. Maybe many in what is now called the West took us for granted, and maybe many forgot when it wasn't that important. But we did it out of a conviction that we were doing the right thing for our nation, and believing we belonged in a family of free people throughout the world.

Stern: Several times in your history you have had to take a really difficult decision, and I'm just wondering how you prepare for that. When I asked the former Turkish leader, Bulent Ecevit, about this he said that he would turn to classical poetry, and when I asked former West German Chancellor Helmut Schmidt, he said he turned to music. What about you?

KH: I enjoy music very much indeed, but it takes me a long time to make a decision if it is an important decision, and that is why when I discuss it with other officials in Jordan I have usually done my homework quite well. But there are nights when I can't sleep at all. I dream of the problems, I wake up with them, feeling more tired than I did when I turned in, but responsibility is a very heavy burden.

Stern: You sometimes go into the desert, don't you? Do you do that at moments of great stress?

KH: Well I go out, I visit people, I try to change the environment I'm in. This last year I think I've ridden a motorbike more than I've done for all the years that have passed. But I found when pressure was so heavy, and so intense, it was a way of just concentrating, because I tried to do something that would take me off the subject I am on. I know when I'm tired, I know when I need a break or a holiday, but unfortunately it is not easy to take breaks, so I try to distract myself. I fly (then you have to concentrate of what you are doing). I do amateur radio and contact friends all over the world. Well, then I return to the problem and try to resolve it with the help of others.

Stern: Let's look at one of those very difficult problems that you had to tackle. In 1956 there was the Anglo-French intervention in Egypt and the second Arab-Israeli war at the same time. Bearing in mind that Britain had been a friend and Nasser's Egypt had been close to being an enemy, how did you arrive at an appropriate strategy for Jordan?

KH: Well clearly we were against the intervention and the way it took place. This might not have endeared us to our friends in Britain for obvious reasons, but it was wrong and we stood against it.

Stern: Yet within two years of that that you called on Britain as well as the United States to help you deal with a threat both internal and external to your regime. What was the nature of the threat and is it the case, as some people have argued, that had there not been foreign assistance your regime might have gone under then?

KH: That might have been the view of some, sir, but if you remember we referred to the way the tide was moving in this area towards the East at that time, and that we resisted that. We were unable to influence royalist Iraq to look at the dynamics of the situation realistically until it was too late. We had the union created and. . .

Stern: ...That was the union with Iraq?

KH: Yes, sir. And in the aftermath of that there was the revolution in Iraq in 1958 (and by the way, Iraq at that time was the seat of the Baghdad Pact, as many would recall). I was the second leader of the union, so we called for help and assistance when we were almost in a state of siege, and at the same time wondering what had actually happened in Iraq, and whether there was any reason for us to intervene from here to try to save the situation there. So the call for help was really in a sense a call to prevent threats developing against Jordan while we looked at the possibilities of doing what we could. But once we realised that the family had been lost, and that the people had their own feelings and their own aspirations, we decided against intervention ourselves. The forces that came were very welcome, but they never interfered in the internal scene and we were able to reorganise ourselves very soon, and they left with our gratitude.

Stern: Were you afraid that what had happened in Iraq could also happen in Jordan?

KH: No. I was not afraid of that, although we had discovered a plan for a coup in Jordan which led us to discover that there was a plan for a coup in Iraq about which I warned them. But they said: "This is the kind of thing that could happen in Jordan. It could never happen in Iraq". But unfortunately, it did.

Stern: I wonder if we could look at your most fateful decision perhaps, and that was to join Egypt and your other Arab neighbours in a coalition against Israel in June 1967. This of course had a disastrous outcome for Jordan. You lost your air force, thousands of troops, the West Bank, East Jerusalem. How in your view did this war come about? And did you have any doubts about entering it?

KH: I had very serious doubts, but I had a commitment, as did Jordan, sir. We were a member of the Arab League, we had an Arab League Charter, we had a joint defence agreement. But I knew full well what the results would be, as happened recently in the case of Iraq and Kuwait. The Arab leaders had met at the summit where Arab military experts were able to come up with the conclusion that the Arab world was way behind Israel in terms of even a balance of strength and that it would require another year and a half, even if the Arabs provided the resources and the coordination for the entire Arab world, to be on a par or to create a balance with Israel. All this came about when Israel had actually diverted the waters of the River Jordan to the Sinai. So, when one day in Aqaba I heard that the late President Nasser had closed the Gulf of Aqaba and put his troops in Sinai, and that the UN troops were moving out, I said: "Oh, here we are. It's going to happen". Throughout we had believed that we were one nation and that whatever threat one country faced, it could never cope, except collectively, through the charter of the Arab League and joint defence agreements. I went to Cairo and spoke to the late President Nasser, and said: 'What's this?' And he said, 'Don't worry; the thing is clear'. So the decision I had to take was to hand over, as I was expected to do, the command of the armed forces of Jordan, to the unified Arab Command (which was effectively an Egyptian command), as the Syrians did, and within days the war broke out and the worst suspicions and fears that we had had developed into the disaster of 1967.

Stern: Are you saying that you thought that you would lose?

KH: Oh yes, we knew, we knew that.

Stern: So you were basically in a no-win situation?

KH: It was a no-win situation.

Stern: If you had your time over again, would you have to make the same decision?

KH: The situation was that Israel would have moved in anyway. We either would have had to react to its attack on Egypt, since it was in command of our forces, or the country would have disintegrated and Israel would have moved in. It was as simple as that, unfortunately. And it was repeated again in the case of the recent disaster in the Gulf. Again, we didn't know; we were not involved; it happened. We had to do whatever we could to prevent the deterioration of the situation. But that's why I feel so strongly, much more than ever, that it's only through Jordan being an example, and others emulating it, where you share power, where people are involved, that such mistakes can be avoided. They've occurred in this region, they've occurred in Germany at a certain point, they've occurred elsewhere. But it's about time they stopped.

Stern: But you are also saying that Jordan is to a large extent at the mercy of events.

KH: It has been, but it has held its head high, and has tried its best. I remember 1967, going around, seeing our troops and saying: "I believe that war is imminent and that we are a major target. You'll have to do your best". Unfortunately, I also saw the destruction of the Jordanian army and the West Bank, and everything that we had built for 15 years.

Stern: Did you at the time tell Nasser that you thought he was making a mistake?

KH: I certainly posed the question very, very clearly. It was fairly obvious. I mean, the time the choice was made to move – effectively falling into a trap – was a year and a half before the arrangements agreed on the material and the military side would have brought us to a position of comparability, or balance with Israel – so how could we expect otherwise?

Stern: You helped draft United Nations resolution 242, calling on Israel to relinquish occupied territories in return for Arab recognition. What did you understand by return of 'occupied territories'? All of them? Most of them? Some of them?

KH: I understood all of them, sir. I understood that regarding the West Bank, which was a part of Jordan, there might be some reciprocal minor border rectifications because, after all, it was a cease fire line rather than an international boundary, as was the case with other Arab states. When the union took place between Jordan and Palestine, the first session of the Joint Parliament declared the West Bank a trust to be returned once the Palestinian problem was resolved for people to then decide what their future was. On the other hand, Arab Jerusalem was a part of Jordan. However, this was only recognised by Great Britain and Pakistan. All the Arab states, all the Moslem states, all the rest of the world spoke of an international city. I struggled, when I was responsible for the return of Arab sovereignty over the Arab part of the city of Jerusalem, for the city to be a united city and for no borders to exist there, and for it to be the symbol of peace between the followers of the three great monotheistic religions. And I still do.

Stern: Did you think the Israelis would comply with 242?

KH: Both we and the Egyptians were talking at the time to the United States at the highest levels, and we were led to believe that it would be implemented within six months.

Stern: Now as a result of the troubled events of the past 40 years in this region, more and more Palestinians have been fleeing to Jordan and playing a full life in the politics and the economics of this country. But why did you turn against the PLO in September 1970 and launch what's often called Black September?

KH: At that time, sir, one could not draw a line between Palestinians and Jordanians. I think on both sides there were Palestinians and on both sides there were Jordanians. But the choice, after trying everything possible to avert that clash was either chaos, anarchy and the destruction of the entire country, or law and order. And those who were for law and order prevailed eventually.

Stern: But didn't Black September and its aftermath jeopardise your own role as spokesman for the Palestinians of the West Bank?

KH: I have never claimed to be a spokesman for them beyond my immediate responsibilities. When the right time came we handed over that responsibility in response to a Palestinian demand, an Arab demand, an Islamic demand, and we were very supportive

181

of them. We feel the closest of all Arabs to them and will always feel that way. As far as we are concerned here in Jordan, we are one family and the overwhelming majority of people here were for law and order, and for the unity of this country. I believe many mistakes were made, and maybe that's a chapter that we'd like to close and leave behind us.

Stern: Let's go back to something that you touched on a little earlier, namely Jordan's policy a year or so ago when Iraq attacked Kuwait. You have said that Jordan's policy has been much misunderstood. But was it ever clear? Could anyone have known at the time precisely what Jordan's policy was?

KH: Sir, in the late forties and early fifties, Jordan did more regarding the recovery of Palestinian territory and Palestinian rights and the sharing of everything with our brethren who suffered then, and who have suffered since, than any. But others more powerful in this region, who did far less, chose to absolve themselves of their responsibilities by putting a lot of blame on Jordan. Jordan chose not to answer, nor to put the facts on record for history. And maybe some of the ill feelings created over the years have festered until now. Having learned from history, therefore, we have issued a white paper to spell out all the facts and it has come out and it is available. I hope people read it who still don't understand where we stood.

Stern: Well, I'll need to read it because I don't quite understand. But I'm just wondering whether you feel you'd handled the situation well, or do you think you could have handled it better? Or were you placed in an impossible position, that whatever you did would have been regarded as wrong?

KH: Well, let me give you one example. I think this white paper has caused us to be unpopular with the Iraqi leadership as well as others, so there you are.

Stern: Well now, a year later people are talking peace. US Secretary of State James Baker is hawking around his plans for a Middle Eastern Conference and he has the backing of the USSR and as far as I can see of many Arab states, including your own. But is there still an important role for Jordan as peace maker, and if so, what is that role?

KH: We are told it is a pivotal, vital and important role, sir. We believe it may be, and after all, we are the closest people to the Palestinian people, and we have been ever since the great Arab revolt. Here in Jordan we were blamed for many years for having shared everything with our brethren – all rights, including nationality and the right to live. So our future is intertwined and inter-related as in the past. Yet I believe that what we are seeking is a comprehensive peace with the involvement of all the concerned countries around the area of Palestine and Israel. There has to be a Palestinian/Israeli dialogue to resolve the Palestinian-Israeli dimension of the problem. We have offered the possibility of a joint delegation, if that is the only way for dialogue to be achieved – but essentially people selected by the Palestinians themselves who are Palestinians will represent the Palestinian dimension of the equation. The rest of us here in Jordan will deal with our problems with Israel, and jointly we will have to deal with problems as they relate to many issues, such as water and other rights and so on. And then there is a regional group. Here I would like to say that this is a very important development because if you look at the land mass of Jordan and Palestine, including Israel, there is no way by which this area can cope with all the Palestinians in the world, and all the Jordanians in the world, and all the Israelis in the world, and all those who are coming to Israel as well. So peace is the way out. At the same time it is important that Palestinians have their rights, the rights that have been denied on their legitimate soil and denied everywhere else, including the Arab world. After the Iraqis moved into Kuwait and then the liberation it caused more than 250,000 Palestinians to move back here. This is the third wave into Jordan. Many of them had been in Kuwait for three generations, but while an Israeli has the right to have a dual nationality (an Israeli nationality and maybe an American one), a Palestinian, under the circumstances that have passed in this region as a whole (with the exception of Jordan), unfortunately has no rights. This has got to stop, and to be addressed, and this is part of the regional context that we are searching for to resolve this problem.

Stern: Your Majesty, you've now been in office for over 38 years. You are one of the world's longest surviving leaders. Now given that many people didn't even think you'd survive for 38 days, how did you do it?

KH: I honestly don't know. The will of God, I suppose, sir. And never thinking about it.

Stern: Although the domestic situation is changing, you've said yourself you've had a great deal of power. Lord Acton once said that power tends to corrupt. Has it had a corrupting influence, or are you able to avoid any corrupting influence that power may have?

KH: I think that power has a tendency to corrupt people who may be weak in some ways. I have noticed that the greatest people I have met in my life have been those who have enjoyed great humility. And it is really the weak and the insecure that have let power appear as a shield behind which they hide.

Stern: For people within and without the country you are Jordan. When you go, do you think the monarchy will go with you?

KH: I hope Jordan will survive, sir, that is the important thing.

Stern: Yes indeed. Looking back on your period of office, what's your proudest achievement?

KH: There isn't one single one that I can point to. But being a Jordanian, being a part of this country, being a part of the struggle of the people I have loved, and the people I have been proud to belong to.

Stern: You have also said that some mistakes have been made. What do you think was the greatest mistake that Jordan's made recently?

KH: I think that if there are mistakes, they were not the result of any conscious desire of any of us to make them. But we are living in a dangerous and very difficult area, and if there are mistakes maybe their origin is more general than just Jordan itself. I am sure there are many, but others could probably see them much better than we do.

Stern: What do you think in the end the history books will say about you? What will they see as your role?

KH: I hope that the judgement will be for me and not against me. That's what I have striven all my life to try to achieve and, as a person who has tried his best, I hope they'll judge me kindly.

Leaders and Foreign Policy-making

Until recently, the distinction between domestic and foreign policy seemed to be clear cut. Food regulations, sales restrictions and penalties for civil offenses were matters of domestic concern: alliances, treaties, diplomatic negotiations and trade were the stuff of foreign policy. Today, however, in an age of international interdependence, of global environmental concerns and of multiple unofficial and informal economic and political ties across frontiers, some claim that the traditional differentiation between domestic and foreign issues can no longer be sustained.[1] After all, the decision of the Bundesbank to maintain comparatively high interest rates has profound international ramifications though presented as a domestic policy; 'ethnic cleansing' in Bosnia has even more profound international implications, in terms of migration and the plea for 'humanitarian intervention'; while a policy to close British pits gives a boost to the coal industry elsewhere. By the same token a policy directed at other states can affect a country's own economy – currency reserves, balance of trade or payments, interest rates, welfare provisions – its domestic stability or even the popularity of its government. At the same time, EC directives on such subjects as food hygiene, the conservation of fish stocks, Sunday trading, employment law and corporal punishment may be said to defy the conventional categorisation of external and domestic realms. On the other hand, those Americans who in 1992 chided President Bush with neglecting domestic as distinct from foreign concerns had an arguable point, and it is still possible to identify foreign policy as an activity of government both directed at and implemented largely in an environment external to the state in question.

But what kind of activity is foreign policy making? Does it resemble the creation and implementation of a grand design, as in architecture? Is it best understood in nautical terms, as the navigation of a course towards some given destination? Does it concern itself with diagnosis and prescription, as in medicine? Or is it more akin to some mechanical contrivance whereby a given stimulus produces an automatic respose? In fact the foreign policy process encompasses planning, analysing, steering and reacting to international circumstance – and more besides! But the degree to which political leaders involve themselves in it, at what level and in what capacity varies. Some adopt a 'hands on', others a 'hands off' attitude. Yet others are content with a collegiate approach in which they are at most *primus inter pares*. Sometimes the leader's influence on the formulation or execution of external policy has been so decisive that it is difficult to recall precisely who their foreign ministers were (unless they reserved that portfolio for themselves). Most readers of this volume would probably have little difficulty in recalling the names of the leaders who have dominated the politics of North Korea since the '40s, Cuba since the '60s, Syria and Iraq since the '70s, yet might be hard put to name the foreign ministers of those respective countries. But by the same token the names of some foreign ministers – among them Talleyrand, Metternich, Castlereagh or even John Foster Dulles – are so imprinted on history that it is sometimes difficult to recall which political masters they served.

What makes the relationship between leader and foreign minister all the more complex is that the balance of influence can shift over time. In 1957, for example, Khrushchev is reported to have said of the new Soviet Foreign Minister, Andrei Gromyko: 'He does exactly what we (meaning the Politburo) tell him. If he doesn't, we get a new foreign minister.' And in his memoirs, Henry Kissinger quotes Khrushchev's boast that 'if Gromyko were asked to sit on a block of ice with his pants down he would do so unquestioningly until ordered to leave it'.[2] However, three decades later when in quick succession Brezhnev, Andropov and Chernenko were all elevated to the 'Great Politburo in the Sky', Gromyko had by all accounts become the country's chief decision maker on foreign affairs, which is, presumably why at the start of his 'revolution without shots' Gorbachev moved rapidly to have the veteran Foreign Minister 'kicked upstairs' to the Presidency.

But, of course, people other than Presidents, Prime Ministers and Foreign Ministers can be key players in the foreign policy process. In West Germany, the late Defence Minister, Franz-Josef Strauss, played a crucial role in external affairs for well over a decade, and Professors Kissinger and Brzezinski virtually dominated American foreign policy when each served as National Security adviser. There may also be key players behind the scenes – wives, personal private secretaries and others with whom political leaders may share intimacies. There is more than anecdotal evidence to suggest that, for example, Eleanor Roosevelt, Rosalynne Carter, Nancy Reagan, Imelda Marcos and, of course, Eva Peron, had ideas and interests that percolated into the foreign policy process. Hillary Clinton has made no secret of the fact that she intends to play a key political role in her husband's administration. At times, moreover, academics, strategically placed civil servants and representatives of interest groups and lobbies may have a greater influence on the foreign policy agenda than those officially charged with the task. Early this century, the geopolitical theories of the then LSE Director Sir Halford MacKinder, concerning the critical importance of the European Heartland,[3] and the 'Memorandum on British policy' in which Foreign Office official Sir Eyre Crowe counselled a 'balancing' role for Britain among the nations,[4] probably helped to shape British policy for more than a generation, while till recently Zionist, cotton and oil lobbyists exercised on American external policies not to their liking the kind of veto power that religious leaders or service chiefs seem to have in many a developing country.[5]

It will be recalled that the leaders interviewed for this volume were generally of reflective disposition, and from their answers it is clear that several had fashioned a clear framework of policy priorities even before taking office. Dominating the agenda for Edward Heath, Helmut Schmidt, Lee Kuan Yew and Kenneth Kaunda, propelled into politics largely as a result of the traumas, respectively, of war, defeat, occupation and the colonial experience, was the need to ensure that the conditions producing such national adversity were never repeated. The other leaders acquired or strengthened their international orientation largely through the responsibilities of office. For Bulent Ecevit, Mieczyslaw Rakowski and King Hussein, induction into foreign affairs came in the form of a sudden crisis which demanded an immediate response. The Greek-instigated crypto-Fascist coup in Cyprus in 1974 seemed to necessitate some precautionary move from the Turkish government on behalf of the Turkish Cypriots once it became clear that Britain was not prepared to act. The mounting pressures on Warsaw by its neighbours as the rise of Solidarity in 1980 exacerbated the country's growing law and order problem, appeared to make decisive action imperative, while the precarious geographical position of Jordan in relation to both Israel and its Arab neighbours was constantly posing unpalatable foreign policy dilemmas for King Hussein.

In contrast, both Garret Fitzgerald and Malcolm Fraser had the good fortune to be in charge when changes in the international configurations of power presented new opportunities for foreign policy – in the case of Ireland in relation to the European Community: in the case of Australia in relation to Asia and the Pacific. And if for the remaining leaders domestic problems took priority, foreign policy had to be directed towards their alleviation. For General Obasanjo and Benazir Bhutto, the immediate task was to prevent other countries from exacerbating domestic regional tensions. In Sri Lanka, Junius Jaywardene sought the support of Indian troops to help deal with the communal violence in his own country. For Michael Manley, who saw Jamaica as the victim of a destabilisation campaign organised from abroad, the need at least in his first two administrations was to court radical nationalist states, including Cuba, as a counterweight to US pressure.

Given that each leader sought to make an impact on foreign policy how far were they equipped for the task and how significant was their contribution? It is instructive that of the thirteen leaders featured above, seven – Benazir Bhutto, Bulent Ecevit, Garret Fitzgerald, Malcolm Fraser, King Hussein, Junius Jayawardene and Michael Manley – came from political families and though that in itself is no guarantee of political sophistication, it is at least suggestive of some familiarity with the dilemmas of statecraft. Two others – Kenneth Kaunda and Lee Kuan Yew – were the architects of their countries' statehood and as they indicate in their memoirs needed to be especially mindful of their respective nations' international as well as domestic circumstance. Two more – Edward Heath and Helmut Schmidt – had already held foreign or defence portfolios prior to their further elevation, while a third, Olusegun Obasanjo, having been in charge of the Federal Government's military campaign during Nigeria's civil war, clearly had had to consider the international ramifications of his military strategy. And though Mieczyslaw Rakowski had never held a foreign or defence portfolio, as a journalist of repute he had had ample time to reflect on matters international and to suggest improvements to existing policy.

The extent, however, to which such leaders succeed in putting a personal stamp on foreign policy is less easy to assess than might appear. It is not just that even in the most 'democratic' of states foreign policy making has always tended to be far more secretive than domestic decision-making, and the relevant archives locked away for decades. It is also the fact that though it is frequently portrayed as a rational and purposeful activity in which identifiable individuals devise, amend or pursue a set of national objectives, assess possible options in the light of perceived constraints and opportunities and select those most likely to achieve priority goals at the least possible cost, the reality is often far more complex.

In the first place, in an increasingly interdependent world, in which the foreign affairs arena is broadening to encompass a host of political, economic, military, diplomatic, legal, scientific, technological, cultural and even sporting activities, decisions of consequence traceable to particular personalities probably account for a decreasing proportion of the total number of foreign policy outcomes. Nowadays in a rapidly changing international environment, foreign policy-making tends to involve so many different hands – informants, advisers, envoys, negotiators as well as official decision-makers – that it is sometimes difficult for even the participants to discover who precisely is responsible for what.

Moreover what appears to be a 'decision' may in fact lack that element of conscious choice and selectivity that the term normally conveys. It may be the resultant of habit, inertia, or of mindless routines and standard practices, as when a given aid programme is maintained regardless of significant changes in economic circumstance and bilateral relations. It may be the product of a fragmented process in which officials exercising their discretion according to their field of competence make a series of minor decisions the cumulative effect of which is to produce a momentum in favour of a particular course of action, but which no-one in particular has willed. For example, the unplanned and unwelcome chill in East-West relations in the wake of President Nixon's fall in 1973 appears to have been the product of a combination of actions, none particularly significant in itself, following the Watergate break-in by Nixon's aides. And even where policy-making is more concentrated, say in a Cabinet or Foreign Office, 'decisions' may be the product not of a careful consideration of alternatives, but of a bargaining process between key individuals that produces an outcome which, in the words of Herbert Simon, "satisfices" – that is, one to which no decision maker takes strong exception, even if it fails to give total satisfaction to anyone. Alternatively it may stem from a refusal to recognise that any choice exists.[6] "There is no alternative" has become an all too familiar refrain!

Nor do the verbal or written recollections of leading officials necessarily clarify the issue as to who makes the operative decisions since they will often exaggerate their own role in getting things done as well as take the credit for popular or successful policies instigated by others. (So readers beware!). And even where particular foreign policy outcomes can be readily attributable to particular individuals it cannot be assumed that either rationality or the 'the national interest' will necessarily have prevailed. All too frequently, rational desision-making is impaired by erroneous intelligence and further vitiated by misperception, prejudice, lack of understanding or empathy, wishful thinking and the kind of intellectual myopia that goes under the name of 'tunnel vision'. What psychologists term 'cognitive dissonance', in which any information conflicting with cherished beliefs, values or desires is rejected and the facts distorted to fit in with pre-existing notions, can add a further impediment to rational policy. Moreover, where leaders have a potent influence on external policy, their relevant acts and utterances can sometimes be animated or distracted by private, family, Party or other considerations or interests. The desire to be seen as 'doing something', to enhance their personal standing in the polls, to boost their Party's domestic fortunes or to appease a particular interest group may be the mainspring for a foreign policy pronouncement, overseas trip or adventure. Doubtless we can all think of recent examples of leaders whose penchant for overseas summits appears to have grown in proportion to their domestic unpopularity.

Leaving aside what leaders are apt to claim for themselves, in point of fact their room for manoeuvre tends to be more limited in external than in domestic policy. Often they are circumscribed by a host of geopolitical, technological, military, economic and psychosocial factors, to say nothing of the legal, political and what are perceived to be moral obligations by which states are generally deemed to be bound. As the late Professor F.S. Northedge put it: 'Effective freedom in foreign affairs...is the capacity to choose between relatively few options'[7]. In consequence, leaders are apt, perhaps after an initial attempt at setting the foreign political agenda, to become pragmatic operators rather than grand strategists. If they have a foreign political role, it is frequently confined largely to adjusting commitments to capabilities and aspirations to practicalities. Here, short term expedients in order to buy time, to sow confusion amongst enemies and reassure friends or simply to avoid having to take a decision at all may have to be substituted for principle – all essentially behind-the-scenes exercises and often masked by an official rhetoric designed to suggest purposeful activity, progress and continuity.

On the other hand, that there are still leaders able to devise and implement plans for creating new nations, uniting ethnic or religious kinsfolk across frontiers, spreading a particular gospel or establishing novel international institutions cannot be denied. After all, the roll call of great statesmen and world politicians did not end with Cavour, Bismarck, Ataturk, Masaryk, Woodrow Wilson and Lenin. In a world, moreover, in which the forces of international integration are constantly vying with the factors of national disintegration, opportunities for high profile political activity are not lacking, even if they are not necessarily taken advantage of. And, of course, in crisis situations when there are heightened threat perceptions and serious time constraints, leaders are often well placed to, as it were, 'make history'. Sadly, it is often at such times that they are at their least rational, and are either paralysed or, alternatively, driven into misplaced hyperactivity by either a dearth or a surfeit of relevant information.

Yet, notwithstanding the continuing ability of leaders to 'grab the headlines', there does seem to have been a perceptible shift away from the kind of high profile leadership much in evidence from the mid-nineteenth to the mid-twentieth century, perhaps due not just to the complexities of modern statecraft but also to the fact that a post-colonial, post-Communist era leaves comparatively little scope for political messiahs and charismatic rulers. Moreover, as time seems to have dented the reputations of many of the 'giants' of recent times, and from J.F.K. to Gorbachev and from Gandhi to Mao, of whom so much was expected, the idols crumble under scrutiny, there is not the same incentive as before for political heroics. Perhaps those bearing responsibility for our well-being would serve their own and the general interest best if they kept popular expectations within reasonable bounds so that if they managed at least to 'keep the ship [of state] on an even keel', as

Helmut Schmidt claimed to have done in the case of his country, they will have achieved something to their credit. In the final analysis, however, perhaps the most that the kinds of leaders interviewed and profiled in this volume can hope for is that they may have earned at least that 'footnote in history', that Lee Kuan Yew feared might be denied his country, and that each will be remembered, in the words of King Hussein, 'as a person who has tried his best', often in very difficult circumstances.

NOTES

1. See, for example, John Burton *World Society*, Cambridge: 1972, especially chapter 4.

2. Henry Kissinger *The White House Years*, New York: 1979, p.788.

3. See his *The Geographical Pivot of History*, London: 1904.

4. The 'Memorandum' will be found in G P Gooch and H Temperley (ed) *British Documents on the Origins of the War, 1898-1914*, London: 1926.

5. See, for example, M P Petracca *The Politics of Interests: Interest Groups Transformed*, New York: 1992 and also R A Bauer, I de Sola Poole and L A Dexter *American Business and Public Policy*, New York: 1972.

6. See, for example, Michael Clarke 'The Foreign Policy System' in M Clarke and B White (eds) *Foreign Policy Analysis*, Ormskirk: 1981.

7. F S Northedge (ed) *The Foreign Policies of the Powers*, London: 1974, p.16.

PROFILES

BENAZIR BHUTTO

Benazir Bhutto was born in 1953 into a Sindhi landowning family. She is the daughter of former Pakistan Peoples Party (PPP) leader and Prime Minister, Zulfiquar Ali Bhutto, who was overthrown in a military coup in 1977 by Army Chief-of Staff, General Zia-Ul Haq, and hanged in 1979. She was educated first in Karachi, and went on to complete her education at Harvard and Oxford, where she was elected President of the Union. She returned to Pakistan to act as assistant to her father on foreign policy issues, and was with him in 1972 when the Simla Agreement on maintaining the status quo over Kashmir was signed between India and Pakistan.

Somewhat in awe of her charismatic father, Benazir Bhutto did not begin to think in terms of a political career until well after and in part because of his death. Then, jointly with her mother, the Begum Nusrat Bhutto, she became the leader of the PPP, but persistent harassment from the Zia government, including long periods of house arrest, limited her effectiveness. In 1985 she left for London to join her mother who had already taken up residence, and continued to organise the PPP from there. In 1986 she returned to Pakistan and assumed a prominent role in the Movement for the Resumption of Democracy, boosted by a wave of popular support throughout the country. When Zia bowed to popular pressure and announced an election in May 1988, Benazir Bhutto was able to successfully challenge in the Supreme Court his 1985

Voters Registration Act, under which the PPP was threatened with a ban prohibiting its participation in the election. Although her support had waned since 1986, a reorganisation of the PPP confirmed her in her position as its leader, and the party went on to win 92 out of 207 seats in the legislature, making it the largest single party.

After negotiating a coalition government, Benazir Bhutto was sworn in as Prime Minister in December 1988. Thereafter, she attempted to reform the economy, to widen educational opportunities, to improve the nation's health, raise the status of women and also, where possible, to defuse tension with India. However, the hostility of the Army and increasingly of the President, regional problems, divisions within the PPP, together with mounting accusations of corruption, particularly against Asif Ali Zardari, whom she married in 1987, undermined the government's authority, and it was dismissed by President Ghulam Ishaq Khan in August 1990. In the elections of October 1990 the PPP lost power, after which Benazir Bhutto and her husband were put on trial for alleged corruption and abuse of power, her husband being held in custody on some of the charges. Whether or not the victim of a malign conspiracy, as she claims, her fall may well have been attributable in part to her position as a woman in a society strongly under the sway of conservative Mullahs. Though she now agrees to a permanent role for the Army in areas such as foreign affairs, defence and internal security she still sees herself as a moderate force in Pakistani politics. The current (1992) infighting within Premier Nawaz Sharif's crisis-prone ruling coalition, as well as recent defections and expulsions from the ranks of the government, have buoyed the PPP and led Benazir Bhutto to conclude that her period of political isolation and what she sees as official harassment may soon be coming to an end.

BULENT ECEVIT

Bulent Ecevit was born in Istanbul in 1925, the son of a professor of medicine and member of parliament and of a noted painter. He was educated at the American-sponsored Robert College, Istanbul, and then at the universities of Ankara, London and Harvard, studying a variety of subjects, from English literature to linguistics and from art history to Sanskrit. After completing his education, he worked in the government press and publications department and served in the Press Attache's Office of the Turkish Embassy in London 1946-50. On his return to Turkey he worked as a journalist on the Ankara-based 'Ulus' newspaper until 1961, where he was at various times foreign news editor, political news editor and managing editor. He also contributed a regular political column for the newspaper between 1956 and 1961.

Ecevit's career as a politician began in 1957, when, as a protege of the elder statesman, Ismet Inönü, he won a seat in parliament for the centre-left Republican People's Party (RPP). After the dissolution of parliament in the military coup of 1960 his next office was as a member of the Constituent Assembly of 1961, and when Parliament reconvened later that year he again became an MP, and remained in Parliament for the next 19 years. Ecevit won rapid promotion in his party, and in 1961 was appointed Minister of Labour in the coalition government headed by Inönü, which lasted until 1965. Under his ministry a liberalising reform of the country's trade union laws took place. When the conservative Demirel government came to power in the elections of 1965, Ecevit returned to journalism, becoming political columnist of the *'Milliyet'* newspaper. At the same time he continued to be active within his party and was appointed its Secretary General in 1966, and Chairman in 1972, but as leader of a leftist faction within the RPP he was coming increasingly into conflict with Inönü. When the general election of October 1973 failed to produce a clear winner, Ecevit successfully and surprisingly negotiated a coalition between the RPP and the Islamic traditionalist National Salvation Party, and in January 1974 became Prime Minister.

In July 1974 Ecevit took the most controversial decision of his political life when he ordered the Turkish army into Cyprus in the wake of the coup on the island, which threatened to lead to a union ('Enosis') between Cyprus and Greece. Though Turkish troops are still entrenched on the island, Ecevit maintains that their presence in Northern Cyprus has helped to avert a communal bloodbath. Back in September 1974, the RPP's all too evident differences with its Right wing coalition partners led Ecevit to resign. He returned to power briefly in June and July of 1977 as leader of a minority government, and then again in January 1978 as head of a new coalition. However, escalating political violence, together with mounting economic problems, undermined support for the coalition, and in October 1979 Ecevit was again obliged to resign, having lost a working majority in parliament. In the military coup of September 1980 Ecevit was briefly detained, and was later imprisoned again by the military regime from December 1981 to February 1982.

Since that time Ecevit has maintained a presence largely on the fringes of Turkish political life. In January 1989 he was elected Chairman of the Democratic Left Party, and has recently been very critical of Western policy, especially in relation to Iraq. Meanwhile he continues his trenchant columns for *'Milliyet'* and is constantly expanding his written output, which includes translations and books on subjects as diverse as politics and poetry.

GARRET FITZGERALD

Garret FitzGerald was born in Dublin in 1926 into a prominent political family which straddled the Irish divide - his mother being a Protestant from the North, his father a Southern Irish Catholic. Educated in Bray, Waterford and at Belvedere College, Dublin, he went on to University College, Dublin, and took a first-class honours degree in History, French and Spanish, and after completing a law course he was called to the Bar in 1947. Yet despite an impressive academic background, he chose to work as a research and schedules manager for Aer Lingus until 1958. Then, after a short spell as Research Assistant at Trinity College Dublin, he became a Lecturer in Political Economy at University College Dublin where he continued to teach until 1973. He also carried on a successful career as a journalist on economic affairs throughout this period, writing for a wide range of domestic and foreign publications.

FitzGerald's political career did not begin until 1969, when he won a Dublin constituency for the Fine Gael party. He rose quickly through the party ranks, and in 1973 was appointed Minister for Foreign Affairs under the leadership of Liam Cosgrave. The Cosgrave government lasted from 1973-1977 and was marked by intense efforts on both sides of the Irish Sea to find a solution to the problem of Ulster. In 1975 when Fitzgerald became EC president he used his position to try to bring the two halves of Ireland closer together through promoting greater cross-border economic cooperation. In fact the search for a solution to the Ulster question was to dominate his political career. For him, a United Ireland could only materialise if the South became more secular and less dominated by the Catholic Church. Only in this way could Protestant fears of the consequences of unification be removed. It was a view which earned him the respect of many in Northern Ireland – Republicans and Unionists alike – but it brought him into conflict with conservative opinion in the South. Outside of Ireland, FitzGerald played an important role in EC politics, particularly over negotiations for the Lomé Convention of 1974, which established a series of preferential tariffs and other assistance measures between the EC and 49 states from the developing world. During this period, FitzGerald also succeeded in maintaining friendly ties both with Israel and the Arab states, and at the same time was one of the most consistent campaigners against South African apartheid.

Following Fine Gael's defeat at the 1977 election, Fitzgerald was appointed Party leader. While in opposition he oversaw the drawing up of the Fine Gael scheme for an Irish confederation, which was published in 1979. The election of June 1981 brought Fine Gael back to power, and FitzGerald took up office as Taoiseach declaring that he would lead a 'crusade' to make the Irish Constitution more acceptable to the Protestants. In November 1981, after a meeting with the British Prime Minister,

Margaret Thatcher, he announced his intention of setting up an Intergovernmental Council, but the scheme foundered as his government was brought down by a budgetary crisis in January 1982. An inconclusive election in February left Fine Gael out of power until a second poll in November 1982 returned a Fine Gael - Labour coalition. Following FitzGerald's meeting with Margaret Thatcher at an EC summit in March 1983, he announced the setting up of a Forum for a New Ireland, and prolonged negotiations with Westminster resulted in the Anglo-Irish Agreement of 1985, which for the first time gave the South a say in the affairs of the North.

Fine Gael's failure to deal with the country's economic problems and the antipathy of conservative Catholics to government policy over divorce and contraception led to political defeat in the 1987 election. FitzGerald immediately resigned as Party leader, since when he has returned to writing and journalism, and is much sought after as a speaker on national, European and world affairs.

MALCOLM FRASER

Malcolm Fraser was born in 1930 into a family of wealthy graziers with a long tradition of involvement in Australian politics. He spent most of his childhood on his family's 8,000 acre farm in Victoria, and later attended Melbourne Grammar School. In 1948 he followed the example of his father in going to Oxford to complete his education, gaining an honours degree in politics, philosophy and economics. In 1952 he returned to Australia and for the next three years worked on the family farm, until winning a seat in Parliament for the Liberal Party in the general election of 1955, making him the youngest MP in the House.

Fraser spent the first eleven years of his political life as a backbencher, only coming to prominence with the resignation of Prime Minister, Robert Menzies, on whom he is believed to have modelled his later paternalistic style of leadership. Menzies' successor, Harold Holt, appointed Fraser Minister for the Army, and after Holt's death in December 1967, Fraser was promoted to Minister for Education and Science, which gave him a seat in the Cabinet of the new Prime Minister John Gorton. The first of a series of well publicised political rows followed. Accusing Gorton in 1971 of failing to support him over a newspaper article alleging disloyalty, Fraser resigned his recently awarded Defence portfolio, thereby precipitating the fall of Gorton. Rescued from the backbenches by Gorton's successor, William McMahon, Fraser served again as Education Minister until 1972, when the Liberals were defeated by the Labour Party.

Between 1972 and 1975 Fraser gradually strengthened his position in the Liberal Party, and in March 1975 was able to mount a successful challenge for the party leadership against the then incumbent 'Billy' Snedden. The following months were the most controversial of Fraser's career, as he used the Liberal majority in the Senate to block the radical legislation of the Labour government and challenged its leader, Gough Whitlam, to go to the polls. When Whitlam refused, the Governor General Sir John Kerr dismissed the Labour Premier and appointed Fraser head of an interim government which then won a victory in the general election of December 1975. Arguments over the constitutionality of Whitlam's dismissal still continue.

Fraser's period of office lasted until 1983, and was characterised by greater pragmatism, a *laissez-faire* approach to the business of government, which reversed much of the legislation brought in by Whitlam, and a strongly anti-Communist, pro-Commonwealth and increasingly regionally based foreign policy. The government's loss of power in 1983 was blamed largely on its failure to stem inflation and rising unemployment.

After losing office, Fraser continued to increase his stature on the international stage by becoming one of the most effective voices within the Commonwealth for the movement against South African apartheid. His frequent calls for economic sanctions against Pretoria brought him into conflict with Margaret Thatcher, a figure with whom he otherwise shared considerable ideological affinity, and as a member of the Eminent Persons Group on Southern African affairs, he had a perceptible influence on international opinion. As a business consultant he continues to travel widely, and as elder statesman his political expertise is still much in demand.

EDWARD HEATH

Edward Heath was born in Broadstairs, Kent, in 1916, and educated at Chatham School in Ramsgate. Awarded a music scholarship for Balliol College, Oxford, he chose instead to read Politics and became an active supporter of the Conservative Party and President of the Oxford Union. His first involvement in national politics came with the 1938 Oxford City by-election, when he campaigned against the official Conservative candidate, Quintin Hogg, in opposition to the then government's policy of appeasement towards Nazi Germany. After wartime service, Heath worked as a civil servant before winning the seat of Bexley for the Conservatives in the 1950 general election. He continued to hold Bexley until the seat was abolished in the 1974 redrawing of constituency boundaries, since when he has been the Member for Sidcup.

After eight months in parliament, Heath was given a position in the Whip's office and promoted to Chief Whip in 1955. It was a post that required great skill, especially in the years following the Suez debacle of 1956, but with the emergence of Harold Macmillan as Prime Minister in 1959, Heath was appointed Minister of Labour. After only a year he was transferred to the office of Lord Privy Seal and given the task of negotiating Britain's entry into the European Community. His enthusiasm for European unity had been evident even before his entry into the House of Commons and it formed the subject of his maiden speech. In this sense, de Gaulle's rejection of the British application in January 1963 came as a bitter blow. On the other hand, appointed to the Board of Trade, Heath scored a notable victory with the success of his controversial bill on resale price maintenance. The Conservative defeat in the 1964 election precipitated a leadership contest in which Heath, representing, as it were, a new breed of 'classless' technocrat, was to triumph. Following another Conservative defeat in 1966, Heath revamped Party policy so as to present a clearer alternative to the policies of Harold Wilson's Labour Party. The Conservatives were beginning to return to the idea of the free market.

His reshaping of the Party in the late 1960's is widely credited as a major contributor to the Conservative victory in the 1970 election. But his years in office were marred by mounting economic difficulties. Faced with the possibility of recession and of widespread factory closures, he turned away from the free market approach and in the 1972 Industry Act gave the state wide powers to intervene and rescue ailing firms. However, the decision of the OPEC oil producers to quadruple prices in 1973 and the opposition of the National Union of Mineworkers to the government's incomes policy only compounded the country's economic problems. When the miner's strike of 1973 led to a three day working week, Heath called a general election in an attempt to win public backing for his opposition to the miners. The ensuing election produced a minority Labour government and a majority Labour administration in October 1974, by which time Heath's tenure of the Conservative leadership was coming to an end. The lasting achievement of his period at Downing Street had been to secure Britain's membership of the European Community in January 1973.

Since relinquishing the Party leadership, Heath has remained in parliament as a backbencher. He was a consistent critic of his successor, Margaret Thatcher, for her over-reliance on market mechanisms and negative attitudes towards the European Community. On the other hand he finds John Major's approach more congenial and in 1992 was knighted for his services to the country.

JUNIUS JAYAWARDENE

Junius Jayawardene was born in Colombo in 1906 into a large, wealthy, middle class family of lawyers and politicians. Educated at the Royal College in Colombo, at Ceylon's University College and finally at the Ceylon Law College, from which he graduated in 1932, he became a barrister at the Supreme Court of Ceylon. Shortly after, he also began his career in organised politics, joining the Ceylon National Congress Party (CNC).

From 1940 until 1947 Jayawardene was honorary general secretary of the CNC, and from 1940 to 1943 was active in local politics as a member of the Ceylon Municipal Council. But on winning a by-election for the constituency of Kelaniya, which gave him a place in the State Council – the supreme legislative body in Ceylon at the time – he gave up the municipal seat.

In February 1948, just prior to Ceylon's independence, he followed the leader of the CNC, D.S.Senanayake, into a merger with several smaller parties, resulting in the formation of the politically centrist United National Party (UNP). Meanwhile the State Council was transformed into the House of Representatives, where Jayawardene continued to act as the member for Kelaniya, and after the UNP election victory of February 1948 became minister of finance.

In the post-war period Jayawardene also began to make a name for himself internationally. He acted as Ceylon's representative at the Commonwealth Prime Ministers' Conferences in London every year between 1948 and 1952 and played a similar role at the Commonwealth Finance Ministers' Conferences. From 1947 until 1952 he was a governor of the World Bank, and in 1950 he helped put together the Colombo Plan, under which financial and other assistance was to be provided to the developing countries of Asia. At the 1951 Japanese Peace Treaty Conference in San Francisco, his anti-Soviet stance brought approval from the US and its allies.

In 1953 Jayawardene moved from the finance ministry to become Minister of Food and Agriculture in the cabinet of the new prime minister Dudley Senanayake (son of D.S.Senanayake). In 1956 the UNP was defeated at the polls and Jayawardene moved to the opposition benches, where, except for a brief period in office in the UNP government of March to July 1960, he was to remain until 1965. The UNP victory in the 1965 general election returned him to the cabinet as both minister of state and parliamentary secretary to the prime minister. Two years later he was elected Vice President of the developing countries' Group of 77.

In 1970 the UNP again lost power, and when in 1973 Dudley Senanayake died, Jayawardene was elected party leader. During the period of Mrs Bandaranaike's government, Ceylon (renamed Sri Lanka in 1972) was wracked with increasing political and ethnic violence, and this, together with the reports of mounting corruption and nepotism, helped to restore the UNP to power after the 1977 election. In 1978 he used the UNP's overwhelming parliamentary majority to amend the constitution, creating a presidency modelled on the French system, and in February 1978 he was duly elected President. An ambitious programme of reforms to stimulate private enterprise and cut back the civil service followed, and their apparent success led in October 1982 to Jayawardene's re-election as president for a six-year term.

In the 1980s Sri Lanka continued to achieve economic growth under Jayawardene, but this was increasingly offset by growing ethnic violence between the island's Sinhalese majority and the Tamil minority. His vigorous response to the terrorism from both sides led to criticism from human rights bodies, including Amnesty International. Yet despite the two year intervention of Indian troops initiated by the Indo-Sri Lanka agreement of July 1987 and Jayawardene's retirement from active politics in January 1989, at the age of 83, the conflict between Sri Lanka's two ethnic groups remains unresolved.

KENNETH KAUNDA

Kenneth Kaunda was born in 1924, at a Church of Scotland mission near Chinsali in what was then known as Northern Rhodesia. His father, a member of the Nyasa tribe, was an ordained priest who, like his mother, worked on the mission as a teacher. After graduating from a local secondary school, Kaunda wanted to become a doctor, but lack of money forced him instead to train as a teacher. Whilst training in Lusaka, he witnessed the violent dispersal of a crowd of black women protesting against meat prices, and this incident is said to have contributed to his vegetarianism as well as his anti-racist attitudes.

After qualifying in 1943 Kaunda returned to the mission, where he worked as a teacher, and then moved to a school in Tanganyika. Later he worked in the Welfare Office in Salisbury, the Rhodesian capital, which brought him in touch with the daily problems of urban Africans. In 1949 he returned to Northern Rhodesia to become an official interpreter, and at this time began his career in organised politics by joining the African National Congress (ANC). His decision to found a new branch of the ANC in Chinsali hastened his rise to prominence, which was further enhanced in 1952 by his appointment as Organising Secretary of the ANC for the Northern

Province. When shortly afterwards he was appointed Secretary General of the organisation this made him the second most powerful black politician in the country after the ANC's President, Harry Nkumbula.

Kaunda worked alongside Nkumbula for the next 6 years, amongst other things, organising the (unsuccessful) opposition to the British plan for a federation of Rhodesia and Nyasaland. During this period he was imprisoned for two months, then travelled abroad to Britain and India, and almost died of tuberculosis. Nkumbula's failure to react effectively to the British rejection of the proposed amendments to the constitution in 1958 led to Kaunda's becoming leader of a breakaway movement. When this movement advocated a boycott of the next elections, Kaunda was sent into internal exile and then imprisoned again. Released in January 1960, Kaunda soon became President of the United National Independence Party (UNIP), which began to press for the independence of Northern Rhodesia under the name of Zambia. He went on to participate in the talks in London which resulted in the elections of 1962 in which the ANC and UNIP between them won 21 out of the 37 seats in the Northern Rhodesian parliament. The result strengthened their hand, and the British gave a sympathetic response to their demand for withdrawal from the federation, the adoption of a new constitution and free elections in the National Assembly. In 1963 the British granted the right of secession and in January 1964, after an election giving UNIP 55 out of 75 seats in the Assembly, Kaunda formed the country's first indigenous government and proclaimed full independence in October.

Kaunda ruled Zambia until October 1991 according to the principles of what he describes as 'Christian humanism'. Though his country was a base for anti-apartheid guerillas, he also attempted a dialogue with the leaders of the white minority regimes of Southern Africa, and while his efforts to bring about economic and social development within the country had positive results, notably in the field of education and health, the country suffered from the volatility of copper prices and from the violent political and racial conflicts in the region he had sought unsuccessfully to mediate. Many also hold Kaunda's policies of central control and state intervention responsible for some of the country's economic woes. Declaring Zambia a one-Party state in 1972, Kaunda had gradually strengthened his hand, but after failing to stem either economic decline or mounting corruption in the '80's, he gave into pressure for a return to multi-Party politics. As a result of Zambia's first contested election in 19 years, he became the first 'Father of the Nation' in Africa to peacefully hand over power. In the end he had served his country well by accepting the will of the electorate and by proving once again that he preferred dialogue to confrontation.

KING HUSSEIN

King Hussein was born Hussein Ibn Talal in Amman in 1935. He was educated in Amman at an Islamic School and then received a British style education both in Amman and Alexandria. The assassination of his grandfather and mentor, King Abdullah, and the attempt on his own life at the Al Aqsa Mosque in July 1951 precipitated his removal to Harrow School for a year. But with his father's abdication due to illness, Hussein was proclaimed monarch in August 1952 at the age of seventeen. Unable, however, to exercise regal responsibilities until reaching the age of maturity, he spent the final year of his education at the military academy at Sandhurst.

The international tension which marked the first years of Hussein's rule had profound repercussions on his small kingdom. Hussein's Hashemite family had been associated with the Arab nationalist movement since his grandfather led the Arab revolt against the Ottomans in World War One, but by the early '50's, Egypt's President Nasser had come to represent the new face of Arab nationalism. Hussein with his British officered army and close links with the West was a natural target for left-wing nationalists, as was his cousin, King Faisal of Iraq. In order to appease the radicals, Hussein in 1956 dismissed General Glubb, the British commander of the Jordanian army, and went on to remove the other British officers in the wake of the Anglo-French 'Suez' invasion, replacing them with Jordanians. In March 1957 a group of the newly promoted officers led a revolt against him but he was able to survive by making a successful appeal to the troops over the heads of their mutinous officers. The decisive confrontation with the supporters of Nasser's brand of Arab nationalism came one year later, after the same forces had deposed King Faisal. Again it was loyalty from the army rank and file which saved him at home, while British and American support helped to ensure that the much feared invasion by neighbouring states did not materialise. The early years of Hussein's reign cast the die for what was to follow, as Hussein was forced to play for advantage between the forces of Arab nationalism on the one hand and those of the West and of the more conservative oil rich Arab states on the other.

Hussein's second major crisis came with the Arab-Israeli war of 1967. Jordan's participation in the hostilities was a foregone conclusion, given that nearly a half of its population were Palestinian refugees, whilst anti-Israeli sentiments were running high amongst the rest. But for Jordan the war was a military disaster. It lost the West Bank, East Jerusalem, many of its troops and all its air-force. Politically, however, the war strengthened Hussein's hand at home and helped him to deal with the threat posed by the increasingly powerful groups of Palestinian guerilas based in Jordan. In 1970 in an operation which came to be known as 'Black September', he ordered his troops against them and emerged victorious after several months of virtual civil war.

The years which followed were relatively peaceful and saw the achievement of steady economic growth,together with improvements in areas such as education and health. Much of the credit for Amman's achievements in these areas belongs to Hussein who, together with his brother, the Crown Prince Hassan, has taken a close personal involvement in Jordan's transformation.

As King of a small, vulnerable state in a geopolitically sensitive area, Hussein has not hesitated to go against the interests of Western or of regional powers as he felt the occasion demanded. His refusal to be a co-signatory of the Camp David accords put him at loggerheads with both Washington and Cairo, but succeeded in placing Amman firmly back in the Arab fold. More recently he attracted widespread condemnation for what was seen as his ambiguous stance in the crisis following the Iraq's invasion of Kuwait, though few could deny the seriousness of the economic and political dilemmas the conflict posed to Jordanian policy.

Among most observers, Hussein has won himself the reputation of being a moderate whose ability to move easily between apparently conflicting forces derives primarily from a wish to avert the triumph of extremism.

LEE KUAN YEW

Lee Kuan Yew was born in 1923 into a family of middle-class Chinese Singaporeans who had been resident in the British colony for three generations. He won a scholarship to Raffles College where he was regarded as an exceptionally gifted pupil, but under the Japanese occupation he was obliged to curtail his education and work for the authorities. It was during the occupation that he became politically aware, resolving to play his part in extricating Asia from colonial rule. In 1946 he went to Cambridge to study law, and graduated with a double first degree. Whilst at University he had become involved in socialist politics and had met Kwa Geok Choo, another Chinese Singaporean, who was to become his wife after successfully completing her studies.

After being called to the Bar, Lee returned to Singapore in 1951 where, together with his wife, he soon established a flourishing law practice. He became legal adviser to a number of trade unions and well known in left wing circles. He was a founder member of the Peoples' Action Party (PAP) in 1954, and as its General Secretary represented the PAP in the Legislative Assembly from 1955 onwards. In the period up to and following Lee's election as the first Prime Minister of the newly independent Republic of Singapore in 1959, he was involved in a series of power struggles with the Communists and eventually suppressed their political activities altogether.

In 1963, Lee led Singapore into a federation with Malaysia, but a range of political and ethnic difficulties arising from the problem of power-sharing between the Chinese and Malay communities led to his country's exclusion from the federation in 1965. In the following years Lee won widespread acclaim for his role in creating a dynamic and prosperous new city-state, but also some criticism for his paternalism, ruthless pursuit of efficiency and intolerance of opposition, often using legal niceties to silence his critics. His critics claim that under him the country was overgoverned. Lee's reply was that the alternative was disorder bordering on chaos and, possibly, Communism.

Lee won eight general elections, the last one in 1988, and developed a virtually unassailable hold on power. In the 1988 poll the PAP attained seventy percent of the popular vote and won 64 of the 65 seats in parliament. For many years Singapore continued to achieve one of the highest economic growth rates in the world and has generally been successful in overcoming setbacks, such as the slump of 1985-6.Lee has long played a prominent, if at times controversial role on the international stage. When he hosted the 1971 Commonwealth Leaders Meeting in Singapore he declared that the Commonwealth could not continue in the face of differences over the question of arms sales to South Africa. He consistently used his country's membership of the Association of South East Asian Nations (ASEAN) as a platform for his strongly anti-Communist views, and any criticism in the West over the number of political detainees in Singapore would be vehemently and indignantly rejected.

In November 1990, after thirty years as Prime Minister – making him the world's longest serving elected leader – he handed over power to a personally designated successor, Goh Chok Tong. Nonetheless many observers continue to see him as the dominant figure, wielding effective power behind the scenes having groomed his son, Brigadier Lee Hsien Loong, who entered politics in 1984, as an eventual successor.

MICHAEL MANLEY

Michael Manley was born in Kingston, Jamaica, in 1924 of a middle class family. His father, Norman, was a politician and later prime minister, his mother, Edna, an artist, and in the mid-1930s he attended the island's prestigious Jamaica College. After graduation in 1943 he joined the Royal Canadian Airforce and served as a wireless operator and gunner. After the war he went to the London School of Economics, and on completing his studies worked in London as a freelance journalist and broadcaster. In 1952 he returned to Jamaica to become a trade union organiser for the National

Workers Union, which was affiliated to the People's National Party (PNP), led by his father. He was to remain a trade union activist for the next twenty years.

On Jamaica's independence from Britain in 1962 Manley's father appointed him senator in the upper house of the island's bicameral parliament. In 1967 he won by a slender margin the Central Kingston seat in the House of Representatives, and two years later he became leader of the PNP, following his father's resignation from the post. In 1972 the PNP ended ten years on the opposition benches and Manley became Prime Minister. He embarked on a series of radical reforms at home, and abroad shifted Jamaica away from the US and closer to the non-aligned countries, in particular Cuba. His left-wing policies caused a serious rift with Washington, which embarked on a policy of destabilisation of Jamaica, contributing to mounting political violence in the country and a serious shortage of investment funds. Despite increasing divisions in Jamaican society, Manley succeeded in retaining the support of the poor, black majority, and this was instrumental in winning him another victory in the elections of 1976.

As one of the most outspoken leaders of the Non-Aligned Movement in the 1970s, Manley argued for more equitable trade relations between the Third World and the developed countries, and lent his vigorous support to the movement for the decolonisation of Africa. His contribution to the anti-apartheid movement won him a United Nations gold medal.

Meanwhile as Jamaica's economic and political situation deteriorated in the period up to 1980, the International Monetary Fund demanded tighter economic policies in return for loans, but Manley's difficulties in coming to terms with those demands contributed to a decline in his Party's support even from the poorer sections of the community. The election of 1980 gave a substantial victory to Edward Seaga's Jamaican Labour Party, and marked the beginning of what was to become a nine-year period of opposition for Manley and the PNP.

Manley's opposition to the Seaga government was conducted from within the House of Representatives, but in 1983 the PNP boycotted the elections, allowing Seaga to win every seat in the House. Meanwhile the failure of Seaga's policies to solve the country's economic difficulties brought about a gradual return of popular support for the PNP, as registered in a convincing series of victories in the local elections of 1986. The general election of 1989 confirmed the resurgence of PNP support, giving the party a comfortable majority in the House of Representatives.

In his post-1989 government Manley eschewed much of the ideology that went with his former periods of office, and adopted a more pragmatic, centrist approach to politics. This involved a pro-business stand and close links with the US. In March 1992, however, ill-health compelled him to resign the premiership and to bow out of politics, thus ending a political dynasty that covered more than fifty years.

OLUSEGUN OBASANJO

Olusegun Obasanjo was born in 1935 at Ota in Nigeria's Ogun state and educated at local Baptist schools. Though he originated from a farming community in the heart of Yorubaland, he distrusts tribalism and has always regarded himself as a Nigerian first and foremost. He began his military career in 1959, when, after training as an officer cadet in Britain, he was commissioned into the Nigerian Army, and in 1960 he was seconded to the United Nations peace-keeping force in the Congo (now Zaire). Returning to Britain for further training – this time as a military engineer – he won rapid promotion in the Engineering Corps, and was appointed its Commander in 1963. During the Nigerian Civil War he acted as General Officer commanding the Third Marine Commando Division, and in January 1970 as head of the Division he accepted the surrender of Biafran forces, and was a strong advocate of national reconciliation. For the next five years he returned to his post as Commander of the Engineering Corps, but after a course at Britain's Royal College of Defence Studies he received in January 1975 his first political appointment – Federal Commissioner for Works and Housing. Later that year he became Chief of Staff, Supreme Headquarters, and in effect de facto Prime Minister in the government of General Murtala Mohammed. Following the latter's assassination in the abortive coup of February 1976, Obasanjo became head of the Federal Military Government and Commander-in-chief of the armed forces.

Obasanjo had come to power with the promise of returning Nigeria to civilian rule. The first stage of the process began with popular elections for a newly instituted system of local government (Nigeria's first elections for 11 years), in December 1976. In August 1977 a Constituent Assembly was elected to approve a newly written draft American-style constitution in which the country was to be divided into 19 federal sub-states. Obasanjo oversaw the gradual wind-down of military rule in the provinces, and in September 1978 he lifted the ban on political parties. In October 1979 he handed over power to Shehu Shagari, the man who had emerged as victor in the elections earlier that year. His period of office is best remembered for its serious attempt to come to grips with Nigeria's intractable political, economic and social problems. In the cultural sphere Obasanjo is remembered for his role in promoting the Second World Festival of Black and African Arts and Culture (FESTAC) – the largest event of its kind ever to take place – which he opened in January 1977.

After surrendering political office Obasanjo also left the army, and returned to Ogun state to become a chicken farmer. Since then he has also led an active life on the international political stage as a member of numerous organisations. In 1985 and 1986 he was a member of the Commonwealth Eminent Persons Group on South Africa, charged with persuading the white minority government to share power, and in 1988 he hosted a meeting of 50 experts and former heads of government on his farm, which led to the formation of the Africa Leadership Forum, a body which aims to provide training in statesmanship to promising young Africans.

Sadly, following General Obasanjo's withdrawal from active politics Nigeria's experiment with civilian administration was short-lived. He claims, however, that he built a 'bridge' to civilian rule, and hopes to see that 'bridge' rebuilt before the end of 1993.

MIECZYSLAW RAKOWSKI

Mieczyslaw Rakowski was born into a peasant family near Poznan, in Western Poland in 1926. He grew up in his native village, but after the German invasion, which touched off World War II and led to his father's execution by a Nazi firing squad, he went to Poznan and worked in a factory. Following the Red Army's defeat of the Nazi occupation in 1945, Rakowski joined the Polish army as a political officer, and in 1946 became a member of the Communist Party. He went to study journalism in Cracow University in the same year, followed by a course in history at Warsaw University. In 1949 he started working for the Party Central Committee as a writer of propaganda material. In the period following Stalin's death he developed an increasingly critical attitude to the regime, and this led him to found the political journal *[*, together with a group of other like-minded journalists. Though a Party journal, it soon won the respect of non-Government intellectuals and dissidents, and in 1958 he became its editor-in-chief – a position he continued to hold until 1982.

Rakowski's political career began in earnest with his nomination as a candidate member of the Central Committee of the Communist Party in 1964. His reputation as both a moderate and a loyal apparatchik stood him in good stead during the turbulent '70's, which saw the virtual overthrow of Party leader, Wladyslaw Gomulka, and in 1975 he became a full member of the Central Committee. As the opposition to Party rule gathered strength, leading to the downfall of Eduard Gierek in 1980, Rakowski came to be seen as a man who could mediate between the Party and the new political forces. In February 1981 he was appointed deputy prime minister with special responsibility for negotiating with Solidarity – Eastern Europe's first independent trade union. After the failure of the negotiations with Solidarity leader, Lech Walesa, and amid growing acrimony and distrust between the two men and the organisations they represented, the Communist leader, General Jaruzelski imposed martial law. Notwithstanding his earlier reputation as a reformer, Rakowski emerged as a prominent spokesman for the Jaruzelski regime, appearing to regard martial law as a necessary short term measure to ward off a Soviet attack and Poland's retreat into chaos. After martial law was lifted in 1983, Rakowski's political fortunes waned, but with the ascendancy of his friend Mikhail Gorbachev in the Soviet Union, Rakowski was returned to favour. Nonetheless his appointment as Prime Minister in 1988 was seen by many people as a last ditch attempt by Poland's divided and discredited Communist Party to maintain a measure of control, after the Jaruzelski government's failure to cope with the country's economic crisis or to work alongside Solidarity.

In a bid to bolster his regime's authority, Rakowski prepared the country for multi-Party elections in 1989 – the first free elections in Eastern Europe since the Communist takeover. To Rakowski's surprise, the Polish electors decisively rejected Communism and Rakowski accepted the result, handing over power to a Solidarity-led administration, though with certain safeguards to guarantee continued Communist influence. However, the defeat of the Party in Poland was to precipitate the downfall of Communism throughout Eastern Europe and the collapse of Soviet power.

After his Party's fall from power, Rakowski became its First Secretary, but his tenure was short lived as the Party dissolved itself in January 1990. Since leaving mainstream politics, Rakowski has been accused by his detractors of accepting Soviet financial favours, using Soviet funds on behalf of the Social Democrat successor to the Communist Party and when in office closing the Gdansk shipyards, where Solidarity was born, not for economic reasons, as he claimed, but out of personal spite – charges Rakowski vigorously denies.

HELMUT SCHMIDT

Helmut Schmidt was born in 1918 and raised and educated in Hamburg, the son of a teacher. In 1937 he was drafted into the army, where he remained until 1945, winning promotion to the rank of Oberleutenant and being awarded the Iron Cross. In the meantime because of the Nazi persecution of the Jews, his family was obliged to conceal the fact that they were of partly Jewish ancestry. Shortly before the end of hostilities he was sent to a prisoner of war camp for four months, where he first came into contact with social democratic ideas, and joined the Social Democratic Party (SPD) shortly after his release. In 1946 he enrolled in Hamburg University, and on graduating in 1949 took up a position in that city's Transport Administration. But he had also been an active political worker, and in 1953 won a seat in the Bundestag for the Social Democrats, which he held until 1962. After losing his seat he remained outside the political arena for three years, but in 1965 he was again elected to the Bundestag and served in a variety of capacities until 1987.

Schmidt's first political office was as Chairman of the SPDs parliamentary Party, a position he held from 1967 until 1969. In 1968 he was elected the Party's Vice Chairman. From 1969 to 1972 he was Minister of Defence and during this period he made proposals for arms control based on the principle of maintaining a balance between East and West – ideas which were to serve as a basis for the subsequent detente between the superpowers and for Bonn's 'Ostpolitik' of the 1970s. Between 1972 and 1974 Schmidt served as Minister of Finance and played a major role in introducing the anti-inflationary policies as well as the round table talks between managers and union leaders which were credited with bringing Germany out of the economic difficulties occasioned by the OPEC oil price rises of 1973. Schmidt's success at handling the economy increased his popular standing and was a major factor behind his elevation to Chancellor in 1974.

As Chancellor at the head of a coalition government with the Free Democrats (FDP), Schmidt quickly established himself on the world stage. At home he enjoyed some success in combating the rise of terrorism and won widespread acclaim for his courageous decision to send in a commando unit to rescue the German hostages held at Mogadishu airport. Describing the central aim of his foreign policy as 'kthe political unification of Europe in partnership with the US', he was one of the architects of the European Monetary System in the late 1970s, and through his close ties with French premier Valerie Giscard d'Estaing he inaugurated the regular meetings of the EC's Council of Ministers. His decision to deploy US Cruise and Pershing missiles in response to the Soviet Union's new SS-20 weapons proved controversial, and though it divided the SPD and fuelled the growth of the anti-nuclear movement in Germany, Schmidt's coalition won the elections of 1976 and 1980 and survived until 1982. It was finally brought down by popular discontent over the stringent economic measures he introduced in the wake of the second oil price 'shock' of 1980-1981.

Following the collapse of the thirteen and a half year coalition Schmidt progressively distanced himself from the SPD and in 1984 quit as the Party's Vice Chairman. In the meantime he devotes himself to writing and has more than a dozen volumes to his credit. Moreover since the mid-80's he has been both co-publisher and senior editor of the newspaper 'Die Zeit'. Regarded by many of his contemporaries as the doyen among elder statesmen he is much in demand at international conferences and is the leading light in an informal association of former leaders.

BIBLIOGRAPHY

GENERAL

Bunce, Valerie - *Do new leaders make a difference?*, 1981

Czudnowski, M - *Does who governs matter?*, 1982

Grauman, C F and Moscovici, S (eds) - *Changing conceptions of leadership*, 1986

Heller, F A - *Decision making and leadership*, 1992

Janis, I - *Crucial decisions: Leadership in policy making and crisis management* 1989

Lindblom, C - *Charisma*, 1990

McIntyre, Angus (ed) - *Aging and political leadership*, 1988

Margach, James - *The Anatomy of power*, 1979

Pekonen, K - *Charismatic leadership and the role of the image in modern politics* 1989

Riker, W - *The Art of political manipulation*, 1968

Roskill, S W - *The art of leadership*, 1964

Rustow, D (ed) - *Philosophers and Kings: studies in leadership*, 1968

Wijewardene, W (ed) - *Leadership and authority*, 1968

Willner, A R - *The Spellbinders: Charismatic political leadership*, 1984

BY LEADERS

Bhutto, Benazir - *Daughter of the East*, 1989

Bhutto, Benazir - *The way out*, 1988

Ecevit, Bulent - *Ortanin Solu (Left of the Centre)*, 1966

Ecevit, Bulent - *Bu Duzen Degismelidir (The system must change)*, 1968

Ecevit, Bulent - *Ataturk ve Devrimcilik (Ataturk and Revolution)*, 1970

Ecevit, Bulent - *Dis Politika (Foreign Policy)*, 1975

Ecevit, Bulent - *Siirler (Poems)*, 1976

211

Fitzgerald, Garret - *Thoughts on two cultures*, 1988

Fitzgerald, Garret - *All in a life*, 1991

FitzGerald, Garret - *Unequal partners: North-South dialogue*, 1979

Fitzgerald, Garret - *Towards a new Ireland*, 1972

Fitzgerald, Garret - *The Israeli-Palestinian issue*, 1990

Heath, Edward - *Old world, new horizons*, 1970

Heath, Edward - *The state of Britain to come*, 1986

Heath, Edward - *An Atlantic approach to North-South relations*, 1982

Heath, Edward - *Our Europe*, 1990

Heath, Edward - *Euro-Unity over the next ten years*, 1988

Heath, Edward - *The place of sovereignty in an interdependent world*, 1984

Ibn Talal Hussein - *My war with Israel*, 1969

Ibn Talal Hussein - *Uneasy lies the head that wears the crown*, 1962

Jayawardene, J R - *Ceylon: the new dominion*, 1948

Jayawardene, J R - *Disturbances in July*, 1983

Jayawardene, J R - *Men and memories*, 1992

Jayawardene, J R - *Selected speeches*, 1979

Kaunda, K D - *Black government*, 1961

Kaunda, K D - *Zambia shall be free*, 1962

Kaunda, K D - *Humanism in Africa and its implementation* 1967

Kaunda, K D - *Letter to my children*, 1977

Kaunda, K D - *Dear Mr Vorster*, 1971

Kaunda, K D - *Africa's economic independence*, 1979

Manley, Michael - *Up the down escalator: development and the international economy*, 1987

Manley, Michael - *The politics of change*, 1974

Manley, Michael - *Jamaica: Struggle in the periphery*, 1981

Manley, Michael - *The poverty of nations* 1990

Obasanjo, Olusegun - *My command: an account of the Nigerian civil war*, 1990

Obasanjo, Olusegun - *Africa in perspective* 1987

Obasanjo, Olusegun - *Challenges of leadership in African development*, 1990

Obasanjo, Olusegun - *Africa embattled*, 1988

Obasanjo, Olusegun - *Foundation for stability*, 1979

Rakowski, M - *Partnerstwo (Partnership)* 1982

Rakowski, M (ed) - *Efficiency of investment in a socialist economy*, 1966

Rakowski, M - *Polityka zagraniczna PRL (The foreign policy of the Polish People's Republic)*, 1974

Rakowski, M - *The Polish Upswing 1971-1975*, 1975

Rakowski, M - *Ein schwieriger Dialog*, 1986

Schmidt, Helmut - *Balance of power*, 1970

Schmidt, Helmut - *A Grand Strategy for the West*, 1986

Schmidt, Helmut - *Menschen und Machten*, 1987 (Engl. edit. Men and Powers, 1988)

Schmidt, Helmut - *Ways out of the crisis*, 1983

Schmidt, Helmut - *The Soviet Union: challenges and responses*, 1984

Schmidt, Helmut - *The Anachronism of National Strategy*, 1966

Schmidt, Helmut - *Perspectives on politics*, 1986

ABOUT LEADERS

Zakaria, Rafiq - *The Trials of Benazir*, 1990

Smith, Raymond - *Garret* 1985

Ayres, Philip - *Malcolm Fraser*, 1987

Renouf, Alan - *Malcolm Fraser and Australian foreign policy*, 1986

Head, B W and Patience, A - *From Whitlam to Fraser*, 1989

Weller, Patrick M - *Malcolm Fraser PM*, 1989

Roth Andrew - *Heath and the Heathmen*, 1972

Dann, Uriel - *King Hussein and the challenge of Arab radicalism*, 1989

Lunt, J - *Hussein of Jordan*, 1989

de Silva, K M and Wriggins, H - *J R Jayawardene of Sri Lanka (a political biography) Vol 1 1906-56*, 1988

Ranganathan, M A - *The political philosophy of President K D Kaunda of Zambia*, 1986

Hatch, John - *Two African statesmen*, 1976

Chan, Steve - *Kaunda and South Africa*, 1991

Morris, Colin (ed) - *Kaunda on violence*, 1982

Minchin, James - *No man is an island*, 1986

Caldwell, Malcolm - *Lee Kuan Yew: the man, his mayoralty and his mafia*, 1979

George, T L S - *Lee Kuan Yew's Singapore*, 1973

Loy Teck Juan et al (ed) - *Lee Kuan Yew on the Chinese community in Singapore*

Levi, Darrell - *Michael Manley*, 1989

Nwanko, Arthur A - *Before I die*, 1989

Carr, Jonathan - *Helmut Schmidt*, 1985